GERMAN EVASION

As he roared earthward at 650 m.p.h., Gentile's earphones flapped with another pilot's urgent cry:

"*Break,* Gentile! *Break* you damn fool!"

But guns flaming, Gentile continued to dive until the Hun he was chasing fell to the ground.

A second and then a third Hun plane flew above his port wing. Gentile was cold with fright. He squirted what little ammunition he had left and then pulled away . . . defenseless.

His hand began to sweat on the throttle. He realized, then, that his only chance for survival was to evade German fire until their ammunition was also exhausted.

"Help! Help! I'm being clobbered!" Gentile screamed as the Germans began to close in on him.

He honked his plane up and stood it on its prop until it quivered and was ready to stall out. Then, for the first time, Gentile moved above the Huns. He'd forced them to fire all their ammunition, turn their planes around and then peel off.

When Gentile bounced down the runway at Debden, he didn't bother to gun the motor before switching it off. The intelligence officer jumped on the wing of his plane to interrogate him, but Gentile couldn't answer. He was spent, worn; he just stared back at the officer blankly and panted . . .

DEATH SQUADRON

BY GROVER C. HALL, JR.

ZEBRA BOOKS

KENSINGTON PUBLISHING CORP.

ZEBRA BOOKS

are published by

KENSINGTON PUBLISHING CORP.
21 East 40th Street
New York, N.Y. 10016

Printed in the United States of America

CONTENTS

About this book ...

As did many ex-servicemen, after the war I began reading about the momentous events which changed the world between 1939 and 1945, seeking the overall view. The ordinary soldier scarcely appreciated his small corner of the picture, let alone the grand objectives and strategy. One account of fighter flying—this book—was frequently mentioned as exceptional, yet no rare bookseller could unearth it. A lengthy search turned up a copy in the New York Public Library; I read it in an afternoon.

I wrote the author—would he allow me to republish it at my risk? He immediately accepted and thus began a long and rewarding association. Grover Hall, an Alabama newspaperman who served as Public Relations Officer with the 4th Fighter Group in England, had written a shorter account, *Mr. Tettley's Tenants,* as the war ended. Back home, he expanded the story into *1000 Destroyed* and printed 2,500 copies, most of which went to former members of the unit. He was interested in people rather than planes, which is what set his recollections apart. Then he took up duties as editor-in-chief of the Montgomery Advertiser. In 1957 he won the National Headliner Award for "consistently outstanding editorial writing."

During his visits, we talked for hours about the war in general and the men of the 4th in particular and I wish it all had been taped. Grover was an astute observer, a gifted writer, a great southern gentleman, a warm and valued friend. He passed away in 1971 after a long illness.

It is with the cooperation of his heir and Aero Publishers that this remarkable story of remarkable men is again made available.

—Len Morgan
15 August 1978

24 April 1946

MEMORANDUM:

TO   : All 4th Ftr. Gp. Alumni.

1. It's been seven months now since I saw Debden, pearl of the E.T.O., where it was rough, brother, rough. In fact, I now have about 14 points as a civilian. But I'm not bucking for rotation back into the army anymore than the rest of you. Just now it's late afternoon of a lush spring day in the Deep South. Beside me is a slug of Kentucky straight bourbon, such as could be had in England at Debden only by those with access to the operational whiskey or through friendship with the medics or with that series of youthful colonels who had the distinction of serving with us, the Debden hired help.

2. A great wisteria vine is trying, as it has all spring, to burst through my window with the intention, I suppose, of resting its coiled greenery and ineffable lace lavender sweetness on the sofa. A mocking bird—that superb Southern songster of which you yankees know naught, but which is to any of your northern thrushes and even the Essex County nightingales, those feathered Sleepy-time Gals, and, indeed, to all the world of avifauna, as Lily Pons to Betty Grable—is perched in that wisteria arbor, making the air throb and the leaves to quiver with his incomparable vesper serenade.

3. In my front yard, the Kentucky cardinals and jay birds are well and truly trained to shut their beaks when my matchless mocker is rendering. And that male cat squirrel, who resides in the same wisteria tenement with the three birds, has also been taught proper deference and reverence for my gray-frocked Caruso—to the extent that when he sings, the squirrel, a mere rat but for a fluffed-up tail, ceases his tempestuous pursuit of his tabby cat-squirrel and stands at parade rest . . . at parade rest, suh, until the last golden echo of flute and reed and siren song ripples across the rubescent horizon to such heavens as may have been provided as repositories of immortal auditory classics . . . Brother! It *is* true what they say about Dixie! . . .

4. But to what purpose are these flat notes on a vibrant subject addressed? Only a Southerner can comprehend the quality of an April afternoon in the South, and, of course, they know anyway. Furthermore, I encounter the peril of desecration in writing of such matters in prose, for only poetry is adequate. But preparatory to getting my wheels down for a landing, I look out on all this and I see my beat-up, 1939 Hudson. Right this minute I can drive it off and across the continent to Red Dog's home in Montana without any care of improvising a fabrication strong enough to induce Clat to okay a trip ticket off the station. All of which is to say that a lot of T.S. with oak leaf cluster has been left behind by most of us, and I take it that you all join with me in hoping that it's perpetually behind. Cheers. Buy bonds.

5. But although I would yield to none among you in my abhorrence for army life, I am amazed to find myself looking back with pleasure and even fondness on some aspects of our life at Debden. You know, sometimes in April and August we had soft days in England—when the sun shone and the clouds were

10

just platinum fleece wafting swiftly down Cambridge way. Remember those little apple trees in front of the officers' quarters and Station Headquarters and the stunted little nubs they bore? The baseball game out front halted for retreat? The waitresses lolling on the bermuda behind the mess, chewing a sprig of Johnson grass and lapping up the snow jobs of the Junior Birdmen? A Mustang, aloft for slow-timing, rifling across the Aero Club and honking its scarlet nose up in a peel-off, the sinking sun shimmering on its aluminum hide? An RAF Lancaster towing a glider over the drome? An AT-6 taking off, sounding like 50,000 horses and looking ridiculous beside the wicked beautiful P-51 bullets? McKennon standing 335th's red pickaback on its tail like a drunk goldfish? The men in green coveralls coming off the line to eat, their mess kits giving off flashes like a windshield The Audley Inn transport at the main gate? Bubbles the publican taking the wraps off the mild & bitter pump and the Waggon & Horses putting out its bottle of spirits for the night, as the brown Army girls make their way across the Saffron common to the town hall hop? A P-51 beating up the field after a test-fire over the Wash? Maj. Heackock surveying his command over the end of his cigaret holder as he cruises about in the Blue Goose? And a new rumor that the 4th was going to be taken off ops, sent home for re-equipment with jets and forwarded to the Pacific?

6. No it wasn't all bad, not at all. In fact, I suspect that we're all enduringly sentimental over Debden and always will be. By King George's lisp, darned if I wouldn't like to catch the 12:50 at Liverpool St. Station and chuff down to see the old place! Wonder what the RAF has done to it?

7. All of which reflections pose a regret. And that is that this is such an incomplete story of Debden. The

11

exploits of many fine pilots are unmentioned. The truth is, there is a story to be written about every pilot who ever made the circuit over "DB". There was not, alas, sufficient space and we had to stop at hitting the high spots.

8. I've become the more sensitive to the omissions and inadequacies of this stunted chronicle lately through correspondence with families of some who were K.I.A. Most of them, I see, cling to a hope that somehow, somewhen, their representative in the 4th Group will show up alive. Therefore, I think it a kindness to say that I hope nothing herein will provide any groundless hope that a pilot may have survived even though listed as dead. I know of no case, I regret to say, where such hope is justified.

April, 1946,
Montgomery, Ala.   —G.C.H., Jr.

1
Eagle Squadrons

The Life & Times of the 4th Fighter Group . . .
The 4th surpassed all other groups in the number of
German planes destroyed in the European Theater of
Operations. It was the pioneer group and the spear-
head of the world's mightiest air force. It had more
"Characters." It—but then that's letting the flaps
down on the take-off.

The first Americans to kill Japs and Germans were
fighter pilots. They started before Pearl Harbor.

In the Orient, it was the fabulous Flying Tigers. In
the Occident, the Eagle Squadrons, also fabulous.

Chennault's Flying Tigers (American Volunteer
Group) baffled and enraged the Japs. The Japs sent
them curses over the radio and expressed their pain
with bombing attacks.

The German radio snarled in guttural frustration at
the Eagle Squadron pilots in England.

"We know where you're based, you Debden air
gangsters," hissed Radio Berlin.

The day Reichmarshal Goering saw red-nosed
Debden Mustangs over Berlin was the day he decided
that Germany had lost World War II.*

The Flying Tigers and Eagle Squadrons had a strikingly parallel development. The same type of fighter
pilot flew the single-engine pursuits of both outfits.
These fighter pilots were different. Otherwise, what

---

*Said Goering after the war.

would they have been doing thousands of miles from their country, swapping cannon bursts five miles above the earth with an enemy superior in numbers and equipment, before America entered the war?

That Eagle Squadron boy out there floating in the choppy, icy English Channel in a rubber dinghy, anguished lest the German launch reached him ahead of the British. He could have been home at a football game. That scion of a rich Long Island family scraping the trees in attacking a gun post? Or that oil company executive, married to a Powers model, parachuting into enemy territory? If the motive was only love of flying, why didn't they join the Army Air Forces, stay home and fly training missions? That one quivering and kissing the ground because it was so wonderful to get back. Why didn't he stay home and continue to fatten his savings by ferrying divorcee candidates from California to Reno, which wasn't necessarily a disagreeable job?

The fact is, they were different from the men and boys of their age group back in the States and they were also different one from the other. Uncommon patriotism and bravery is far from a complete explanation. With some, yes. With others it was restlessness or frustration in civilian life. Most of them had flown civilian planes and joining the air force was a means of getting to fly all they wanted. For some, it was a reach for personal glory, perhaps to show somebody just who the hell they were, or to please somebody. In some cases they came to England to fight the "wily Hun" for the immemorial motives that have impelled men to join the army and leave home since before Scipio Africanus—debt and woman trouble.

Anyway, they did come to England, the Eagle Squadron pilots, and when the Focke-Wulf and Messerschmitt pilots saw them they said, "Achtung, Spitfires." Later on the Eagles transferred to the U. S. Army and the Jerries said, "Achtung, the red-nosed Mustangs!'' They were Jerry's worst enemy.

In 1934 Debden Airdrome was a farm in Essex County, England, largely owned by A. C. Kettley. Its dells and meadows abounded in game, and daffodils sparkled on the hummocks (that is, on state occasions when the sun deigned to come out). Hanger No. 2 was erected upon the bed of a pond so deep that Mr. Kettley never saw the bottom of it, and from which many silvery brook trout were taken. Mr. Kettley was drawing his living from this fruitful farmland as had his father before him. For 83 years and more these acres were owned by Kettleys. As far as Mr. Kettley knew, Kettleys would till it for another 83 years.

Mr. Kettley specialized in the cultivation of sugar beets, and with a skill to which numerous silver trophies eloquently attest. These trophies he showed me before beginning his recital of events of that certain evening in May, 1934.

It was seven o'clock and he stood amid the wheat where the station cinema was subsequently erected. He heard the roar of the RAF's new fighter, the Bristol Bulldog; the pilot was returning from an exhibition at Ipswich. The motor coughed and the wheat patch appeared as good a place as any for a forced landing. The Bulldog glided right over Mr. Kettley's head and cut a long, deep alley in the wheat. The wheat shoots wound around the undercarriage like spaghetti on a fork, and the plane nosed over and buried its spinner in the loam. "What are you doing in my wheat field?'' rasped Mr. Kettley. The pilot tried his legs and exclaimed, "I'm alive!''

"I repeat, sir—what are you doing in my wheat field?''

"Your wheat, huh? If it hadn't been for your blasted wheat my bus wouldn't have overturned!''

However, the RAF type was so rejoiced to find himself among the quick and not the dead that he grew affable and said to the very sovereign owner of the shimmering wheat:

"Sir, let's off to the nearest pub. My treat and my pleasure."

Mr. Kettley acquiesced, first availing himself of the six gallons of petrol he was able to drain from the Bulldog. Doubtless Mr. Kettley would have declined the pilot's invitation had he known what was to eventuate from the incident. But he had no way, alas, of knowing that for years to come he was going to have tenants on the Kettley acres from England, the Dominions beyond the Seas, from Georgia to Rhode Island to California.

That night the local constabulary guarded the wreckage of the Bulldog and next day the Air Ministry investigators arrived to determine the cause of the crash. An official dug a hole and observed, "Wonderful land." Soon thereafter some RAF officers bounced into the Kettley dining room, announcing: "Kettley, we've got good news for you—we've come to buy your farm for an airdrome site."

"To hell with you!" boomed Mr. Kettley.

But this was 1934, the RAF was girding for a war and he was forced to sell. The London *Daily Mirror* reported that, although Essex County belles were willing and then some for the airmen to pervade their midst, Mr. Kettley reacted like "a bear with a sore head."

The first of Mr. Kettley's tenants wore the smoke-blue of the RAF. Next came the mad Free Poles who flew in 23 different directions in forming up over the drome. Finally, came a third set of tenants who wore pink pants and forest green tunics to the amazement of the English. The Americans talked louder than the others, stayed gone much longer when they took off for the day's work across the Channel, and painted bulgy nudes and such-like on their planes. Sometimes the Americans rented rooms in the Kettley domicile so their wives could visit them on weekends. Mrs. Kettley, an unworldly little lady, was sometimes perplexed that the appearance of the wives of the officers seemed to change so radically from visit to visit.

During the 1940 Blitz many an RAF Spitfire and Hurricane took off from Debden Airdrome to fend the onslaught of the Luftwaffe. In fact, it is said that the "first shot in the Battle of Britain" was fired by a Debden interceptor. On a Saturday morning in August, 1940, the German bombers came. One of the bombs fell on the eastwest runway and it always had a rise there after its repair, which made it difficult for No. 2s to avert becoming airborne in the propwash of the No. 1s.

"I lost two cows, three calves, seven hogs, 56 head of poultry, including geese," Mr. Kettley recalled.

"And my two swans," Dame Kettley interposed, "flew away that day and never came back."

Mr. Kettley, who all the time and even now, resides on the fringe of the airdrome, was making a sentimental saunter across his whilom beet patch to ascertain for his wife if the daffodils bloomed as of old, before this spot of bother. Two taut RAF Regiment guards pounced upon him. At the guardhouse:

"Who am I? What was I doing walking around that area? By God, I'm A. C. Kettley! I was walking around for me health. Anything wrong with that?"

The duty officer bade him go in peace. Nix:

"Sir, you brought me here in a car, and you'll jolly well get me back in a car!"

The RAF gave Mr. Kettley a pass granting pratique to walk the station at will and speculated that if This Other Eden had 10,000 such farmers, they could repulse the German invader with their bare crotchets.

By February, 1941 the Spits and Hurricanes made it too costly to bomb England by day and Goering changed over to night attacks, which is mirrored in this entry in the RAF log book for the night of Feb. 14:

19:00—Quiet.

20:00—Flying continues.

20:45—Aircraft bogged up at end of runway.

22:47—Wellington bomber lands ... *German* machine makes circuit of drome. Identified itself as friendly aircraft and landed. Machine taxied up to watch officer and member of the crew got out and talked to duty pilot in German. Duty pilot identified aircraft as Heinkel 111.

22:53—(six minutes later)—German bomber takes off.

23:00—Discussion in watch office reference to firearms.

All of which was to record that the German craft landed at Debden, mistaking it for a French drome. In the darkness the RAF officer mistook the bomber for a British Wellington. A German alighted from the craft as the officer sauntered up. The RAF officer couldn't understand what the airman was saying in the foreign tongue. A Free Czech, no doubt.

"Achtung!" cried the German. Another member of the German crew trained a machine gun on the Limey, and the Heinkel took off. A few minutes later a Heinkel was shot down over the Channel and, like as not, it was the same plane.

Flying Tiger pilots were drawn from the AAF, Navy and United States Marine Corps. The three squadrons of the A. V. G. were formed in 1941. Somebody in the Pentagon Building, or higher, said abracadabra and commissioned pilots were allowed to resign and join the A. V. G. Naturally those who renounced regular commissions in the U. S. Army to go to China had special reasons—dissatisfaction with the army way of doing things, maladjustment, or lust for action.

Those who joined one of the three Eagle Squadrons likewise had reasons for not being in the AAF. Apart from emotional reasons, there were others such as a lack of requisite college training, or inability to pass physical examinations. A good many of their finest pilots had been washed out of American cadet schools for lack of flying ability.

The RAF had scraped the bottom of its pilot reservoir and it was fighting for the life of England. So the RAF opened up its ranks to American fliers by forming an American volunteer outfit—"71" Eagle Squadron. As Americans flocked to the Union Jack, two other squadrons were formed, "121" and "133" Eagle Squadrons. These three squadrons in the RAF were never based together and never flew together. They didn't like each other.

At first Eagle Squadron recruiting was a cloak-and-dagger transaction. The AAF rejected or washed them out, the RAF caught them on the first bounce—but in the beginning, furtively and *sub rosa* so as not to compromise U. S. "neutrality". In fact, one pilot, Col. Chesley G. Peterson, the most celebrated of the Eagles, was fetched back from Canada by G-men. After the country took fright at the impending conquest of England, recruiting came from behind its whiskers and was quite open. At Maxwell Field, Ala., the RAF had an enlistment booth near the Bell Street gate through which washed-out aviation cadets passed in their misery.

These Americans—adventurers, patriots, and not a few of the gentry which follows fire trucks—sailed to England to fight the Germans in RAF uniforms. They wore an "E.S." patch on the left shoulder of their blue tunics and to 45,000,000 Britons, fighting for survival, that "E.S." flash meant a gallant American boy come to shed his blood with theirs in their mortal ordeal. The Eagles got a reception beyond anything accorded the Americans who followed in American uniforms.

The sight of these North American warriors in pubs, on buses and streets gave British spirits a lift as the fire and flame fell upon them in the Battle for Britain. Their presence imparted substance to Mr.

Churchill's: "... Carry on the struggle, until, in God's good time, the New World, with all its power and might, steps forth to the rescue and liberation of the Old."

So the Eagles became the darlings of London. They couldn't buy a mild & bitter in the pubs. In a theater queue a grateful Briton might crush a ticket in the hand of an Eagle Squadron pilot and flee quickly beyond the thank-you. The Eagles were decorated by the King at Buckingham Palace. But they were likely to be turbulent, high-spirited and troublesome. One particular Eagle would quarrel with a fellow pilot and threaten, "You bastard, I'll get you upstairs today and shoot hell out of you!" Three thousand miles from home and facing death daily, the Eagles, as a class, often appeared not to have been house-broken. But they came as deliverers and the most vexatious, chronic prima donna among them could expect clemency when he got into trouble. So they acted as if they owned England, as did the rest of us in the first days after arrival a couple of years later.

2
Little D-Day

The three Eagle Squadrons did not distinguish themselves primarily in the Battle of Britain, for at the height of this shattering collision between the mighty Luftwaffe and the RAF's 40 fighter squadrons, the Eagles were just beginning to wet their feet in combat.

Flying the RAF's knock-kneed little Spitfires 5Vs, so graceful, so maneuverable, and the hump-backed Hurricanes, the Eagles did some scrambles (sitting in a cockpit awaiting German attacks and the "scramble" order). But chiefly their fighting occurred later over the Channel and along the French coast with FW 190s and Messerschmitt 109s.

"71" Eagle Squadron, the first organized, did most of the fighting. There was a lot of convoy patrol duty and many Americans who had come to fight found themselves ignominiously assigned to duty as instructors. Nevertheless, many were soaking up combat know-how that later helped every American airman sent to England. The Flying Tigers in 1941–42 were littering the rice paddies in China and Burma with Jap planes. In England, at the same time, the Eagles were fighting in the gray skies with the best of Germany's pilots, among them Goering's famous Yellow Noses.

It appears whimsical in retrospect, but in 1942 there was a great public demand for a cross-Channel invasion of the Continent. Londoners, not commonly regarded as demonstrative people, were writing "we want a Second Front" on Lord Nelson's statue in

Trafalgar Square.

The Eagles were as eager as the civilians; and when the Dieppe Raid came Aug. 19, 1942, they thought it was D-Day. It wasn't that by a Mulberry, a Pluto and 90 divisions, but it occasioned one of the war's great battles between Allied and German fighter planes. The Eagles never forgot Dieppe, and some continued on combat status for more than a year just to participate in D-Day, so wonderful was Little D-Day, Dieppe.

"71" Eagle Squadron was based at Debden Airdrome with two RAF squadrons. These, together with other wings of the Dieppe air force, took off early that morning. They were briefed to maintain an umbrella over Dieppe, where the Commandos would land. The sky was cloudless and the pilots were to keep it cleansed of German aircraft.

Around Debden and throughout East Anglia, Englishmen watched the swarm of planes fly over and listened as their throb came and went. The Eagles and other RAF squadrons flew three sorties to Dieppe that day. The German fighters and bombers met them over the beaches where the ground troops were hacking each other. Visibility was unlimited. Fighter planes tangled in tempestuous duels. Other fighters attacked bombers, wings quivering to the recoil of their cannon fire. Bombers fell in flaming splinters on the white beaches. The Eagles could see the gladiators grappling as they pulled out of whining dives. There was fire and flame, above and below.

Don Blakeslee, commanding "121" squadron, shot down a couple of Jerries. Roy Evans, once a California railroad fireman, chased the German fighters and blazed away, but couldn't get within range. Don Gentile knocked down a bomber and a fighter.

Chesley G. Peterson, first American to command an Eagle Squadron ("71"), was there in a Spit. He clobbered a Jerry and was then shot down. Peterson was not only cool, but jaunty as he floated down into the

Channel. Peterson carried one of those RAF horse pistols in his flying boot, and thinking he might never have another opportunity to fire it, blazed away as he fell and threw it in the water ahead of him.

That night patrons of the White Heart Pub foregathered early, certain that something momentous had come off. The White Heart was the tavern in the town where "71" Eagles hung around. The basement section was more or less reserved for them and was known to all as Daniel's Inn. Excitement was at a high pitch as the Englishmen swarmed about the Eagles and listened to the shouting Eagles reconstruct the great battle. It was the same as finding yourself in the Brown Derby listening to the victorious Rose Bowl team (probably the Crimson Tide!) jabber how they did it.

The phone rang:

"This is Pete. I'm O.K. They got me out of the drink."

Peterson had been rescued from the Channel.

"Wee" Michael McPharlane, of Hastings, Mich., had likewise been shot down. He phoned and demanded to speak to his roommate, Oscar Coen, a Carbondale, Ill. school teacher.

"Oscar, put those damn boots of mine back where they belong!"

The Eagles never forgot that day or that night. But there were other memorable occasions, and one of them was the British premiere of the movie, *Eagle Squadron*. The English really put on the dog for that. The premiere was to be held in London's best theater and the Eagles were to be honor guests as the movie was allegedly based upon their exploits.

For once, the Eagles shined the buttons on their tunics. With their best English girls on their arms, they entered the theater with dash and smartness and were ceremoniously ushered to reserved seats. Peterson had just wed Audrey Boyes, lovely South African actress, and they sat beside Don Blakeslee. It was the first time Blakeslee had ever seen the famous Peterson.

The lights went off. They unreeled the movie. The movie had been made in Hollywood . . .

"Jesus," groaned the pilots, humiliated by the corn stench.

They ducked out before the lights went on again.

By now it had become time for the Flying Tigers and the Eagles to be repatriated into the U.S. Army. The AAF was forming air forces both in China and in England; it wanted the skill and experience in combat of the only Americans who had it at the time.

The Tigers had begun operations against the Japs Dec. 20, 1941 and transferred from the Chinese Air Force to the AAF July 5, 1942. They had destroyed 297 Jap aircraft. Their high scorer was R. H. Neale with 15½ destroyed.

The Eagles destroyed 73½ German aircraft, or about six German squadrons. Forty-one of the 73½ were destroyed by the original squadron, "71". High scorer was Gus Damon, a fragile looking Hollywood makeup man, with 9; next, Peterson, with 5.

Afterwards these group and individual scores were surpassed by wide margins, but comparisons here can be misleading. The pilots of these two volunteer groups were fighting the cream of the Jap and German Air Forces and they were greatly outnumbered. They were using relatively crude ring gunsights, while the aces who came much later had the magical K-14 gyroscope sight. But beyond all of that was the paramount fact of pioneering. They had to learn to destroy German planes before they could destroy them. The first man to swallow a sword deserves more credit than the second man, even though the second swallowed a bigger sword.

In the summer of 1942 the United States had begun to build the world's mightiest air force in England—the Eighth. It had 185,000 officers and men. But it was only a puny force in its early days. It had a few bombers, but not a single fighter pilot who had been to combat. The AAF got some battle-tried fighter pilots Sept. 29, 1942 when the three Eagle Squadrons met at Debden Airdrome to become officers of the U. S. Army, with ranks commensurate with the rank they held in the RAF.

The pilots fondly hung up their RAF uniforms and transposed their RAF decorations to the AAF's green tunic. Their decorations and AAF silver wings they pinned over the left breast. Over the right breast they sewed the knitted RAF wings.

It was a big day at Debden, but it was lost upon the Eagles because, having been trained in RAF military ways, they didn't know how to ape U. S. Army customs of the service. They saluted with their palms showing; they stamped their feet down as they completed facing movements. Stars, bars, gold and silver leaves revealed rank, but for God's sake, what rank?

Gen. Carl A. Spaatz said to 2nd Lt. "Deacon" Hively:

"My name is Spaatz."

Deacon eagerly replied:

"Mine's Hively."

The Eagles lined up on the parade ground in a drizzle. Air Chief Marshal Sir Charles Portal said:

"On the occasion of the merging of the Eagle Squadrons* with the U. S. Air Corps, I would like to thank them for all they have done during the past two years. The RAF will never forget how the members of the Eagle Squadrons came spontaneously to this country, eager to help us in the critical weeks and months during and after the Battle of Britain."

An RAF band sounded off. Enlisted personnel, including British WACS, paraded. Air Chief Marshal

---

*Probably the only fighter group activated in a theater of war.
For squadron rosters, see Appendix.

Sir W. Sholto Douglas said:

"You joined us readily and of your own free will when our need was the greatest. There are those of your number who are not here today—those sons of the United States who were first to give their lives for their country."

Before Marshal Douglas were the Eagles.† They now belonged to the United States Army. The band struck up the *Star Spangled Banner* and Old Glory was hoisted: The United States now had a fighter base and a fighter group operating in England.

Debden Airdrome: the 4th Fighter group.

3
Gentlemen, the P-47

If they tried hard, the Eagles, whelped in the RAF way and naively convinced it was the only way, could think of perhaps two things they liked about the United States Army Air Forces.

Pay: As a pilot officer in the RAF they drew $76; as a first lieutenant in the AAF they drew $276.

Food: U.S. army rations meant the end of Bubble & Squeak (collards and potatoes) for breakfast.

But they heard that American brasshats—the same gentry that had once considered them unfit for the AAF—meant to bomb Germany in daylight. "Clueless bunch of beggars!" snorted the Eagles. The RAF and the Germans had both tried that and been forced to abandon it in favor of the less costly night bombing.

And, of more personal concern, the pilots were hearing that the AAF also had a new, secret plane on the assembly line, Republic's P-47 Thunderbolt. They anticipated it would probably be about as good as the P-40, which the RAF had sent to the Middle East because it wasn't good enough for combat with German pursuit craft. The Eagles weren't convinced that the game was worth the candle, despite the pay and food. They were disturbed over the prospects of flying any but the finest planes over the Continent, for its skies were deadly even for a Spitfire. They all remembered what had befallen one squadron of Spitfires Sept. 26, 1942.

The squadron was briefed to take a dozen or so Forts to Morlarix on the north coast of France. But due to an error in the weather report, the force had strayed some 135 miles south of the target. There was a 10/10th cloud layer and the Spit pilots couldn't see the ground and its reference points.

Finally Capt. Marion E. Jackson, of Corpus Christi, found a hole in the clouds and saw land. A flak barrage came up, which told the pilots they were not over England. Jackson, leading a section of four craft, anxiously checked his fuel gauge and found he had between four and six gallons left. Those flying on the flanks in No. 2 and No. 3 positions had even less fuel because their turns had been necessarily wider.

As the squadron turned inland to bail out, a swarm of FW 190s pounced upon them and the squadron was broken up. Jackson, trying tö get farther inland before bailing in order to improve his chances of escape, was attacked by a 190 at 200 feet. He turned into the German. The 190's speed was too great and he skidded in front of Jackson's guns. Jackson gave a one-second burst of cannon fire. The 190 rolled over and crashed into a field (probably the second German craft destroyed in the war by an AAF pilot in Europe). Almost immediately thereafter flak riddled Jackson's plane and he jumped.

Next day the Germans buried the pilot Jackson had killed and with him, three of the Spit pilots. What happened to the other eight was never learned.

The memory of this engagement dominated pilot thinking at Debden. It was always remembered that the Continent could open its jaws and devour a whole squadron. Certainly it was not a place in which the pilots wanted to do any guinea-pigging in an untried, unproven plane. The Eagles had been born in Hurricanes and raised in Spits, and they preferred, if it had to be, to go to glory in them.

Then one day the boom was lowered. The man with the eagle emblems on his shoulder (they now knew this denoted a colonel) assembled them. He was the C. O., Col. Edward W. Anderson, of St. Petersburgh,

Fla., and he said:

"We're going to fly Thunderbolts. But under no account must anything be said about this. It must be kept from the Jerries."

Silent groans and curses. "Tell the Jerries? Humph, they'll know it soon enough when they see us crashing all over the place!"

But the pilots got what they regarded as a reprieve. They were to continue operations with Spits for a time as the coffins hadn't been ferried in from the undertaker. The nature and pennyweight size of these pioneer operations of the AAF are striking when compared with those later days when the AAF could dispatch 2,000 bombers and 1,000 fighters any time.

Oct. 2, 1942—Wing Commander R. M. B. Duke-Woolley, sent by the RAF to fly with the Americans, was leading when a small gaggle of FW 190s was encountered at 24,000 feet in the Calais area. Oscar Coen and S. M. Anderson got one each. W/C Duke-Woolley and Jim Clark shared another. Each took half credit. When the Briton left the group he took with him his half credit for addition to the RAF total, while Clark's half was added to the AAF's total. Thus, for a long time the 4th Fighter Group had "½" dangling to its score. Later the group shared destruction of a Jerry with another group, thus making the "½" a whole. But that "½" is still hanging on some group's score; it probably visited around to all of the groups in the course of the war.

Oct. 9—Escorted three (*sic*) Fortresses in a raid on locomotive works in France.

Oct. 14—Twelve Spits attacked three ships off the Hook of Holland.

Oct. 29—Two Pilots, Lts. Anderson and Goodson, took off on a rhubarb mission to attack barges and shipping.

Nov. 4—Mrs. Eleanor Roosevelt visited Debden (natcherly).

Nov. 21—Lt. Roy Evans and Lt. J. J. Smolinsky

went on rhubarb. A Fieseler-Storch trainer was peppered by Evans. Trainer tried to ram Smolinsky. Evans polished off the trainer. Evans had to bail out 500 yards off the English coast. Royal Marines gathered him in.

Dec. 11—Lts. Beeson and Anderson machine-gunned enemy troops parading in France.

And so it went. The Eighth Air Force was to become the world's mightiest, but at this time its fighter strength consisted of the three squadrons of the 4th Fighter Group (48 planes). The Eighth was capable of scarcely more than impudent pecks at the formidable Luftwaffe. Indeed, the operations in the winter of 1942 were inadequate even to portend the grand scale operations of a year later, when the 4th Group alone was capable of savage slashes with 72 planes at the Luftwaffe and insolent swaggering over Berlin.

Nevertheless, the 4th was doing some valuable pioneering by providing a clinic for those who were planning the gigantic operations of a year later. On Feb. 24, 1943, Maj. Gen. Frank O. 'D. Hunter, then chief of VIII Fighter Command, passed out RAF medallions to Debden pilots with the assertion:

"Five months ago I came here when the first group of you were transferred to VIII Fighter Command. You will never know what it meant to us to receive a group of fully trained operational pilots. It has formed a nucleus around which we have built our fighting machine.

"We have been able to select men from among you to send to other units to train and lead them. All this, and everything the RAF has learned in three years of fighting the Hun, has been of invaluable aid."

Maj. Gen. Kepner said a year later:

"The 4th Fighter Group has been the stem whence fighter command doctrine has sprung."

Then one day the P-47 white hope was ferried in to

Debden. To the 4th went the dubious honor of selection as the group to give the Thunderbolt its combat baptism. To the pilots the Spitfire was a sure-footed, graceful little filly; the P-47, a bull-necked, unwieldy stallion.

There were a lot of little things. The propeller on old model Spits turned counter-clockwise, so they would have to grow accustomed to the different torque of the P-47. They liked the Spits .20-mm. cannon, but saw no sense in the P-47's eight .50-cal. machine guns. The cannon is some larger and more explosive; with cannon a pilot could always see when he got strikes on an enemy plane; it gave the exhilarating feeling of tearing the German to bits. They were not impressed by the fact that the .50-cal. machine gun bullets had much more range and that many more rounds could be carried in the wings.

The Spit's legs were knock-kneed and close together, while the P-47's were bow-legged and wide apart like a hawk's, so it could land in places the Spit couldn't taxi. The pilots complained that the mirror and glass canopy on the P-47 made it difficult to spot enemy planes. But the chief thing the pilots abhorred about the P-47 was its great size and weight (seven tons). With their radial engines, the craft resembled milk bottles. The pilots missed the jockey-feeling Spit compactness gave. Early model "T-bolts" had a way of giving off smoke in the cockpit, which fact all but made some pilots bail out. At first, they weren't supposed to go below 18,000 feet in combat with 47s.

The pilots junked the P-47 rear-view mirrors and installed Spit mirrors and bleated, "If they had to change—why couldn't they have given us Mustangs instead of these things? They won't climb, they won't turn tight, they won't do anything but dive."

Remarks they made about the sponsors of the P-47 were unladylike. Said the P-47 sponsors of the pilots: "Prima donnas!"

March 10, 1943 was the day on which Jerry was

supposed to get a look at the wonder plane. On that day the 4th gave the P-47 its combat debut. All personnel watched the take-off. The pilots got almost to the end of the runway before pulling the stick, desiring to remain on the ground as long as possible. They circled the field. The engines gave off a deep-throated roar, but the distinguishing sound of the 47 was the whistling noise created by air flow on its radial engine. To me it's the same sound as that made by doves settling in a baited field just before daylight.

Leading the group was Peterson; he set course over Debden and headed for France. They swept down the French coast. To their exquisite relief, the Luftwaffe didn't come up. When they returned to base, Peterson, eagle of the Eagles, ejaculated, "I don't mind telling you, I was scared."

4
Babies

The first thunderbolt to destroy an enemy aircraft was flown by Don Blakeslee. Flying along the coast of France on April 15, 1943 Blakeslee led 10 Thunderbolts in a dive on three FW 190s flying at 23,000 feet.

Blakeslee opened up with the P-47's eight half-inch machine guns (later guns were reduced to six). At 500 feet the German pilot tried to bail, but he was too low. Corpse and wreckage splattered in an Ostend backyard. Blakeslee was congratulated for demonstrating that a P-47 could out-dive an FW 190.

"By God it ought to dive," Blakeslee snorted. "It certainly won't climb."

It got to be the summer of 1943 and the 4th Group fighters were sweeping to and fro along the fringes of the Continent. Sometimes they escorted bombers. Other times they went alone on fighter sweeps in an effort to lure the Huns aloft. But Jerry hadn't won his wings yesterday and he refused to sacrifice his fighters in vainglorious tangles with American fighter craft, which, after all, were relatively harmless as they dropped no bombs. So the 'Bolts roared up and down France without German opposition, just spinning their wheels.

Dry runs though the fighter sweeps were, they did provide a clinic in which the shortcomings, peculiarities and potentialities of the 47 were revealed to tacticians and engineers.

Already the change in the tide of the air war in favor of the United Nations was manifest. Oldsters of the Eagle Squadrons could remember when you didn't

33

have to go and seek Jerry—he came to you spoiling for a fight. Flying a mile out in the Channel was accounted an operational mission. An engineering officer put-putting from one British base to another in a Tiger Moth was subject to prowling FWs which had a way of swooping out of the sun to clobber them to splinters. There was a subsequent phase in which the Channel was divided into more or less equal parts and he who ventured into the German side did so with the assurance of a Jerry reception.

As Allied fighter strength waxed, the Germans pulled their fighters farther and farther back from the coast, surrendering territory in the land battle sense. They would draw their fighter squadrons back and out of Allied fighter range and attack the undefended bombers when the fighters turned back.

But Fighter Command had an answer for that one and the answer was shaped like a giant teardrop. It was slung to the belly of a 47 and in flight it looked like a pilot fish riding 'neath the belly of a shark. Pilots called these extra fuel tanks "babies" and doubtless the literal-minded Krauts were rather confused the first time they heard a U.S. pilot shout to another, "Drop your baby!" These extra fuel tanks gave fighters added range with which they forced the Luftwaffe to retreat farther within its continental lair.

Nowadays drop-tanks are taken for granted like the fourth blade of a prop; not so, then. Pilots approached their first baby mission anxiously and with the usual effusions about the brass up the line smoking a new kind of dope. They walked out to the line to watch their crewmen sling the babies, and their countenances were not less grave than those of the Disciples proceeding to the Last Supper. They observed that the clearance between the explosive babies and the runway was but a few inches, and this sufficed to provoke peristalsis in the most sluggish imagination.

"It makes you think," quoth one.

"It shakes you actually," said another.

Most asked dolefully, "What are they trying to do—kill us?"

They bitched less passionately when it became known that Col. Anderson was going to die with them. At 39, Col. Anderson was well beyond combat age, but on tough shows such as this, he would go along in accordance with the traditions of soldiery. He wouldn't lead the group but would fly unobtrusively as some shavetail's No. 2.

July 28 was the day. It was the first belly tank show in the E.T.O. and also the first time any fighter craft had been briefed to penetrate beyond France into German skies.

Rendezvous with the bombers was made in the vicinity of Emmerich, Germany. A box of Forts was being mauled by from 45 to 60 FWs, 109s and JU 88s. Six of the 190s were queueing up on a stricken Fort which began to straggle. To the astonishment of the German pilots, they found themselves suddenly beset by a swarm of Allied Fighters. Capt. "Spike" Miley, of Toledo, Ohio, with Col. Anderson on his wing, charged down on the six Jerries out of the sun as they were soaring up to attack the limping Fort. Nine German interceptors were destroyed. Anderson got two of these. Back at Debden he asked, "Say, what the hell kind of planes were those I shot down?"

It was obvious that German intelligence officers hadn't told their pilots about babies. And it was some weeks before Fighter Command publicly announced that Germany had been drawn within combat range of the 4th Group.

On Aug. 16 the Thunderbolts of the 4th were just specks or hair-sized vapor trails to the people of Paris. But the throngs in the streets below could tell that something eventful was going on in the blue sky above. They heard the piercing, galvanic whine of powerful aircraft diving and climbing. Sometimes the planes swept low over the Eiffel Tower and Parisians could hear the symphony of Hun cannon and

American machine guns.

But even if the Parisians had neither heard nor seen the falcon gyrations, they would have known something felicitous was in progress because now and then a piece of debris plummeted to earth with a tail feather of flame and smoke and the debris was daubed with swastika markings.

Scores of Forts had careered majestically across Paris—the 47s weaving and criss-crossing above to screen them from attack—to sing their putts on Le Bourget Field, converted since Lindbergh landed there in 1927 to a plane depot. The sky looked as though it had never seen a cloud. As the Big Friends and their pugnacious little trigger guys approached the target a swarm of Jerries swirled up to intercept. The 47s charged the Jerries. Twenty thousand feet above the Arc de Triomphe the American and German varsity squads joined battle.

"I would have given 1,000 damn dollars to have seen that show from the ground!" Jim Clark said afterwards.

What he said was eloquent of the fact that the action is so fleeting and the speeds so great in fighter combat that a pilot rarely sees more than one or two things at a time—the plane in his gunsight and/or the one in his rear-view mirror. The newsreel customer got a better look for two shillings sixpence.

In the course of the battle German craft fell to earth in the outskirts, in the suburbs and in the city. One, downed by Maj. Don Young, of Chanute, Kans., splattered on a block of flats in the city.

"I saw a 190 as it approached the Forts from 9 o'clock," Young recounted, "and I went into a shallow dive and closed to 200 yards. I then closed to 75 yards, seeing strikes and pieces flying from the 190. It rolled over and went into a spiral dive for about 1,000 feet, then into a violent spin with large pieces flying off. It crashed in a ball of flame in a square of houses."

Jimmy Happel was one of the few who got a good look at his own handiwork. He was on the tail of a 190 when it began to climb. Happel gave it what pilots are pleased to call a "squirt".

"I saw the canopy come off, and parts fly off at the same time. I knew he was finished, so I stopped firing and flew off to starboard and then back to look him over. I watched him go down."

Capt. Fonzo (Snuffy) Smith, of Molockoff, Tex.:

"My No. 2 and I went upsun to position ourselves on about six 190s attacking the bombers. At 25,000 feet I couldn't find the Huns and I began weaving back and forth and looking above and below me. Just then a 190 painted black pulled up under me to the right. I took plenty of time to look around, called my No. 2, told him to cover me and slid in dead astern of him. I don't think the pilot got out."

Roy Evans downed a 109 and killed the pilot:

"I saw three 109s start to attack a straggling Fort out of the sun. I was about 3,000 feet above with my section and went down to attack. The first burst him in the tail. I moved my bead up and gave about a two-second burst. I was closing so fast that I flew past very close to the craft, less than 20 yards away. I saw the pilot slumped over the cockpit."

As the 47s and Germans tangled, Blakeslee was orbiting above both, directing the battle. It was a new tactic and Fighter Command would not permit its disclosure in the newspapers.

"Bud" Care got two 190s, both of whose wheels dropped down like the legs of a wounded bird.

"Seeing two flying line abreast almost parallel to the bombers, I attacked from line astern. I gave a two-second burst from 200 yards and saw the undercarriage drop down. One hit and exploded in a small field on the outskirts of Paris."

Maj. John G. DuFour, of Alameda, Calif.:

"I was leading the squadron a mile north of Paris when I saw two 109s making vicious head-on stabs at the Forts. They were out of range, but I took a squirt anyway and saw strikes to my surprise. I dove on two others. I took one last look at the 109 and saw his left wing suddenly peel back and fly off."

It was a new American record for the E. T. O.—18 destroyed for the loss of one. Capt. Joe Matthews was shot down, but he escaped from France and returned to Debden to report that he had bagged a Hun before going down himself. Although they had met Jerry on equal terms and shot down 18 for the loss of but one, the pilots still didn't have a kind word for Thunderbolts, which is a whit difficult to explain on the basis of logic.

Beer was free that night at Debden. And one can imagine that the gallery—Paris' three million—had concluded that there are appropriate occasions for celebration other than Bastille Day.

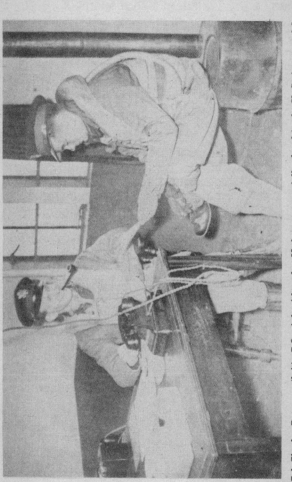

Col. Chesley Peterson (left), C.O. of the 4th and at 23 the youngest full colonel in the U. S. Army, and Lt. Col. Oscar Coen, Carbondale, Ill., a school teacher who became one of the first airmen, to be shot down and escape from France. At times he was under water, breathing through a reed.

BETWEEN-THE-ACTS

Maj. James A. Godson holds forth, as always, in 336th Dispersal. Gentile (leaning on table) does—well, what the photographer told him to do.

A cake cut by Col. Don Blakeslee to mark the 500th Jerry destroyed.
Lt. Col. James Clark watches.
Capt. Shel Monroe, Waycross, Ga.

Debden had a party to mark every hundredth Hun destroyed. Blakes-lee cutting cake; Maj. Gen. Bill Kepner on his right; Brig. Gen. Jesse Auton on left.
Bottom photo is just what it appears to be.

THE PUKKA GEN

Maj. Goodson (finger poised) expounds for Robert Lovett, Assistant Secretary of War for Air. Lt. Col. Walter Clatanoff, ground exec, nearest finger. Brig. Gen. Jesse Auton in extreme left; Col. Blakeslee on right.

Thunderbolts of 335th Squadron off from Debden for their combat debut in early 1943.

by LIFE Photographer Frank Scherchel

Copyright TIME, Inc.

Capt. Joe Joiner (upper left), Corpus Christi; Maj. Leon Blanding (right), Sumter, S. C.; Capt. Carl Brown (left), Huntingdon, Pa.; Maj. Baldwin M. Baldwin, Reno, Nev., group intelligence officer.

Capt. Kenneth (Black Snake) Peterson, Mesa, Ariz.
Lt. Thomas Biel (lower left), of St. Paul, killed in action; Capt.
"Georgia" Wynn, Dalton, Ga.

Capt. Allen Bunte (upper left), Eustis, Fla.; Maj. Hank Mills (right), Leonia, N. J.; Lt. Ray Clotfelter (lower left); Lt. James Dye, Dallas, Tex.

Maj. "Bud" Care (upper left), Angola, Ind.; Lt. James Ayers (upper right), Oklahoma; Lt. Col. Roy Evans (lower left), San Bernardino, Calif.; Lt. Paul Riley, York, Pa.

Lt. Col. Jim Clark (upper left), Long Island, N. Y.; Lt. Aubrey Stanhope (upper right), a Frenchman; Capt. "Dutch" Van Wyk (lower left), Patterson, N. J.; Lt. Steve (The Greek) Pissanos, Plainfield, N. J.

Godfrey, Gentile and Goodson check where it happened on an intelligence map.
Intelligence officers (lower row)—Capt. Ezzell, Capt. Mead, Capt. Leverock, Capt. Croxton, Capt. MacCarteney. Upper row—Lt. Jenks, Maj. Baldwin, Capt. Benjamin, Capt. Ashcraft.

334th SQUADRON

Standing, left to right.—Capt. Ben Ezzell, Capt. Vic France, Capt. Charles Ashcraft, Lt. Alex Rafalovich, Lt. Howard Moulton, Maj. Gerald Montgomery, Lt. H. Thomas Biel, Maj. Mike Sobanski, Lt. Vernon Boehle, Maj. "Deacon" Hively (sitting, left to right), Capt. Archie Chatterly, Capt. "Robert" Williams, Capt. David Van Epps, Capt. Alfred Markel, Capt. Joe Lang, Capt. "Georgia" Wynn, Lt. Robert Hills, Capt. W. B. Smith, Capt. Sheltor Monroe, Capt. "Cowboy" Megura. Personnel naturally turned over in the course of the war. This was posed in the spring of 1944.

5
"I'm Being Clobbered"

The most celebrated name to emerge from the RAF
Eagle Squadrons was that of Chesley G. Peterson. He
was a member of the original squadron and the first
American to command one. At 22, Peterson had been
decorated by King George with the British DFC and
DSO. He also wore the American Distinguished Service Cross, Purple Heart and numerous Air Medals.
"After you get the first one," Peterson used to laugh,
"the others come mighty easy."

Peterson was wed to a beauteous, ebon-haired actress. At 23, he became a full colonel—youngest in the
U. S. Army. He had left home to fight at 19, a boy on
a man's errand. For all of that, Peterson's father—
who not only lived near Salt Lake City but was also
named Brigham—thought, when he returned home for
a visit, that Chesley was a boy returned from a man's
errand.

"Put that cigaret down, son," admonished the colonel's papa, "you can't smoke in my presence." And
throughout his leave, Full Col. Peterson dutifully hid
behind the hen house to smoke.

Peterson fell in love with planes early: "It was 1929
and I was just a button. A couple of barnstormers sat
an old crate down in dad's alfalfa patch and asked if
they could use it for a while as a landing field. Next
day dad talked them into taking me and my kid sister
for a ride. They did. I stuck my arm out and was

53

amazed when the air almost blew it off. When I got down I said to myself, 'This is a damn good thing.' "

Peterson was certain thenceforward that there could be but one life for him, that of an army pilot, and he began to cut his cloth to that pattern. He even eschewed commercial flying because he understood the army frowned on it.

"At the end of my sophomore year at Brigham Young University," Peterson said, "I asked myself why the hell I was still there—the Air Corps only required two years of college. I quit."

At Lindbergh Field in San Diego, Aviation Cadet Peterson was washed out for "inherent lack of flying ability." But the irony of purging a man who was to become a great combat pilot was apparent, not real: A sympathetic instructor employed this means of purging Peterson as a kindness, because the real reason was the discovery that he had been under-age at enlistment.

His life thus hopelessly ruined, Peterson got extensively drunk and maintained himself in that condition for days, taking a trip across the continent as he quaffed. Then he went to work in the Douglas aircraft factory, and was tormented by the sight and smell of the planes. In 1940 he still yearned to become a fighter pilot. Enlistment in the RAF appeared the answer, but G-men fetched him back. He thought he might get overseas by volunteering as ambulance driver for the French Army. Instead, he tried once more to enlist in the RAF. This effort was successful and he was soon in England.

This was a period when others who were finally to meet up at Debden in the Eighth Air Force's most colorful group were about to slip into the traffic stream that led to Debden. Don Gentile was buzzing his girl's house in Piqua, Ohio, in a homemade biplane. Don Blakeslee's Cub had been cracked up by a friend and he had decided to enlist in the RAF as the only means of getting another plane to fly. "Deacon" Hively was initiating himself into the intricacies of a new science called *geo-morphology*. "Goody" Goodson was being torpedoed on the S. S. *Athenia*. Roy Evans was telling the Santa Fe Railroad that he'd rather be a fighter pilot than an engineer. Mike Sobanski, the Pole, had returned to Warsaw to meet his father in the smoking ruins of their home. The Greek was taking $12 flying lessons on a $15 salary. "Mac" McKennon the Ridgerunner was winning tri-state contests with his soulful renditions of Chopin and Mozart. Kid Hofer was winning trophies in the Golden Gloves Boxing Tournament. "Swede" Carlson was ferrying disenchanted matrons to Reno. Freddy Glover, a third baseman, was farmed out by the Cardinals. Johnnie Godfrey was running away to become a Canadian infantryman for the second time—and I was writing a damnfool editorial in *The Montgomery Advertiser* that the Maginot Line was invincible. Really a pregnant time all the way around.

Peterson had arrived in England when plane traffic across the English Channel was mostly in the opposite direction of what it was on V-E Day. The Few were very few. Peterson heard RAF Wing Commander Churchill tell a Vickers foreman one night, "I don't know how—but by tomorrow morning you've got to make us 12 Spitfires." And next morning the Spit short order was ready for scrambles.

In the RAF Peterson strafed, ram-rodded, dog-fought and mastered tactics in such fashion as to become famous in both England and America. With polite aggressiveness he constantly agitated against the defensive spirit.

Peterson was tall, wiry and approximately knock-kneed, with flaxen hair and deep-socketed blue eyes. He was affable and well liked; he was boyish without loss of dignity. But the salient characteristic was combativeness. After he came to Debden as a U.S. officer, a press conference was arranged for him in the army's press relations offices in Grosvenor Square (near the fabled balcony from which a famous actress hurled jewelry gifts at her titled lover below, and he returned the fire with horse droppings). Some 40 British and U.S. correspondents met Peterson for an interview on the state of the air war. Peterson was vexed when the photographers wanted his picture with the flag as a background.

"I take a dim view of this corny stuff," said Peterson, arching his neck. He acquiesced, however, when it was pointed out that Gen. Marshall had condescended to pose similarly.

Then Peterson began his address to the correspondents who had come to perform no greater disservice to him than his further glorification. He said in a tight, low voice:

"I want to say right in the beginning that I'm going to be damn careful in what I say to you. I'll tell you frankly, I expect you people to misquote me. I don't trust reporters . . ."

Some correspondents walked out on Peterson immediately. Others followed as soon as they got their breath back. The incident did nothing at all to detract from the 4th Group's repute at the time as a tribe of snotty prima donnas. The *Stars and Stripes* staff always associated the 4th with this performance, the result being that the paper thereafter had 12-point headlines for the 4th and 24-point type for the derring-do of its rival, the Zemke's Wolfpack. Apart from principles of sound newspaper practice, this making fish of the 4th and fowl of the Wolfpack was quite in order.

By now Peterson had amassed a great log of combat time, he had been shot down once and was showing signs of wear. Then one day he was forced to parachute from a Thunderbolt as he tried to make the English coast. Peterson jumped from less than 1,000 feet and was catapulted into the Channel—his chute had failed to open. However, his chief injury was a black eye.

"I miscalculated the glide of the Thunderbolt," Peterson remarked.

His nerves were beginning to unravel. A little later he returned from a dogfight so exhausted he could scarcely bring the craft home. Whereupon the general grounded Peterson* and from then on Don Blakeslee led the 4th Group in combat.

By the fall of 1943 more and more combat wings of bombers were pasting Germany and their fighter escorts, by means of their drop tanks, were able to escort them further before turning back for lack of fuel. But the fact the fighters had to turn back and leave the bombers at all made it bloody business for the Big Friends, for the Germans had swarms of deadly fighters and they used them with admirable skill and craft.

On Oct. 10, for example, the 4th took the 390th Bomb Group to Munster, Germany. As the bombers approached the target they were so strung out that 50 Thunderbolts could not protect all the bomber boxes. Thirty German fighters soared up as the four-engined planes wheeled over the target. The Thunderbolts ripped into the marauders, but before they could scatter the enemy fighters, Blakeslee was forced to order them to make for England as there was just enough fuel left to make base.

"Horseback to Big Friends," said Blakeslee, "sorry we'll have to leave you now."

For a moment the quiet of the Sunday afternoon was felt as the bomber crews apprehensively watched the fighters make vapor trails for England. The Germans had accurately calculated the time when the 4th

---

*Blakeslee succeeded Peterson Jan. 1, 1944. Peterson helped the Ninth Air Force with its invasion planning and then returned to General Staff and Command School.

would have to turn back. They attacked and an epic battle raged between 10 of the Forts and the Hun swarm. Not until a year later did the AAF release the full story.

The interphone of one bomber exploded with the tail gunner's cry, "Enemy fighters at five, six and seven o'clock, low, hitting the box behind us."

One of the first bombers knocked out of the sky was piloted by Lt. John G. Winant, Jr., son of the U.S. ambassador to the Court of St. James.

A German rocket caught a Fort amidships. It broke in half, and one half nosed up and collided with another Fort. A waist gunner was rocketed out of the flaming, splintered bomber in a grotesque swan dive four miles above Germany. His chest was shot away.

In a short time some 50 aircraft, American and German alike, were burning and crashing to earth. But the majestic Forts—never once in the whole war were they turned back from a target—ground forward on their bomb runs. Still the Germans swarmed in with tempestuous acrobatics. The interiors of the bombers were splattered with blood whose clots froze in the icy blasts screaming through cannon and rocket rents.

"How's the squadron holding up?" asked the bomber leader.

"*What* squadron, captain?" asked the tail gunner. We're up here all alone!"

Another 36 fighters were sighted dead ahead, coming in for a bare-knuckle head-on attack. Bomber ammunition was all but exhausted, the floor was ankle-deep in bullet hulls and wounded gunners bled in them, some dying of their wounds and others dying because they were too weak to connect themselves with oxygen.

A ball turret gunner tracked the Hun fighters with his guns and succeeded in holding some at bay—they didn't know the guns were empty.

White vapor trails appeared to the west, but this time it wasn't enemy fighters. "I felt like yelling and praying at the same time," said a Fort pilot. It was a fresh group of Thunderbolts coming in as part of the relay escort. The German fighters disappeared.

True, 10 of the Forts had been able to destroy 60 German fighters, an amazing performance and far above the average. But eight of the 10 Forts in this one box had been shot down—80 men lost. Had the 4th's Thunderbolts not been forced to turn back for lack of fuel, they could have protected the bombers from this murderous attack. But the Germans had craftily waited for the interim during which the 4th turned back and the next escort relay was on the way. Later, the escort system was worked out so the bombers were not left alone. Meanwhile, the Germans capitalized this fighter weakness and there was talk that the United States would have to abandon daylight bombing the same as Germany and England had.

But by January, 1944 the AAF was completely and irrevocably committed to diurnal bombing. The 4th had become but a small gaggle of the vast air armada marshalled on this emerald flat-top to unleash an air offensive calculated to decimate the Luftwaffe. The undertaking awaited only the pleasure of the weather. By now virtually all of the Eagle Squadron alumni had departed Debden, through enemy action or rotation. The bulletin board in the Officers' Mess had a newspaper photo of Maj. Gus Daymond doing the honors with a butterscotch blonde in Hollywood's Brown Derby. Left were a few Eagles like Blakeslee, Evans, Gentile, Clark, Edner, Beeson and Care. The majority were pilots who had won their wings in the RAF or RCAF but had transferred to the AAF before doing any combat flying.

The Old Grads were likewise disappearing from the scenes across the tracks. For example, the "Abbeville Boys", Goering's own yellow-nosed demons who used to ply their trade in the vicinity of Abbeville, France, were conspicuous by their absence, and Debden heard they had been dispatched to the Russian Front. Luftwaffe pilots were thus very hot in some cases and very clueless, or incompetent, in others. But they came up in growing strength and fought savagely.

One day the 4th's three squadrons were escorting the Big Friends on another mission in the Paris area. Gentile bagged one FW and was pumping away at a second. He roared earthward at about 650 m.p.h., guns flaming. The Hun dived straight into the ground with an orange spray flash and his slipstream almost sucked Gentile into the ground after him. Gentile put the stick in his belly to climb back up to the rest of his squadron.

He had concentrated on his shooting in the dive, serene in the belief that his wing man was screening his tail. As his plane groaned out of the powerful, leaden Thunderbolt dive, Gentile heard the muffled thump of FW 190 cannon fire and saw what is called "corruption" fly over his port wing. Gentile's earphones flapped with the urgent cry of another pilot:

"Break, *Gentile*, break! Break, *Gentile*, you damnfool!" *Gentile* was Gentile's nickname.

Miles away over the Channel, Maj. Gen. Kepner was cruising about following the combat over his radio. To Gen. Kepner the shout sounded like:

"Break, *General*, you damfool!"

General Kepner couldn't imagine who could be flying in combat with enough rank to address him as damfool, but just the same, he told Gentile later, he reefed his Thunderbolt around and broke like mad to port.

Gentile went into a tight turn with the Hun. Not many pilots could turn in a Thunderbolt on the deck with an FW 190, but Gentile had the skill and was too frightened to worry about spinning out. The Hun had his No. 2 glued on his wing and he soon showed Gentile he was a tough adversary. Gentile went shuddering and shaking over the treetops with the two Germans. He was cold with fright, the same as he had been in his green RAF days when he escaped a German assailant with violent black-out turns and pull-outs, thus winning the bet that his body could stand more black-outs than the Germans.

On some reverse turns Gentile squirted what little ammunition he had left after downing the other two Jerries. Now he found himself without ammunition and with two determined, accomplished killers on his tail. In the head-on attacks the Germans discerned that the Thunderbolt's wings were not firing; this made him press the attack that much more resolutely. The Hun peppered Gentile with some 30° deflection shots. Gentile pulled away and flicked down.

One of the Germans had been lost in the maneuvering and Gentile found himself going around in circles over the trees, rawhided by the German. Gentile was defenseless without ammunition; his one chance of surviving the vendetta was to evade the German fire until his ammunition was also exhausted. The German kept pressing for the one brief opportunity of lining the thunderbolt up in his sights. Gentile's hand got clammy on the throttle.

"Help! Help! I'm being clobbered!" Gentile screamed in near panic.

Somewhere above in the clouds the rest of his squadron was flying about. Until this day Gentile remembers the imperturbable drawl of Willard Millikan answering:

"Now, if you will tell me your call sign and approximate position we'll send help."

Gentile shot back, "I'm down here by a railroad track with a 190!"

But Millikan couldn't find Gentile. The duel—cannon vs. flying skill—went on down below. Characteristically, Gentile began talking to himself: ". . . Keep calm, Gentile . . . don't panic."

Gentile still managed to keep one jump ahead of the

German, but his desperation mounted. The Hun was lathered and remorseless, having seen the American clobber the two 190 pilots, his acquaintances and perhaps his friends. He knew by now that the American with the "Donnie Boy" insignia was a superlative pilot; this was a chance to blast an American ace out of the sky without risk. He kept firing, but the American always climbed or banked just inside his line of fire.

Gentile felt like giving up; he was going to be shot down anyway; it would be better to get some altitude and bail out. But he had some last words:

"Horseback, Horseback! If I don't get back—tell 'em I got two 190s!"

The two fighters were flat-out on the deck, down by the railroad track, the German on the American's tail firing. The German began to close the gap. Gentile suddenly honked his ship up and stood it on his prop until it quivered and was ready to stall out. For the first time Gentile had gotten above the Hun and could have swooped down on him for a kill had his ammunition not been exhausted.

Gentile had preserved himself. He had made the Hun fire all his ammunition without hitting him. The German suddenly peeled off and sulked home, his two FW *kamerads* unavenged.

Gentile bounced down the runway at Debden. He didn't bother to gun the motor before switching it off. He was spent and worn, his very fingers heavy with weariness. The intelligence officer jumped on the wing of his plane to interrogate him. Gentile didn't answer, just sitting in the cockpit rolling his eyes and panting.

One of the pilots composed a song to be sung to the tune of *Tramp, Tramp, Tramp, the Boys are Marching*. It became a Debden theme song. The chorus:

Help, Help, I'm being clobbered,
Down here by the railroad track,
Two 190s chase me 'round
And we're damn near to the ground
Tell them I got two if I don't make it back!

6
The American Male at Debden

This particular Red Cross girl wasn't really pretty, but there were compensations. Swimming and tennis had made her brown, firm, smooth. She was nearing 30, but bobby socks and a shrill gaiety helped her appear young enough for the 22-year-old pilot. Too, she was one girl among 1,500 men—a circumstantial belle.

They were jitterbugging to a waltz. He said, "Gee, you're smooth." And she answered, "You're kinda cute yourself."

So he was. When he wasn't flying, he was playing cowboy and Indian over the station on a motorcycle. He didn't hang his .45 automatic up in the locker after a mission as the others did, but dashed about the Officers' Mess with the weapon thumping his leg.

They walked outside by the roses growing on the clubhouse and kissed. He had the kind of skin that grows lobster-red in the course of such interludes. The eyes of both glistened and it would be hard to say whether it was the stimulation of the mating gestures or anticipation.

"Tonight's the night," he said.

"Is everything," she asked, "all fixed up?"

"Yeah, let's get started."

"But not dressed like this," she objected. "I'll go to my room, and get into something else and meet you at the place."

She preceded him to the rendezvous out in the green darkness where 334th Squadron parked its planes. She nimbly climbed into the cockpit of a fighter plane. Soon he appeared and she raised up so he could get beneath her in the seat. She thus sat in his lap and he lashed her to him and both of them to the seat with the safety belt. The motor roared and the throttle grazed her brown knee as he gunned the craft down the runway. The fighter pilot and the Red Cross girl were airborne in the moonlight.

Over Cambridge and out to The Wash the couple flew, close-packed in the metal-smelling little cockpit. He pushed the stick forward and they dived on a barge. The girl pressed the red tit on the stick and the wings of the silver craft flashed orange. She felt the craft bucking to recoil of the six half-inch machine guns. The pilot might not be Gable, but she was certain that few American girls had ever been courted in this fashion.

She gaily turned her blond head to his and kissed him. To express reaction, the pilot stood the plane on its prop. It was not a circumstance which led the pilot to consider such abstractions as the number of court-martial offenses he was committing.

As they taxied up the runway on their return, the pilot's crew chief halted the plane to warn that the squadron commander was waiting. The girl, dressed in G. I. clothes for disguise, jumped into a truck and sped back to the Mess, while the pilot taxied on around to where the major was waiting.

The major jumped up on the wing and poked his head into the cockpit without pausing to speak.

"What's up sir?" asked the pilot sweetly.

"Where've you been and how come these guns have been fired?"

"Well, major, this is my new kite and I just took it out to test-fire the guns."

The major looked into the cockpit again. Then he growled and stalked off to find the joker who had lied that the pilot was flying about with a girl in his lap.

Debden, one soon gathered, was not altogether like

other army establishments. It was the ancestral home of the 4th Fighter Group and its inhabitants were often different from those on other bases, a fact on which all agreed, though not always with the same reasons in mind.

Debden Airdrome, which had become such through the fortuity of a plane crash a decade before, was located in Essex County some two miles from Saffron Walden, which village, we heard, had served Oliver Cromwell as headquarters in the Civil War. It was 45 miles north of London and 15 miles south of Cambridge, and doubtless the dreariest town in all the United Kingdom.

Most of the other 14 fighter groups of the Eighth Air Force were established in dismal Nissen Hut stations, metal tent cities where you slept around a pot-bellied little stove in one county and went to the can in the next county. Debden, contrarily, was a permanent RAF station, which meant steam-heated brick buildings, tennis and squash courts, billiard room, napkin rings, flowers, waitresses, civilian orderlies called batmen and RAF silverware. Both were primitive beside the mahogany furniture, oak paneling and battalions of slave labor servants on permanent Luftwaffe stations in Germany; but nobody knew about that until the war was over, so Debden existed as an oasis of luxury and comfort.

As seen by William F. McDermott of *The Cleveland Plain Dealer:*

AN AMERICAN AIR FORCE FIGHTER BASE, ENGLAND—After having taken board and room in several different bomber stations I thought I ought to get around to a fighter base and see how the other half lives . . . A slightly alcoholized bombardier recently put the prevailing sentiment: "Everytime I see a fighter pilot I want to kiss him. A lot of us wouldn't be here if it wasn't for those babies."

There are photographs and drawings of their former officers on the walls, some long dead, some happily alive and thriving. A famous British artist has his studio in one of the mess hall rooms. The first shot in the Battle of Britain was fired from this post . . . I did not expect the additional comforts this station offers . . . You can have your breakfast as late as 8:30 in pleasant contradistinction with the infantry's stoic 7 a. m., and if you sneak in at 9 o'clock you still have a good chance of being fed. The food is superior to that offered by some de luxe London hotels. It was the first time I had looked an egg in the eye for the several months I have been in England. For the first time on a visit to an air force station I was able to sleep without shivering in the usual sleeping garments . . .

Debden, fair Debden.

A squadron of B-26s landed at Debden once because their field was socked in. One look around and the bomber pilots didn't care if the weather never lifted. Six days passed and the Marauders were still parked around the control tower, looking like great wasps sitting on a clod of clay. The pilots sent G. I. crew members by jeep to fetch their blouses and toothbrushes from their base. The G. I.s returned with many other G. I.s from their station lamely explaining that they were mechanics needed to work on the bombers.

The fog continued to prevent the bombers returning to their base, but over at Debden it was sunny and the fighter pilots and bomber boys would go up to play cops 'n robbers, calling it "bomber affiliation." Lightnings and Thunderbolts from adjoining stations came over to take turns bouncing the bombers. *The Plain Dealer* correspondent had come to chronicle the prowess of the crack 4th Group pilots, but presently the bomber boys, taking full advantage of Debden facilities, had the reporter doing stories on themselves.

Debden had its own chicken farm and the mess secretary had been withholding a fried chicken spread until the bombers who came to dinner went away. But the bomber boys were able to say when they left, "Well, anyway, we stayed until you killed your damn chickens."

The population of the 4th Group at Debden consisted of some 1,500 officers and men, three Red Cross girls, the waitresses in the Officers' Mess, an unending stream of dignitaries bucked down by higher headquarters for a look-see, a detachment of newspaper correspondents and the RAF's *clark* of works (there to see that the Americans didn't improve the place too much).

Of the 1,500 men in a fighter group—a group is the counterpart of a regiment—relatively few are pilots. A group ordinarily is composed of three squadrons, which commonly fly 16 planes each. Each of these squadrons has more than 200 enlisted men—mechanics, armorers, cooks, drivers, clerks. To the three fighter squadrons is added a "service" group of three squadrons; they maintain station utilities and do the third echelon repair work on planes. Working with the enlisted men are non-flying administrative officers, otherwise "paddlefeet", "ground types" or "penguins"—a gentry of O.C.S. hearties without pride of Air Medal or hope of D.F.C. Said Lt. Col. "Stormy" Davis, Lubbock, Tex., of his category: "The only reason they let us in was because there was a war on."

When the Eagle pilots transferred to the AAF in September, 1942, the remainder of the 4th's personnel was RAF. In November some 600 enlisted men and O.

C. S. graduates, erstwhile, "Luper's Troopers"* with officer-candidate do-or-die still gleaming on their gold bars, debarked from the Queens Mary and Elizabeth in the River Clyde. Upon their arrival in this, the land of Cor Blimey, the ground personnel was assigned to the 4th.

In time the RAF personnel moved out, with the exceptions of the WAAFS who married Debdenaires, but the RAF aroma lingered on. Everyone used "actually", even "ectuelly", several times to the Limey's one. "Thank you," "hot darn," "that's good"—all these phrases disappeared from Debden parlance and the word "cheers" served as a lingual universal joint. "Cheers" had many connotations; with the Britons it was a wonderfully pleasant idiom; the same was true in American usage, except that the robust craving for slang among Americans often imbued it with a sardonic overtone. For example, when a soldier was told his pass had been cancelled so he could be put on K. P., he might respond grimly—"Cheers". When he took a drink with someone, glasses were clicked and each quaffer murmured, "Cheers." Somebody lent you a "poon" until payday and you expressed gratitude by saying "Cheers." You met a friend and the greeting was "Cheers, Sheila." Or if taking leave of a friend you would say, instead of so long, "Cheers, Sheila." Or to congratulate a man on a promotion, "Well, cheers, Brown One."

To illustrate both the shades of meaning of cheers, and at the same time the nature of life and the pursuit of happiness in the E.T.O., we have this joyous outburst of a sergeant:

"Cheers, friends. My gal friend's husband has just got the Distinguished Flying Cross! Ain't it wonderful?"

The cliche with the most operational hours was, "It's rough in the E. T. O." Mostly that meant the

---

*After Col. James Luper, widely known in the AAF as a martinet.

weather. England's weather comes from the North Sea and its air is moisture-laden, with months passing and no sight of the sun. *Stars and Stripes* was only half-kidding with a photograph of a sunlight shaft captioned, "That Stuff is Sunshine." The Limeys were always saying, "We had lovely weather the summer the war broke out." The winds are gales and the fog is so thick that London traffic can be immobilized at high noon. No one at Debden could give a plausible explanation of why anybody inhabited England. Caesar wouldn't stay in 55 B.C. The Germans didn't invade in 1940 and who is there to say it wasn't the climate, as much as the Royal *Nivey,* that changed their minds?

Withal, Debden denizens could not but feel a tingle when they debarked in England, for the country was associated in their minds with so much deathless history, from Nell Gwynne to Guy Fawkes, from Runnymeade to No. 10, from the Duchess of Windsor to the Battle of Britain. As they landed, almost everyone could hear the echoes of Mr. Churchill's broadcasts in 1940, the ones they had heard at Sunday dinner, with those phrases that glowed like phosphorous bombs and those lisped, rusty-hinged perorations with the authority of St. Peter's trumpet ... * "We shall go on to the end, we shall fight in France, we shall fight on the seas, and oceans, we shall fight with growing confidence and growing strength in the air, we shall defend our island ... we shall fight on the beaches, we shall fight on the landing grounds, we shall fight in the fields and in the streets, we shall fight in the hills; we shall never surrender, and even if, which I do not for a moment believe, this island or a large part of it were sub-

*Has anybody written a book since June, 1940 without finding a place for this excerpt?

jugated and starving, then our Empire beyond the seas . . . would carry on the struggle, until, in God's good time, the New World, with all its power and might, steps forth to the rescue and the liberation of the Old.''

Every man, however "non-operational" his job might be, felt a sense of participation in this rescue of the Old World by the New. He knew he was in England to play a part in history's most spectacular military operation. Meanwhile, officers and men settled down to life in England, approaching that activity in much the same way as Englishmen had set about colonizing America. Slang for England was Goat Land.

Romances got started in a vapor of boasts. Americans boasted of toilets that flushed, sinks that drained, clean kitchens and sunlight. The English girls chided the "Yanks" for their boastfulness—then boasted of their own modesty! The Americans were at first given to slurring the British currency, belittling the wagon-sized freight cars (goods wagons), moaning about the weather and groaning about the insipid beer—a generally raucous, tiresome bunch of visiting firemen who had forgotten Lt. Gen. Ira Eaker's classic: "Until we've done more fighting, we won't do much talking. We hope that after we're gone, you'll be glad we came." But as time went on, the soldiers lost their sense of being strangers; they adapted themselves to British customs and folkways as no other army could have and blended easily and naturally into the civilian mass. When months later newly arrived soldiers conducted themselves as they had done in the beginning, the veterans frowned on them as foreigners. After the war the Limeys debated whether the Yanks had not influenced the '45 Labor Party landslide. They never became completely reconciled or at ease in the face of American boisterousness and gritty impatience with formalities, but neither were they completely reconciled to the Americans leaving their country. After the war, one English town,

Baldock, had been without G. I.s for two weeks. When others came in, publicans held on to their raincoats to make sure they would return next night. As I saw it, Americans generally felt like shaking Englishmen by the neck to rout them out of what was seen as their "rut"; they refused to give England a full measure of credit for its wonderful war role, but they answered "nobody" when asked: "Well, if you don't like England as an ally—then what country would you choose in her place?"

The first thing the Debden soldier did was to make for the local at the Rose and Crown to order a scotch and soda.

"Sorry," the barmaid would answer, "you've had it."

"Had it, did you say? I just got here."

Somebody would then explain that "had it" is RAFese for you're out of luck, or it's all gone there ain't no more.

At Audley End Station he bought a ticket for Liverpool Street Station for his first 48-hour pass to London, and squeezed on the 5:15. There was standing room only on the trains, a condition which would have prevailed even if the Britons had put their newspapers down. At first the soldier didn't know West End from The City, so he queued up for one of those faded blue cabs that sit up high and gadabout like a maiden aunt come *vis-a-vis* with a long lost lover. Later, when it was ruefully discovered that a British pound sterling is not equivalent to a dollar bill green, he learned to ride the Underground, savoring the names of the stops as he went . . . Eastling Broadway . . . Knightsbridge . . . Marble Arch . . . Chancery Lane . . . Elephant and Castle . . . Charing Cross . . . Oxford Circus . . . Piccadilly Circus . . . East Acton . . . Bank.

On the first trip he started out to do all the historic spots, like the haunts of Dr. Johnson, Goldsmith and

Rare Ben Jonson. He viewed the Blitz scars but was forbidden by the censors to write home about them. He sauntered through the ineffable Piccadilly Circus, capital of America-in-Britain, Leicester Square, the Strand and tiptoed through Westminister Abbey. He took a gander at the Mother of Parliaments and set his watch by Big Ben. He progressed along Birdcage Walk to Buckingham Palace to see the changing of the guards. He whistled up a taxi, the approved method being a trumpeted tax-HEE.

"Take me to 221-B Baker Street."

This archness is old stuff to the driver, but he drives there anyway. The fare found neither Dr. Watson nor Holmes at home, which is probably elementary anyway. Probably out getting the usual 7% cocaine pick-me-up.

If he were an officer, he had more or less had it insofar as sightseeing went. On subsequent 48s he headed straight for the Jules Club on Jermyn Street, or to any of a most formidable array of places he was able to establish himself in. It's just possible that he proceeded to a lecture on the early history of the Belgian Parliament, but if a quorum were needed, it was best to start searching at the Cracker's Club—that dingy little Piccadilly hole with the smell of a "Y" gym through which half the Allies' fighter pilots passed and wrote their names on the walls—and wind through the Studio Club, Lansdowne House, the Garter, Wellington, Embassy and Astor Clubs.

Ah, but the enlisted man on furlough—he covered England like the dew covers Dixie. He was an authentic grassroots plenipotentiary. He was everywhere and stood short nowhere. With less money to spend but with just as much time off as officers, the enlisted soldier saw twice as much of the country and knew its people that much better.

In Piccadilly Circus, about Rainbow Corner, you couldn't see even the big "Bovril" sign for the American olive drab. They walked about with the girls of many nationalities on their arms. White-helmeted M. P.s—a source of ceaseless delight and fascination to Englishmen—stood in the entrances to the Underground, which blew its dank breath into the street, and lay in wait for G. I.s with unbuttoned blouses or one more mild and bitter than they could carry. Through the incredibly congested Circus the lavender-and-old-lace cabs would rage, packed with Americans. You could tell the new arrivals because they rode in clusters of five to eight with the top down, waving a bottle of Scotch and causing the Limeys to remark, "See? The Americans are the reason spirits are in short supply."

Night would fall and Piccadilly would assume the shape which will always be a flashing memory with those who did time in the E. T. O. The blackout was rigid, or at least it would have been had it not been for thousands of G. I.s hurrying about with their torches (Limey for flashlight). You could tell an American from any other in the dark because their flashlights were larger and more powerful. From Lower Regent Street, they made Piccadilly look like a jar of fire-flies in a closet. The Leicester Square theater queues would grow even longer, reaching down Shaftsbury Avenue almost to Piccadilly. At first blackout the celebrated "Piccadilly Commandos" would begin walking the night, as much a part of the scene as the doorman in front of the Regent Palace Hotel. Inappropriately, the famous statue of Eros, God of Love, was crated during the war. They were more an institution than a facility, and few G. I's, (I speak for Debden), permitted themselves a conclusive encounter. They were as alert as a bell captain and aggressive, approaching everything in olive drab with a parroted American slang greeting which was ridiculous when conveyed on a British accent. Their honorariums were enormous (and downright incredible when they walked under a light). But they were an integral part of Piccadilly's teeming, fetid pageantry. A Debden corporal wrote a

73

song, *Lilly from Piccadilly*, which the E.T.O. sang.

Soon the soldier began to feel at home, the first sign being that he spent two days in London without gawking at the barrage balloons loafing over the city. He got caught in air raids and learned to tell the big ones from the little ones by the whistle. He became allergic to exposed lights and blacked them out with reflex action. He began counting British currency as easily as U.S. There was just one thing whose hatefulness never diminished, the weather. Every day he felt as though his skin had accumulated another layer of mold.

Isn't there some Kipling about "single men in barracks don't grow into plaster saints?" Anyway, there were 1,500 officers and men at Debden, for the most part high-spirited American males between the ages of 20 and 30, some 3,000 miles removed from home and trying to forget the fact. Some arrived as virtuosos of the secular life, while others maintained the pretense until they got the hang of it.

Personnel of the 4th Group variously bled and sweated for two and a half years to prove themselves the worst enemy the Germans had among American fighter groups. Generally they relieved the pace with boozing, roistering and giving the girls a break.

Consider a party night on pay day.

In the late afternoon the public address system in the Officers' Club would reverberate with a clarion call:

"There will be a small crap game in the game room."

You would see them bounce up and soon, perhaps $1,500 in sweaty pound notes would be swapping hands.

The approximately 250 officers at Debden bought 700 bottles of throat-scratching whiskey a month (at 75 shillings the blackmarket bottle, that came to $10,500). The Colonel got what few bottles there were of pre-war Haig's Pinch Bottle; majors got the wartime Pinch Bottle; the rest of us got Dennison's.

Girl guests at the dance began arriving at 6 o'clock, from London to Land's End, some on bicycles. They had to sign names and addresses at the guard post at the gate for reasons of military security (this appeared a less pointless precaution later when we learned about German intelligence operations at Debden). They would go into the dining room with their dates for dinner. The girl waitresses tried not to stare at the girls, but having served the officers daily they took a possessive interest in appraising their tastes. Others had a more basic interest. Naturally they were generally disapproving and were not always inarticulate about it.

The enlisted men would likewise be having a party at the Red Cross Aero Club. From miles about groups of girls, most of them British WACS, were fetched in truck convoys. The men were not allowed to take the girls out of the building for walks or talks, one reason being that the Colonel was responsible for getting them back to their stations by midnight. So everything outside the building was off-limits, and especially the air-raid shelters. But love, and its reasonable facsimiles, find a way and the favorite escape exit was a window in the girls' room. There was an unending stream of traffic through this lavatory window, which often brought squeals from girls who had not repaired to the water closet for the purposes of egress.

News of the party at the country club of the E. T. O. spread with the swift pervasiveness of a peace rumor. Many came by plane, among them some privileged girls not subject to rules against civilians in army planes.

One such was a Netherlands ferry pilot. She didn't have a pretty face, but she had some other unforgettables. She was tall, lithe and moved on her long legs with the springy grace of a panther. Not freckles, nor even slacks made her less than an object of mating ardor among the officers. The chief obstruction was a truculent full colonel who squired and attended her with the fierce closeness of Cerberus guarding the gates of Hell.

She and her colonel would roar in over Debden at full throttle in a twin-engine mosquito. Being a ferry pilot she was privileged and able to fly fighter planes. So she would get in a plane and it always appeared that the crew chief was taking an uncommonly long time to help her with the chute harness. Her colonel would get in another craft and they would streak down the runway together. Over the field at low altitude, the two would dog-fight, twisting, twirling, turning, diving, climbing—each trying to get the other in his gunsights. Venus and Adonis had their meadow and glades; Hero and Leander had their Hellespont; Antony and Cleopatra had their houseboat on the Nile—the Colonel and the lady ferry pilot had the blue sky and platinum cloud fleece over Debden.

Still another Red Cross girl from a neighboring field would arrive in an AT-6. Her pilot-chauffeur would allow her to handle the dual controls. A few hours later she would be in the bar holding court for the Junior Birdmen, saying quite seriously, "I have 11½ hours flying time now—how many missions have you flown?"

Debden, fair Debden.

The drawing power of Debden balls could best be seen by the visiting aircraft parked about the control tower. There were P-47s, Lightnings, Mustangs, Marauders, Forts, Libs, Tiger Moths, Lancasters, Typhoons. Even the Navy was represented—PBY Catalinas. Cafe society of the E.T.O. was assembled.

The tone of Debden parties had been handed down by the RAF, whose pilots first occupied the Officers' Mess. Just before the RAF turned the base over to the Americans, an RAF fighter pilot rode down the 150-yard corridor through the building on a motorcycle. The RAF's American successors had no idea of letting Debden's old traditions perish or even languish. On many nights, with a tough show coming up at dawn, everyone would go to a movie, grab a buffet snack, write the folks and go quietly to bed. But other times, especially when weather kept the pilots grounded, you might hear one emptying a clip of .45 calibre slugs into the walls of his room. A pilot whose nerves were on edge with too much combat might be seen to empty his pistol at a roscoe machine that refused to pay off. There were two roommates who sometimes lay on their backs in bed and shot the lights out as the pistol was closer than the light switch.

Most of the parties were conventionally shrill, jitter-buggy and raucous, but undistinguished. On unpredictable occasions, however, overwrought pilots would embark on a binge calculated to take the place of air battles which the weather was precluding. One particular night several of the pilots left the party to commandeer an ambulance, which they filled with flares and smoke pots. All around the perimeter of the flying field they sped in the ambulance. The officer-of-the-day charged after them in a jeep. The back door of the ambulance came open like a bomb bay and the pilots began firing Very gun flares at the pursuing law. The ambulance was the only vehicle on the station without a governor and it pulled away from the O. D.'s jeep like a rum-runner from a revenue agent.

Over flower beds and lawns and smack through rubbish cans the ambulance raced. Before the officers' quarters the ambulance buckled to a stop and one of the occupants opened up on a second story window with a fire extinguisher. The milky stream splattered on the wall just above the head of a North Carolina officer, Capt. Jim Levi. He leaped from the bed, grabbed another fire extinguisher and returned the fire. The stream drenched the assailant below, who murmured, "Gee, light flak."

77

In the dormitory where some of the girl guests stayed for the night and in the building next to it, the pilots placed smoke pots. The girls awakened to see great smoke billows and fled onto the lawn as they were attired at the time, *décolleté* and less. The chubby chaplain sleeping in the adjoining building was likewise awakened, and seeing the ambulance outside the window, concluded that it was an eight-alarm fire. In fact, he decided the staircase was probably blocked by a wall of flame and he would have to leave by the second story window. He ran frantically to the window and looked down.

"Hey, Red!" squeaked the chaplain.

The man looked up and growled, "Aw, I ain't Red."

The chaplain joined the girls in their starboard orbit on the lawn below in what had been the hush of the moonlit night. The pilots sent a salvo of parachute flares up to flood-light the spectacle, which had some similarity to the afternoon of a faun.

In another building, a warrant officer and his wife slept soundly. The dense smoke didn't awaken them immediately, but presently he was waked by an irresistible nausea. He apparently had not thoroughly masticated the ham sandwich he ate before retiring, for when he regurgitated, he looked and decided that about half his liver or some other major organ had left its abdominal moorings.

"Jeez!" he bawled to his wife, "get the medics—I'm dying!"

Then they saw the smoke coiling up at them. They climbed atop the roof, huddling in a blanket beside the chimney. Flares were coming up like star shells.

"Aw, c'mon down," they were told.

"Hell no, we won't come down—just send us some more blankets!"

Cutting your best friend out of his date was considered entirely ethical and elsewhere that night an officer got awfully sore about being rolled. A sinister light gleamed in his eyes. "Hah, I'll fix 'im," he said.

78

Whereupon he went to the upstairs bedroom of the interloper and threw his bed out of the window. He ran downstairs, hauled the bed away and placed it beside the owner's aircraft.

Next day the Colonel ordered the bar closed for 10 days and strafed the ambulance boys with 104s.

Debden, fair Debden.

The greatest American fighter pilot to lead a group into combat with the Germans?

When pilots debated that, nominations were usually closed with the mention of two men. They commanded the two most famous fighter outfits in the U.S. Army. They were:

Col. Hubert Zemke, of Missoula, Mont., commander of the 56th Fighter Group, otherwise the Wolfpack.

Col. Donald James Matthew Blakeslee, 26, of Fairport Harbor, Ohio, commander of the 4th Fighter Group.

One day Lt. Col. Claiborne Kinnard, Jr., of Franklin, Tenn., at the time deputy commander of Blakeslee's group, told 4th Group pilots at a briefing:

"There is not the slightest doubt that Herb Zemke is the most brilliant, gifted and able air leader in the United States Air Corps."

Fourth Group pilots dissented with a snort: "And a pig's sciatica!"

So it is seen that a pilot saw Blakeslee or Zemke as the greater according to which one he had flown with, and certainly that makes it a case of honor for all. Both of them led many pilots who were more deadly at clobbering a Jerry. Zemke was stiff and tense at the controls; Blakeslee couldn't shoot. But each had a fine gift of leadership and generalship that placed them above the others however deadly they may have been. Each shot down a formidable string of Jerries, but their forte was leadership. Each was the generator of his group. Zemke was a well-rounded officer, energetic, relatively polished, reticent but not forbidding. Contrarily, Blakeslee was ill at ease in the administrative sphere of his command. He was rapacious, explosive, easy to drink and jest with, but difficult to understand. Zemke was a student of tactics, whereas Blakeslee played by ear. In some respects Zemke was Tunney to Blakeslee's Dempsey.

This much, however, was not debatable. Blakeslee flew more missions and fought the Luftwaffe longer than any other American pilot. He had more than 1,000 hours of combat operations and a total of between 400 and 500 missions. Other pilots went home for rehabilitation leave when they completed 200 or 300 hours. Blakeslee didn't because home to him was the cockpit of his plane. Blakeslee had been in it so long that one day Cpl. John Cowman, of Sapulpa, Okla., looked out of the window at the planes parked in the gray mist and mused, "I guess Col. Don must have been born under one of those planes."

If, as they say, an institution is but the lengthened shadow of a man, the 4th Group can be explained in terms of Don Blakeslee. In the first place, being a fighter pilot was like nothing else in the war. It could yield an exhilaration such as an infantry man couldn't get from firing a bazooka into Hitler's mouth. One day the group was racing back to Debden after leaving 50 German planes burning and exploding on the ground. A transmitter button got stuck and the pilot didn't know the whole group was listening to him talk to himself. His soliloquy buzzed in the earphones of the other pilots, irritating as a snorer's wheeze. They could hear his panting breath as he mumbled ecstatically:

"Gee those kites really burned . . . Yes, they sure as hell really burned . . . Hah, hah, hah, I sure had a good day today . . . Yes, sir . . . Those bastard planes really burned . . . I looked sharp on that last pass . . . Hah, hah, hah . . . Say, that Me. 109 looked like a P-19 . . . Boy, whatta day I had today."

Doubtless, this same pilot was tight-lipped and reticent when the intelligence officer interrogated him, possibly saying, "Nothing much—just a lot of flak." But inside he was jumping with lumpy excitement. Blakeslee spoke for himself and for the 4th Group's star performers when he said:

"We *love* fighting. Fighting is a *grand sport.*"

Can you imagine a bomber pilot, an infantryman or a medic saying that fighting was a "grand sport"? Their only thrill came with surviving another day's combat. The fighter pilot, Blakeslee in particular, found dogfighting six miles above the earth about the same as knights jousting and breaking lances before the ladies of the court in a tournament. At 7 A.M. a Debden pilot might be eating fresh eggs and reading the *Daily Express*; at 9 A.M. diving on a Focke-Wulf atop a cumulus cloud at 600 m.p.h. and splintering him; at 8 P.M. standing in the glitter of the bar at the Savoy Hotel in London telling his Goat friend how he did it.

A fighter pilot flew a plane such as no civilian could hope to own regardless of purse. The propellers cost something like $3,000. The plane was valued at $65,000. It had cost about $50,000 to train the pilot. In civilian life, the counterpart would be something like Groton, Harvard and a yacht or a polo pony for a graduation present.

Fighter planes are wicked looking and beautiful. Pilots developed physical feeling for them as a cowboy might for his horse. Sometimes they could be seen to pat their planes like a horse, and some said they cared more for their planes than they did for their wives. The pilots got frightened a lot. One of them, whose plane was blasted by a Jerry on his first mission, could never thereafter get into a cockpit without puking and they sent him home. They ate lightly as a class and many couldn't sleep at night. Sometimes they got so tired they wanted to cry. Their nerves became tatters. One pilot would sit at the table and bend the knives and forks double. They might abruptly leave the combat area on seeing a friend crash in a ball of whirring flame. But the thrill of flying a fighter craft and firing its guns was usually enough to nullify the fright and overcome the strain. They got the supreme thrills without the dogface's dirt and squalor.

Their medals accumulated systematically on their tunics and photographers were there to snap the "gong" ceremony. They took the ring out of their hats and, to impart those operational folds and creases, soaked the caps in water or jumped up and down on them. They were acceptably "beat-up" when they began looking like the ear of a hound dog. Fighter pilots were the warrior dandies of the services.

Blakeslee went wild over flying as he watched the Cleveland Air Races. With earnings from the Diamond Alkali Company in Fairport Harbor, he and a friend were able to buy a cub and fly from Willoughby Field. His friend cracked the plane up, however, and the only way Blakeslee could get another was to join the RCAF. He trained in Canada, wonderful days in which he flew over the plains buzzing foxes in a trainer. He had relieved his mother's anxiety by assuring her that he would always be an instructor and never go to combat. He maintained this kind delusion long after he had shot his first German planes down.

Arriving in England May 15, 1941, Blakeslee was assigned to the RAF station at Digby. Soon the RAF commander, Wing Commander Pitcher, told Blakeslee it was his turn to march the enlisted men to Sunday morning worship. Blakeslee insisted that only non-flying officers should have that chore.

"You'll do it or else," said Pitcher. "I'm not joking."

"I won't do it," said Blakeslee.

The "or else" was posting Blakeslee to Biggin Hill,

the RAF's most famous fighter base. Blakeslee quickly demonstrated his ability and got some Huns on the diffident sweeps into France. When he completed his operational tour of 200 hours, they told him he'd have to rest up for a while as an instructor. The only way Blakeslee could remain on combat status was to join "133" Eagle Squadron. Blakeslee had studiously avoided contact with the Eagles.

"They were punks,"* Blakeslee always said. "They would play sister in making their claims."

Flying with them later, Blakeslee shot down a Jerry and bellowed over the radio, "There, you bastards! you see him burning, don't you?"

Flying with "133", Blakeslee served briefly as its commander and brought his combat time up to 400 hours. When the 4th was formed, Blakeslee was commissioned a pilot, whereas Peterson and three others got majorities. This soured Blakeslee.

Blakeslee succeeded Peterson as commander of the 4th Group only on the understanding that the job would in no way curtail his participation in the Grand Sport. Blakeslee fought the Germans almost daily for more than three years with none of the rests pilots normally take. His career extended from the days when fighters were being bold if they flew 10 miles into enemy-held Europe to the day he led the 4th from England to Russia. He came back from a mission with 71 cannon holes in his Thunderbolt. Upstairs and downstairs, the Germans shot at him for more than three years. His spoor was on every major air battle field from Dieppe to Berlin.

Said the Germans to some 4th pilots who had been shot down and captured:

"How's old Don Blakeslee? Guess we just never will get him. But we'd swap all you fellows for him alone."

Blakeslee was Old Man River, he just kept rolling

---

*As a matter of fact, he used another four-letter word.

along. His rapacious enthusiasm for combat seemed to flourish on the dangers and strains that killed or exhausted other pilots. He had some sort of durability and resilience denied the others.

With respect to physical capacity, Blakeslee was a Paul Bunyon sort of a man. Stories abound of his capacity at the bar. For three years he confounded fellow flyers by an ability to drink all night and fly all day. Back in his RAF days he was making for his hotel in London's gray daybreak when he encountered a Bobby.

"Have a drink with me," Blakeslee said.

"Thank you, sir, but I'm just coming on duty," the Bobby said.

"Now, look, if I can drink all night and take a drink, you can certainly take just one after a night's rest."

He got the Bobby drunk.

The mess secretary came wringing his hands, complaining that the Junior Birdmen were smashing the beer mugs on the bar as they emptied them. "Good show," said Blakeslee. "Shows their spirit." With that, he cracked a few himself.

Blakeslee never painted swastikas on his plane to show the number of Germans he had shot down, he never painted a name on his craft and never wore a white scarf except once, of which more anon. The "WDC" letters on his kite and the "Don Blakeslee" stamped on his leather flying jacket were eloquent enough in his case.

Blakeslee was a handsome man, a six-footer with pale blue eyes, ruddy face, wavy hair and very small feet. His shoulders were so square they seemed to own a dyhedral angle. He was quick and vigorous in his movements. His personality was magnetic. He spoke rapidly and violently in a baritone voice that always stood out from the magpie jabber on the radio. A *Cleveland Plain Dealer* correspondent saw Blakeslee this way:

"He's a reticent fellow of shy and modest demeanor. You felt that words came to him with effort and that he blushed like a boy when he told of matters related to himself. I asked him if he ever felt like quitting. Blakeslee paused soberly and said: 'The first time I saw a plane falling in flames, I was hard hit. It was a good friend of mine. What am I doing here? I asked myself. That's the first and last time that's happened to me. You miss a man when he goes, but it doesn't affect you in the same way.' "

Top-flight pilots of the 4th could shoot better than Blakeslee. "Hell, I can't hit the side of a barn," he would laugh. "There's no sport in it for a guy who can shoot straight. The sport comes when somebody like me has to pull up behind 'em and start shooting to find out where the bullets are going—like spraying flowers with a garden hose."

Blakeslee's worth lay in his matchless capacities as an air leader. He was everywhere in the battle, twisting and climbing, bellowing and blaspheming, warning and exhorting. His ability to keep things taped in a fight with 40 or 50 planes skidding and turning at 400 miles an hour was a source of wonder. On one Berlin attack, Blakeslee was chosen to direct all the fighter planes in the Eighth Air Force, the magnitude of which assignment is understood when one considers that even No. 1s and 2s had difficulty in staying together in combat. That was approximately 800 planes. Taking a group as a regiment, Blakeslee was commanding 15 regiments—an army.

Having engaged the Germans more often perhaps than any other U.S. soldier, ground or flying, Blakeslee had no superstitions connected with survival. Many pilots refused to have their picture shot at the take-off lest it jinx them. "That's kid stuff," Blakeslee once snapped. "It's whether your number is up."

In three years of absorption in killing and averting death, Blakeslee had been living at 400 m.p.h. amid Hun cannon fire and he was not, therefore, geared to restraint and the techniques of tact. When he was considering the Army of Occupation, it was pointed out that he didn't speak German. To which objection he snorted, "Hell *we're* the conquerors—let the Germans speak *our* language!

Blakeslee went about leading his group of pilot-pariahs into battle with inexhaustible zest. The qualities that made him an outstanding leader were those that have made leaders in all wars: decisiveness, boldness, personal magnetism and zest for battle. Others flew 200 or 300 hours of combat and retired to instructing; Blakeslee flew more than 1,000 and never thought of quitting.

"You don't have to worry about pilot fatigue," Blakeslee said, "as long as you've still got your enthusiasm."

And so Blakeslee was up early in the morning to lead every mission, and if he hadn't been to bed he went just the same. No other pilot at Debden had his stamina. What accounted for his durability, the ability to go on and on while others flagged or dropped out?

One thing was his physical endowment; he appeared to be made of cast iron laced together with steel cables. There was some Finnish blood in him and perhaps from that he got some of the stamina that makes Finns great marathon runners.

Another quality was will. An intimate once said: "I don't care what it is, if that man just wills it, it will happen." A girl once held a lighted cigarette to his cheek and kept moving the red ember closer to his jowl to make him turn his head. He had bet he couldn't be made to move. The fire touched his cheek. He didn't turn his head. This is perhaps not an adult means of employing one's will, but it was the same quality which kept him fighting the Germans for 3½ years.

A third thing was, Blakeslee found the maximum outlet for his talents and personality at Debden. He wanted to stay in the army always so "I can fly hot planes." At Debden Blakeslee led the life of a feudal baron. Debden was a duchy. Blakeslee was lord of all he surveyed and the pilots were his admiring lieges and retainers who hunted wild boar with him. Blakeslee led them in hunts in the skies over Europe. Then he returned to sit by the fire, surrounded by his lieges, court jesters and equerries, rehearsing and discussing the intricacies of the hunt and draining numerous hogsheads, often until it was time to brief for the next hunt—a "grand sport".

Blakeslee

WEREWOLF OF THE WOLFPACK

Col. Hubert Zemke, Missoula, Mont., a great fighter pilot, leader and outstanding professional soldier. He led the rival 76th Thunderbolt Group. Every man at Debden admired "Hub" Zemke. So did every man in the Luftwaffe.

Col. Blakeslee on return from the first Berlin attack. He was chosen to lead the spearhead.
Maj. Godfrey and Maj. Glover rehearse the way in which Glover talked Godfrey out of bailing. Note Godfrey's hand. He wore the meat off pumping the primer to get back to England.

335th FIGHTER SQUADRON

(On Prop) Maj. Pierce W. McKennon, Ft. Smith, Ark., commanding.

(Left to right—top row) Lt. August W. Rabe, Yonkers, N. Y.; F/O Lucian W. Freeman, Norwich, Conn.; Lt. Hugh W. Lindsay, Paoli, Pa.; Lt. Thomas H. Elffner, Fowler, Kan.; Lt. Calvin W. Willruth, Lancaster, Mass.; Lt. Mack D. Heaton, Piedmont, S. C.; Lt. Kenneth Green, Trafford, Pa.; Lt. Robert Hunter, Jr., Johnstown, Pa.; Lt. George D. Green, Whittier, Calif.; Lt. Robert L. Couse, Asbury Park, N. J.

(Left to right—second row) Lt. Orval C. Miles, Cloverdale, Oreg.; Capt. William H. George, Orlando, Fla.; Lt. Charles L. Brock, Lockhart, Tex.; Lt. H. Stanley Rasmussen, Oakland, Calif.; Lt. Enoch Jungling, Carlton, Ore.; Capt. Albert J. Davis, Ogden, Utah; Capt. Shelton W. Monroe, Waycross, Ga.; Lt. Robert A. Cammer, Houston, Tex.; Lt. Loton D. Jennings, Wayne, Me.; Lt. Robert C. Buchholz, Oaklahoma City, Okla.

(Left to right—bottom row) Capt. George H. Davis, Berlin, Md.; Lt. Charles E. Konsler, Utica, Ky.; Lt. Olin A. Kiser, New Philadelphia, O.; Lt. Stanley W. Conners, Albany, Calif.; Lt. Robert J. Mabie, Marshalltown, Ia.; Lt. Paul J. Lucas, Jr., Shamoki, Pa.; Lt. David R. Allen, Saddle River, N. J.; Lt. Henry A. Lee, Hampton, Va.; Lt. Leslie L. Burgess, Norwich, Conn.; Lt. Robert C. Hawley, Portville, N. Y.; Lt. Charles B. Greenlese, Memphis, Tenn.; Lt. James E. Halligan, Jr., Boston, Mass.

[Picture posed in January, 1945.]

336th FIGHTER SQUADRON

(Left to right—in prop) Maj. Fred W. Glover (C. O.), Asheville, N. C., commanding; Capt. LeRoy A. Carpenter, Jr., Austin, Tex.

(Left to right—top row) Lt. Maurice W. Miller, Jr., Jackson Heights, N. Y.; F/O Donald P. Baugh, Sioux City, Ia.; Lt. Robert O. Davis, Tallahassee, Fla.; Lt. William H. Ayer, Egypt, Mass.; Lt. Richard E. Moore, Barstow, Ill.; Lt. Douglas N. Groshong, Selma, Calif.; Lt. John W. Izant, Cleveland Heights, O.; Lt. James F. Hileman, New Kensington, Pa.; Lt. Van E. Chandler, Waxahachie, Tex.; Lt. Harry N. Hagan, Yorkville, O.; Capt. Joe H. Joiner, Corpus Christi, Tex.; Lt. Donald J. Pierini, Trenton, N. J.

(Left to right—second row) Lt. Harold H. Frederick, Oakland City, Ind.; Lt. Thomas A. McCord, Oracle, Ariz.; Lt. Wilmer W. Collins, Lyons, Ga.; Lt. Benjamin L. Griffin, Jacksonville, Fla.; Lt. Woodrow W. Schaefer, Yoakum, Tex.; Lt. Richard J. Corbett, Madison, Wisc.; Capt. Carl R. Alfred, Atwater, O.; Capt. William D. Riedel, Ault, Col.; Lt. Earl F. Hustwit, Pittsburgh, Pa.

(Left to right—third row) Maj. John D. McFarlane, Calais, Me.; Lt. Harold R. Crawford, Jr., Seattle, Wash.; Lt. Douglas P. Pedersen, Long Beach, Calif.; Lt. Paul M. Morgan, Lexington, Ky.; Lt. B. O. Brooker, Jr., Columbia, S. C.; Lt. Henry A. Kaul, Oak Park, Ill.; Lt. Francis M. Grove, Hanover, Pa.; Lt. Franklin W. Young, Marmora, N. J.; Lt. Melvin N. Dickey, Tampa, Fla.; Lt. Robert J. Cavallo, Wilmington, Ill.; Lt. Harry L. Davis, Cotulla, Tex.; Lt. G. E. Ridler, East Orange, N. J.

(Left to right—bottom row) Lt. Melvin C. Franklin, Middletown, O.; Lt. John P. Murchake, Jr., Annapolis, Md.; Lt. William H. Hastings, Washington Court House, O.

[Picture posed in January, 1945.]

334th FIGHTER SQUADRON

(Left to right—top row) Lt. Charles W. Harre, Brownstown, Ill.; Capt. Thomas R. Bell, Shawboro, N. C.; Lt. Carl G. Payne, San Antonio, Tex.; Lt. Robert S. Voyles, Belle Fourche, S. D.; Lt. Clarence L. Boretsky, Milwaukee, Wisc.; Lt. Kenneth E. Foster, Oil City, Pa.; Lt. Andrew C. Lacy, Sullivan, O.; F/O Alvin L. Hand, Newton, Pa.

(Left to right—second row) Lt. Arthur R. Bowers, Tiskilwa, Ill.; Lt. William J. Dvorak, Western Springs, Ill.; Lt. Lewis F. Wells, Quitman, Ga.; Lt. Jack D. McFadden, Brookville, Pa.; Lt. Paul E. Burnett, Cushing, Okla.; Lt. Calvin H. Beason, Anderson, Ind.; Lt. James W. Ayers, Tulsa, Okla.; Lt. Michael J. Kennedy, Philadelphia, Pa.; Capt. William F. Hedrick, Redondo Beach, Calif.; Lt. Timothy J. Cronin, Oconomowoc, Wisc.; Capt. Ben Q. Ezzell (I.O.), Harlingen, Tex.

(Left to right—third row) Lt. Raymond A. Dyer, Glassport, Pa.; Capt. Robert H. Kanaga, Harbor Beach, Mich.; Lt. Kenneth G. Helfrecht, Madison, Wisc.; Lt. Joseph E. Gallant, Chelsea, Mass.; Lt. William O. Antonides, Carbondale, Col.; Capt. David W. Howe, East Hickory, Pa.; Lt. Jerome E. Jahnke, Los Angeles, Calif.; Lt. William B. Hoelscher, Indianapolis, Ind.; Lt. Donald M. Malmsten, Burwell, Nebr.

(Left to right—bottom row) Lt. Conrad J. Ingold (I. O.), New York, N. Y.; Maj. Louis H. Norley, Conrad, Mont., commanding; Capt. Gerald E. Montgomery, Littlefield, Tex.; Lt. Edward J. Woznaik, Girard, O.; Lt. Leo C. Garcin, Bay City, Mich.; Lt. Alan Skirball, Columbus, O.; Lt. William C. Spencer, LaGrande, Ore.

[Picture posed in January, 1945.]

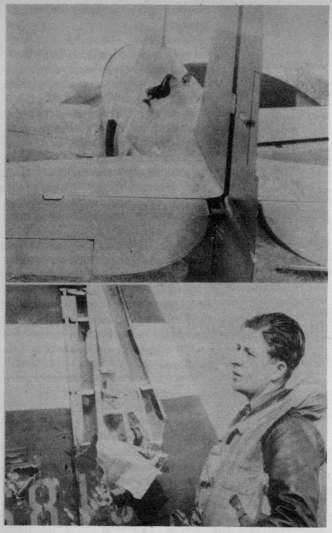

A Hun pumped 68 cannon shells into Blakeslee's Thunderbolt before Goodson clobbered him.
Beeson wonders how he flew this flakked-up Mustang back from Germany. So do we.

End of the trail: Col. Blakeslee is greeted by Maj. Gen. Kepner, C.O., 2nd Air Division, on return from history-making escort from Britain to Russia. Blakeslee went to London for relaxation amid B-bombardment.

Acknowledgment: These shot almost all the pictures in this journal. They are (back row, left to right): Sgt. Raymond Bogenschultz, Eggertsville, N. Y.; Lt. Albert B. Olson, Niagara Falls, N. Y.; Cpl. Edward Gilman, Somerville, Mass.

Front row—Cpl. John Mooney, Crystal Lake, Ill.; S'Sgt. Isadore Swerdel, Perth Amboy, N. J.; Sgt. John Roback, Rochester, N. Y.

Virginia Irwin of the St. Louis Post-Dispatch interviewing the "Salem Representative", otherwise Kid Hofer, and Duke. She was a premier war correspondent, was discredited for preceding armies to Berlin—and given a year's bonus by the boss, Joseph Pulitzer.

"BEE"

Lt. Col. Duane W. Beeson, Boise, Idaho, after his release from a German prison, where he was put in solitary for calling a German a Hun. He was a master of deflection shooting. His combat films were close-ups of burning splinters and deceased Germans.

"THE COWBOY"

Capt. Nicholas Megura, Ansonia, Conn., one of the most violent pilots in combat. He once got in the circuit over Tempelhof Airdrome at Berlin and flew around with the Jerries like he was an FW 190 pilot. He once screeched at a fellow pilot: "Attack that Jerry, you son-of-a-bitch, or I'll have you court-martialed!"

"KING OF STRAFERS"

*Maj. James A. Goodson, Toronto and New York, now representative,
Aviation Division, Goodyear.*

SIX ACES

Lt. Col. Duane Beeson (clockwise), Capt. "Cowboy" Megura, Maj.
John Godfrey, Maj. James Goodson and (center) Maj. Don Gentile.

Maj. Willard Millikan with daughter and English wife, Ruby, with
whom he lived between missions in a nearby village.
"Tonight and Every Night", you remember, was about the Windmill
Theater in London. Here is the chorus on a visit to Debden. (It was
rough, brother, rough in the E.T.O.)

Debden Officers' Mess

Where Bubbles held forth in Saffron-Walden. Wonder if the spirits are still in short supply? They can't blame it on the cheeky Yanks any more.
Station Headquarters.

North Gate entrance to Debden Airdrome.
Officers' Mess.
Officers' Quarters.

G. I. MESS
1. *In.*
2. *Out.*

HAPPY RETURNS

A Debden party on the occasion of Col. Stewart's birthday. A circus tent (above) was rented for the occasion and erected on the greensward in front of the Officers' Mess.

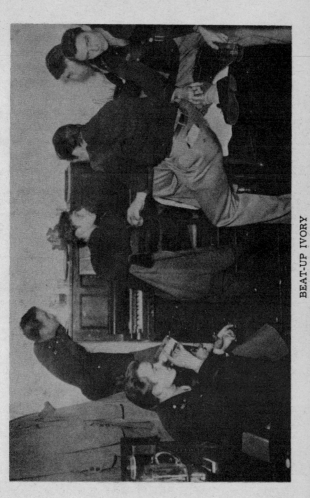

BEAT-UP IVORY

McKennon at boogie-woogie console. Without McKennon—why, without him we might have gotten some sleep.

Blakeslee Briefing . . .

Courtesy ILLUSTRATED

Tea for seven after a rough mission. Cheers, mite.
E.T.O. cafe society foregathered at Debden.

British WAAF learning whatever the sergeant is trying to teach her at this Aero Club do.
Lt. Henry S. Sedmak, of Detroit, the provost-marshal, marries a British WREN.

Debden was 40 miles from London and this is Audley End Station, from which departed the 1:20 for Liverpool Street Station.

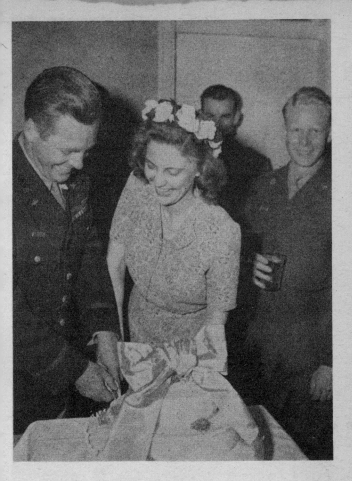

Lt. Col. Sidney Woods, Somerton, Ariz., married Sally, the Red Cross representative, at Debden.

Mrs. FDR visits Debden. Shakes hands with Maj. Gus Daymond, an Eagle Squadron luminary, and Col. Edward Anderson, first C.O. of the 4th Fighter Group.
Col. Everett W. Stewart briefs the 4th on the morning the Allies smashed over the Rhine.

Ram-rodding one of the six half-inch machine guns carried in the wings of the P-51 Mustang.

Capt. Vermont Garrison, Mt. Victory, Ky.

8
The Blakesleewaffe

The men flying with Blakeslee, among them some of the AAF's outstanding aces, were "characters" and as dissimilar in personality and background as Andrew and Judge Hardy. Other groups were largely composed of youngsters fresh out of high school or college, but in the great days of the 4th the pilots were in the soldier-of-fortune mold.

There was, for example, the austere Lt. Col. Roy W. Evans, of San Bernardino, Calif., 29 years old and barren of a single thing suggesting the callow, downy-lipped-hot-rock-fighter-pilot type. He never affected a white scarf and the cowling of his plane was as bare of names and pictures as a Lady Godiva with page-boy bob. Evans had been a fireman for the Santa Fe Railroad and was about to get his engineer's papers when railroading began to interfere too much with his private flying. Santa Fe said it was the other way around. Howbeit, Evans quit and joined one of the Eagle Squadrons.

Sinewy, tall and powerful, Evans had the look of a stiff-necked Eagle about him. Again, he looked like a truculent school teacher who was ready to thrash fractious pupils two at a time. A rather harsh man with a propensity for starchy discipline, Evans was a teetotaler who had no patience with pilots given to drinking and who saw no sense in the dances sponsored by the Officers' Club. He removed the tubes from his radio when on leave. Withal, he was very well liked and highly respected as a pilot. Crafty and fierce in combat, Evans professed to feel like a spent

121

old man in the club at night, but never too spent for a game of checkers or snooker. Later he was shot down while escorting bombers over Dresden and imprisoned by the Germans. After his liberation he made for Debden. Somebody asked if it was flak or a Jerry pilot which brought him down.*

"A Jerry shoot *me* down?" Evans replied disdainfully.

There was James A. Clark, Jr., of Howell's Lane, Westbury, L. I., who later became a lieutenant colonel and deputy group commander. Clark could lead the group and carry the courses, altitudes, weather conditions and rendezvous times in his tawny head, but ask him his age (24) and usually he couldn't remember offhand.

Tall, blue-eyed and uncommonly handsome, Clark was the nephew of the famous polo player, Tommy Hitchcock. Hitchcock had had a celebrated career in World War I as a member of the LaFayette Escadrille. He had run away from home to volunteer in this fighter outfit, which was the counterpart of the Eagle Squadrons. Possibly his uncle's example had something to do with Clark's leaving school to join the RAF instead of the AAF, as some of his peace-preferring friends did. Hitchcock frequently visited his nephew at Debden. He was killed in a Mustang the day before Clark married Lady Bridget-Elliot, daughter of an English earl. Clark was an aloof man of strange diffidence who once argued against his promotion to captain and insisted he shouldn't be awarded the D.F.C.

Bee ... Maj. Duane W. Beeson, 22, of Boise, Idaho, 334th Squadron.

Beeson was undoubtedly one of the two or three deadliest pilots the 4th produced. He set the pace for

---

*I saw Evans last in January, 1946 at Maxwell Field, Ala.

destroying German planes and his rivalry with Don Gentile did much to get the group started in its record-smashing.

A diminutive fellow with big hands and wrists, Beeson had the bodily architecture of a boy not quite grown. His voice was strident and his accent harshly western. His manner was aggressive and he was intense to the point of fretfulness. He was intelligent but naive. Once, for example, he was loudly agitated because the local paper made his crew chief out as a flier. The crew chief was embarrassed because he naturally never flew and objected to having the folks at home consider him a hero. Beeson, strongly attached to his crew chief, raised hell. It was explained that the story, written by the Debden P.R.O., had simply been misconstrued by the headline writer, ignorantly but not maliciously.

"Okay, then," said Beeson seriously, "why don't you just make a rule that the newspapers have to use your stuff just like you write it?"

"Look here, Beeson," I exploded, "the President of the United States has been protesting about his treatment in the papers since the latter part of Term No. 1. He's the commander-in-chief of the whole damn thing, and he can't control a newspaper in the slightest degree because the Constitution—"

"Well, just the same," he said, unconvinced, "you could tell 'em."

Beeson had a lot of drive, he was analytic and naturally disposed to bore in at the why of things. He and others referred to him as Bee. He was fastidious and painstaking in everything and not one comma of his combat reports would his intelligence officer, Capt. Ben. Ezzell, of Harlingen, Tex., alter without permission.

Beeson had planned to become a lawyer and, to obtain the money, had sold magazines and hitch-hiked to Oakland, Calif, where he became a hotel clerk. The war deranged his plans and he wound up in the RAF.

123

In the RAF he was always spoiling to go out and kill Germans, having picked up an unaccountable Hun phobia somewhere along the line. The elder statesmen of his Eagle Squadron patronized him and sometimes treated him as a pest. He was said to have cracked up several planes through pilot error. But before it was over, he shot down more than twice as many Germans as the highest scorer among the Eagles.

At Debden Beeson built his own gunnery gadget and practiced deflection shooting. Accurate, deadly shooting was a science he had mastered and the science was a passion with him. He assiduously studied the methods and techniques of the great fighter pilots before him, and braced his elbows against the cockpit when firing after the fashion of "Sailor" Malan, a great RAF ace (32 kills). Beeson was probably the only pilot in the AAF to hold both hands on the stick and to press the tit with left thumb to fire.

Beeson was a passionate assailant and his attacks were made in a fuming frenzy. He worked out a technique for bouncing a Hun and opening fire before the others in the squadron could split-ess. New pilots in his squadron often decided that their idol had clay feet because they saw him overshoot a Jerry in attacking, but the old ones knew that this overshooting was deliberate and purposeful, as the maneuver obviated the necessity of slowing down and making of himself a more favorable target for any Jerry which might have gotten on his tail.

He was deadly, this little man who looked like a boy. It showed in his combat film. Either he'd get so close that the film would show Jerry pieces flying as if splintered with an axe, or so close that oil from the Jerry plane would spray and cloud his cine camera in the wing so it couldn't photograph the pieces.

Kid Hofer ... Lt. Ralph Hofer, of Salem, Mo., 334th Squadron. Hofer vaulted from the boxing ring into the RCAF, the resin still on his shoes. Hofer won a trophy in 1940 in the light-heavyweight division of the Golden Gloves Tournament. He also played semipro football in a Chicago league, but his specialty was boxing. He had met Billy Conn in Chicago's Trafton Gymnasium and Conn had gone a few rounds with him. Later, Hofer did some professional fighting under the name of Halbrook. He liked the "scientific angle" of fighting, but he didn't relish hurting anybody, and also vice versa.

In 1941 Hofer was in Detroit, bound for California, where there were some very good purses to be picked up in American Legion bouts. He was waiting around in Detroit for the '42 Hudsons to roll off the line, having made an arrangement through which he was to deliver the car to a West Coast agent in return for the transportation and expenses. One afternoon he crossed over to Windsor, Ontario for a look-see. When he emerged from the tunnel under the Detroit River, an immigration officer stopped him.

"Came over to join up in the RCAF, I suppose?" said the officer, thinking Hofer had come as scores before him.

"Well, I—"

"That building right over there is where you go," cut in the official.

Hofer had never been near an airplane, nor had the slightest interest in them. Inside the building, however, youngsters from all over the U.S. greeted him and infected him with their own enthusiasm. "Wonderful deal," they told Kid Hofer. Somebody shoved an application form Hofer's way. It looked like a darn good idea to Hofer. He signed.

The others went out to lunch. The RCAF officer began calling off names from the list; only Hofer was there to answer. Off he was sent for RCAF cadet training in the States.

One afternoon he was riding down Chicago's Lake Street in a black Nash sedan, the owner of which sat beside him and was pretty. She thought Hofer was pretty, too, in his blue cadet uniform. Suddenly a Buick pulled out in front and caused Hofer to jam on the brakes. The driver jumped out and hurried up to Hofer.

"I've been looking for you!" the man said.

"Who, me? I—" Hofer began, wondering whether he had run a red light or whether the girl was married.

"Tell you what I want. I want to know if that's an authentic RAF cadet uniform and if you are a cadet?"

"The answer is yes."

"Well, that's great. I'm an advertising man. Got a studio over on Michigan Boulevard and Coca-Cola is my client. I want you to pose in that uniform with an American cadet and a Coke bottle. I'll want about five shots and I'll give you 10 bucks for each."

"Naw, I—"

"Oh, go on and do it, Ralph," warbled the girl.

It was to be the advertising man's last job as he was an artillery captain and he had already changed into his uniform to leave. Kid Hofer and the American cadet posed together in such fashion as not to steal the show from the Coca-Cola bottle.

"Okay, sport, that's fine," said the man. "Here's your money. We plan these campaigns a long time ahead, but in about two years you'll see it on our billboards in every place. The slogan will be 'Thirst Knows No Boundaries', Limey and American cadet together—get it?"

"Yes, sir, Thirst Knows No Boundaries."

"Don't forget, you'll be seeing yourself on billboards in about two years."

The man was wrong about one thing—Hofer wouldn't get to see the billboards because he was in England, running up a remarkable bag of Jerries in a remarkably unorthodox way. He would get on the deck and wait for the others to flush the Jerries down to him.

Hofer was tall and powerfully built; it was difficult

126

to reconcile his frame with his chronic smile and guileless manner. He let his hair grow into a chestnut mane and he wore a snake ring and a football jersey with the number 78 on it. Hofer commenced bagging Huns as unceremoniously as he had enlisted in the RCAF. It was an accepted axiom that a pilot flew 10 to 12 missions before his eyes were good enough to even see a Hun, let alone bag one. But Kid Hofer bagged a 190 on his first mission and astonished all by gaily diving down to strafe a flak boat in the Channel. The veterans said pilots could not get a Jerry the first trip, but Hofer had combat film to show for it. It didn't take him long to become the only flight officer in England with five swastikas on his kite.

Hofer appeared to have a gay disregard for all the dangers European skies held. No other pilot in the group would prowl about there without a wing man, and preferably a squadron. Not so Hofer, who was out to see how many Huns he could bag. He got a bang out of the Salem Chamber of Commerce passing resolutions eulogizing his part in the global war and the newspaper clippings. One day he had to turn back from a mission because the wing tank wasn't feeding, but his mechanic quickly fixed it and Hofer took off before he was checked in. He took a spin around Holland and Belgium, scouring for Huns and blazing away at flak posts in the Zuider Zee. On his return he saw Lt. Col. Clark bouncing over the grass towards his plane. "I'm in for it now," Hofer murmured to his crew chief.

"Where the hell you been, Hofer?" Clark angrily asked.

"Sir, I had to turn back," said Hofer.

"But these guns have been fired. Explain that."

"Oh, that, sir, I—well, I did that before I aborted," said Hofer.

Another time he was on the tail of a Jerry blasting away. He could see the half-inch slugs ripping into the Hun, but the Hun suddenly pulled away and left him, for Hofer had used up the gas in his fuselage tank and had forgotten to switch over to his wing tanks, Meanwhile, another pilot whipped in and opened fire on Kid Hofer's Hun.

"Break! Break!" shouted Hofer.

The pilot, led to believe that a Jerry was barreling in on his tail, broke sharply to port and Hofer zoomed in to resume his firing and destroy the Hun.

Millie ... Captain Willard W. Millikan, 26, of Malvern, Ia., 336th Squadron. Millikan, like Beeson, became a great pilot and good officer by perseverance. Pre-war life was a pretty serious operation to Millie because he had to hack his way. To qualify as aviation cadet Millie had to have about $350 worth of dental work. In flying school he got to worrying about how he was going to pay this money back, the result being that he clutched the stick instead of caressing it. And the school—the same Lindbergh Field at San Diego from which Peterson was purged—washed Millie out for lack of flying ability. So Millie gravitated into the RCAF. The RCAF instructor advised Millikan to go in for ferry flying as he was sure to kill himself in fighter craft.

"No thanks," said Millie gravely, "I'll be a fighter pilot." Millie flew 52 missions before he skidded over behind a Hun at Emden and got his first kill. Millie was very studious about his flying and was forever plumping for bigger and better pre-mission consultations between flight leaders and pilots, a province in which the 4th was always weak.

Millie had married an English girl and there was a baby daughter with 3½ teeth. Many of the pilots grew cautious when they married or fell in love; not so, Millikan.

The Greek ... Lt. Spiro (Steve) Pissanos, of Athens, Greece and Plainfield, N.J., 335th Squadron. Steve was a man who talked with feeling and elaborate gestures about whatever he was talking about. He was chronically excited about things in general, and in particular, about the Greek who had become an American officer.

Steve was jet-propelled by impulses, the most consequential of which seized him as a boy of 15 in Athens near the olive groves where Plato and Aristotle exalted cold reason above emotion. A mechanic in Athens on the way to work, Steve stopped suddenly, spellbound by the spectacle of two Greek Air Force biplanes doing acrobatics.

"I was crazy, I guess," Steve would say later, "Instead of going on to my work I walked 20 miles to the airdrome. And I did the same thing every day. I cannot tell you how angry my father was. But I made friends with the pilots and they gave me some free rides. I did anything to get to hang around the drome."

One day the Greek squadron leader asked, "What the hell have you been doing around here?"

Steve said he wanted to fly, but they wouldn't let him on account of his age. But the fliers let him live in the hangar and he started going to school at night. School meant as much to Steve as it would have to Puck and he was promptly flunked out of high school. Thus thwarted in becoming a Greek army flier, Steve reacted with excitement, which was but a loud garb for a strong determination. He called upon Premier Metaxas and described his aspirations. Steve was elegantly explosive in his petition, but he got nowhere.

"So," Steve remembers, "I just went right to the Royal Palace and asked to see King George. I explain I have no money, no nothing—I just wanted to do this flying business. But no soap. I got damn mad with all this foolishness! There was nobody to pay any attention to me and what I really want to do. I say okay, then I leave the country—that's what!"

So Steve left Greece to her fate and signed on as a

129

crew member of a steamship bound for America, but always the vessel docked in a South American port. The seventh crossing got him to New York.

"There I was, boy, I had no money, no friends, but the main thing was I could not speak English, no. Boy, I tell you, those were some days."

On the subway The Greek was mightily gratified if he could read the Gothic streamers in the *New York Daily News*. Maybe someday he would be able to read the stories as well.

"I got a job in a restaurant because that work takes less talk than any other. You know, you can cooperate without understanding much or saying much, you know, boy?"

The restaurant was Hatchitt's, 149th at Broadway. There in the summer of 1938 the mercurial young Greek, pixilated with a desire to become a pilot, became a pantry boy for the next nine months.

"I always find that the best way to learn anything is to copy it down," Steve would say. "So all the words I have trouble with I write down on pieces of paper. The easy ones I put here (tapping his posterior) and the hard ones I put here (tapping his breast pocket just under his DFC). It took me an hour to ride from my room on 33rd Street to Hatchitt's. I suddenly see this is time I should spend well. I studied whatever I had in my pockets, here and here."

Steve started his flying lessons; he made $15.00 a week and the lessons cost $12.00. The proprietor's daughter, Elizabeth, took an interest in his ambition and bucked him up by cooking Greek dishes for him. She offered to lend Steve $500.00, but he declined because it appeared inconceivable that the pantry boy could ever repay such a sum.

"I tell you, boy," Steve would say, "This $12 a lesson was getting me. You know—clobber the Greek! Somebody asked why I didn't take flying at a New Jersey field—cheaper, you know. So this girl Elizabeth and I find out about it. I asked them how somebody could learn to fly around here. I found a field where it was more in my reach to go after the CAA license. I got a job as pantry boy at the Park Hotel in Plainfield, N. J. I was the boy making the seafood cocktails and giving out the desserts. I tell you boy, it was rough. I opened 1,000 oysters—look at this hand here!—from the clams and oysters. By this time my Engeleesh it was getting better, you know. But I still had all this navigation stuff to learn. I discovered that the hotel's menus had a big white space on them. If you come to Plainfield now I bet you find 1,000 menus with my navigation problems scratched on them!"

By October, 1942 Steve was an American citizen, the first to become one under provisions of the modified overseas naturalization law. That night the mirror over the Debden bar bore this Bon-Ami legend:

"TONIGHT THE DRINKS ARE ON STEVE PISSANOS— AMERICAN."

Thenceforward Steve gave his home address as Plainfield and in looking back over it, he often said with mist in his eyes:

"Sometimes I think of those people who laughed because the pantry boy wanted to fly. I'm not much, I know, but it gives me pleasure to think I came to America with $8 and couldn't even speak the language—and now I'm an officer of the United States Army. I don't care who knows, boy—I'm proud of that, I tell you, boy!"

Steve bagged five Jerries to qualify as an ace. When he was shot down, he couldn't jump from the wing of his plane because his chute harness became entangled with the cockpit lever. Standing on the wing of the stricken plane, Steve held the stick and with no rudder control, crash-landed with the plane. He was asked later what remarkable combination of phenomena had permitted him to land a ship while standing on the wing. He rolled his eyes and responded fervently:

"Donta ask me—aska that Man up there!"

Goody . . . Maj. James A. Goodson, 23, of Toronto, Canada, 336th Squadron. Goodson gravitated to Debden by land, sea, and air. Before he could become an aviation cadet, he had to be a pantry boy on a Cunard liner; before he ever flew a Spit or a T-Bolt, he had to be torpedoed at sea.

Goodson had black hair with eyes and mustache to match. His eyebrows were arched, physically and mentally. He was sardonic in German, French, and, I believe, Greek. Goodson was not perceptibly displeased if told he had the countenance of a junior Mephistopheles. He was well-endowed intellectually and, both by nature and cultivation, uncommonly self-possessed. Having seen so much of the world, having lived so adventurously and having addressed himself to the job of being a sophisticate, Goodson probably would have considered it a minor indignity to encounter anything, from the realm of duel with a long-nosed 190 to the realm of metaphysics, that disconcerted him. He loved his sardonic jests. One day he was to lead the group on the longest mission ever undertaken by fighters, actually or in Jules Verne. The course ran off the board and another map of Poland was held up alongside. Goodson told the pilots:

"At this point you will pass within 50 miles of neutral Sweden. Er—not too many, please, unless you have to."

Goodson was born in America of British parents, but came up in Toronto. After high school he felt impelled to see something of the world and, for that matter, to allow the world to see something of Goodson. So he put to sea, of which experience he said:

"Having no money, I traveled from Winnipeg, Canada to Liverpool, England for half a crown, or 50 cents. That, I spent for dinner in Cornwall my first night out. Outside of Winnipeg I was thumbing a ride. A trailer with seven college boys stopped. They were stewed as goats. They wanted to know if I could cook and I lied that I could. Could I drive? I lied again and climbed aboard. However, in the course of the junket I learned to perform acceptably in both capacities. The boys remained drunk and amiable.

"After passing through the States we returned and at Cornwall I set about catching another ride. An automobile dealer came along in a hearse he had bought for the motor in it. When we stopped at night he said I could sleep in the hearse if I wished. I didn't, but where else? Along came two men to open the door of the hearse. The louts opened the hearse door. A corpse suddenly came to life and sat upright. That was me. They retreated in some haste."

Summer of 1939 found Goodson aboard a Cunard liner as pantry boy, bound for England, of which he said:

"I crossed over to France and was in Paris when the Germans marched into Poland. There was very little excitement over the war and at first they didn't black-out the lights about the Arc de Triomphe. I returned to England and found everyone looking for gas masks and preparing for the blackout. I decided that if the English were excited I'd better get the same way."

Goodson booked passage to Canada. The vessel: the S. S. *Athenia.*

Now Scotsmen are supposed to have what is called *fey*, a cross between a crystal ball and clairvoyance. It was this fey which prompted one Scotsman aboard to remark:

"All my life I have been trying to get to America, but even now, sailing here, I somehow feel I won't make it."

"Oh, don't worry, old man," soothed Goodson, "of

133

course you will."

The *Athenia* was off the Hebrides when the U-Boat's torpedo struck. Goodson was below decks, near the third-class dining room.

"The sauce cook," Goodson related with detachment, "was scalded with his hot sauce. The grill cook was thrown against the grill and had striped grill sears on his back. The fish cook was blown to the top deck. As I passed the hatch on which the Scot and I had talked about his premonition, I saw him. He was purple and dead."

After some work with the *Athenia's* medical party, Goodson swam to a lifeboat.

"There were some American college girls in the boat, cool as cucumbers they were," Goodson recounted. "They were put aboard a Norwegian tanker. Wet and scantily clad—and I do mean scantily clad and wet—they were rushed to shelter in the hold, where the seamen were sleeping. The sailors awakened and saw what they saw. They didn't know whether it was a dream or reality—nor cared."

Before the year was out Goodson had gypsy feet again. This time it was an oil tanker, the M. V. *Montrolite*, and he had advanced from pantry boy to steward. On his return to Canada from this junket he was able to enlist in the RCAF. By 1941 he was back in England and found himself occupied with the caprices of gliders. The instructor did not even pretend to know more than his charges about gliders and they set out to learn together.

"At first," Goodson remembered, "we found the slipstream was pulling the tail of the tug plane down. We adjusted for this and the slipstream pulled the tug's tail up. By the time it came my turn to fly the glider, the tug pilots had got where they'd trip their own release at less than the slightest provocation. A friend of mine crashed in a woman's back yard and she said, ' You're just in time for tea.' "

Mike ... Maj. Winslow M. Sobanski, 24, of Warsaw, Poland and New York, 334th Squadron. Sobanski was born in the U.S., but by September, 1939 when the Germans invaded Poland, Sobanski was a student at the University of Warsaw. He tried to enlist in the Polish Air Force, but was told there was no time for training. He became an infantryman instead and boarded a troop train for the Vistula Front. German bombers wrecked the train and Sobanski with it. They pulled him from the rubble and put him aboard another train. Lying on straw, he rode for five days before he arrived at a hospital, where he had to wait two nights for treatment. It became necessary to move on again, for the Germans were advancing. Near Brest-Litovsk, Sobanski and other wounded were captured by the Germans. No one thought Sobanski could walk, so he wasn't guarded, and was able to walk out of the infirmary into the night.

Back at Warsaw he changed to civilian clothes and observed the Huns going over in black waves of 80. He limped to his home in Warsaw and found it had been shattered. Sobanski was joined by his father as he rooted about in the debris for anything he might salvage of his home. News of the sinking of the *Athenia* reached Warsaw, but Sobanski had no way to know that, as he dodged the Gestapo, a future cohort, Goodson, was abandoning the *Athenia.*

Sobanski eluded the Gestapo until April when he was able to obtain a U.S. visa by means of his American citizenship. By summer he had reached members of his family in New York. In the same apartment building resided James C. Cater. Sobanski and Cater didn't meet then, but four years later they met over Germany, Sobanski in a fighter, Cater, in a bomber. Both figured in the news stories of the mission and the *United Press* noted that Cater and

Sobanski both gave 400 East 57th Street* as their New York address. The *U. P.* phoned Debden:

"Tell Sobanski that I just talked to Cater and he said that after seeing what the fighters did to the Jerries he wants to meet Sobanski—and kiss him."

Tall and powerful with a hawkish countenance, Sobanski had a nostril scar to remind him of the Germans. Sobanski was methodical and once after his squadron had dive-bombed a German drome and alerted the golf-ball gunners, he said over the radio with thick and solemn accent:

"I go back down now to photograph the damage."

After he began killing Germans and strafing their trains, Sobanski became more and more mellow, to the point of coltishness.

Gentle . . . Capt Don Salvadore Gentile, 23, of Piqua, Ohio, 336th Squadron. Gentile began to take his flying and courtship seriously at an early age. Until his senior year at Central High School Gentile's life was uneventful. He played football with hope of an Ohio University football scholarship. A nine-cylinder homemade airplane and a blonde complicated matters.

Gentile loved speed. In the family Lincoln-Zephyr he raced the Piqua cops and when he called for his date, her mama was likely to caution, "Now Don, if I let my daughter go out with you, I'll expect you to drive carefully." But one night when Gentile called, the girl had already left with a rival. Gentile tailed the boy home that night and asked for an explanation. It apparently was not a satisfactory explanation as Gen-

---

*This is the address of Sobanski's foster father, Harry Bruno, fighter pilot of World War I, aviation pioneer and celebrated author (**Wings Over America**). After the war I was a guest of the Brunos at this address. Mr. Bruno told me that, due to language difficulties, Sobanski was washed out in Canada by the RCAF. Sobanski phoned long distance: "Harry, dis is Mike. Der **bawstards** have washed me out, what do you think!" Mr. Bruno called his old friend, Marshal Bishop, the greatest of all fighter pilots in two wars. Bishop fixed it and Sobanski got his wings on the second try.

tile beat him up. Nor, apparently, was it a satisfactory explanation that Gentile gave Judge Smith in court next day, for the judge fined him $30 and court costs.

Flying lessons made Gentile crave a plane of his own. He secretly drew $300 from his account, accumulated from wages earned as waiter in his father's Genoa (night) Club, and bought a nine-cylinder crate from a man at the airport. A few hours later the Gentile phone rang and a self-appointed underground in the person of an anonymous female neighbor said to Mrs. Gentile:

"I won't call any names, but there is a man who has just sold your son an airplane and he's going to kill himself. He has just got hold of an airplane a I think it is a crying shame as he's bound to be killed."

"A what—an airplane? My Don?"

"That's right, Mrs. Gentile, an airplane!"

Gentile's parents bounced him when he reached home. His mama boxed his ears and talked with Mr. Gentile about having the man arrested for selling an airplane to a minor, which certainly must be a violation of some law. But Gentile continued to pester his parents until father bought peace by buying him an Aero-Sports biplane.

Gentile buzzed the school house, Gentile buzzed the water tower, Gentile buzzed the blonde's house on Roosevelt Ave., as well the one on Ash St., and Officers Strickland and Studebaker of the Piqua constabulary put the buzzer on the elder Gentile.

"If your son doesn't stop this low flying," they fumed, "we're going to jail him—he's a menace."

And Gentile would beg off in the immemorial fashion of boys, "Aw gee, pop, I won't do it no more, I promise."

In the summer after graduation from high school, Gentile was working for Jackson Steel Mill to take on a little more heft for a football career. He wanted to be an army pilot, but lacked the requisite college credits for enlistment in the AAF. He thereupon persuaded his parents, who were Italian immigrants, to permit him to enlist in the RAF. He came over on the boat with Jim Clark, who was very quiet and couldn't bear crowds.

Gentile and Clark found themselves assigned as instructors, a pain in the sciatica to them. One day Gentile took off in his Spitfire and flew over a stadium where a dog race was in progress. Gentile did a wingover and dived on the track. Up one side and down the other Gentile roared at horseback level. The spectators in the grandstand panicked, some mistaking the Spitfire for a German raider.

The man in the red coat riding the white horse gave a blast of his silver horn, tally-hoed, jumped from his steed and took shelter. The greyhounds reacted variously, some reversing their field, some jumping fences—all of them running faster than ever their ancestors ran. Only the mechanical rabbit carried on as before.

When Gentile landed at his base, he was sharply rebuked and confined to quarters. Being one of the pampered American fliers, Gentile was not court-martialed. Instead, he was posted to another outfit and relieved of his duties as instructor, which was the way he had planned it. The new outfit was "133" Eagle Squadron and the commander was Don Blakeslee.

In January, 1944, just before the Eighth AF undertook its offensive to erase the Luftwaffe, Gentile could be seen on the long winter nights by the fire with a cigar. Gentile sat quiet and expressionless on those nights and you would have put him down as stolid and unresponsive. In fact, he struck me then as a negative, wax-like figure. And, for the most part, most of us judged the book by the cover. Even Blakeslee, who had flown with Gentile for a couple of years, failed to recognize the skill and daring of this languid, seemingly torpid character. Others thought him simple. Truth was, Gentile had decided he was going to shoot down more Jerries than anybody else in the group and he was planning how he was going to do it.

When the squadron commander didn't put Gentile on the board for a mission, he would manage to muscle in by going as a spare, several of which were dispatched on missions to take the place of any who had to return to base because of engine trouble.

Gentile was closer to the The Greek than the others, probably because he was the son of Italian immigrants, and they roomed together. The effusive, bounding Greek loved to muss Gentile's hair, always oiled and preened like Mrs. Astor's horse. Gentile would push The Greek's hand away in peevish irritation—he was seeing gaggles of ME 109's flying line abreast in the blue haze of his cigar smoke. Gentile felt that he had learned a great deal from his tangle with the 190 down by the railroad track and he had developed an almost serene confidence in himself. His confidence was not the blatant, raw cockiness that some displayed, but a calculation that he probably could out-fight any German. Invariably, however, he would say in a high-pitched voice after a mean show, "Man, I sure had a close call today." Once when he was still tense from a bad clobbering, I kidded him because he had destroyed only one Jerry instead of the usual two or three. Gentile responded with a petulant, "Hell, man, I was fighting for my life today!" But a bath and cigar caused the conception of his ever being shot down to spiral-dive right out of his thoughts. This bland, puncture-proof confidence was subtly revealed in the fact that Gentile had saved around $8,000 since entering the service. In short, he wasn't blowing his money because of any we-who-are-about-to-die compulsion.

Capt. John T. Godfrey, 21 of Woonsocket, R.I., 336th Squadron. Godfrey was destined to become an outstanding American warrior, to destroy more enemy aircraft than any other pilot in the 4th and to become a national hero in whose honor factory whistles were blown, military parades staged and war bond rallies held. But at home, in his teens, Godfrey was the subject of many anxious family consultations.

His parents were prosperous people who were troubled because Godrey wouldn't go to college and take his higher learning like a man. In fact, he just would stay in high school. He was moody, reckless and appeared to be shiftless. His salient feature was his set of darting, gypsy-black eyes. They later proved the keenest eyes in the 4th, disciplined, radar eyes that could spot enemy specks in the sky miles away. But in 1940, they had a restless, faraway expression that reflected Godfrey's maladjustment.

At 18, Godfrey ran away from home to Canada to join the Montreal Regiment. His father retrieved him and he went to work in the Navy yard at Providence. Soon he ran again, but this time his father, with a better idea of where to look, overtook him before he got farther than the Boston station.

But Godfrey still rebelled at going to college. Finally, in August, 1941, his despairing parents made a covenant with him. It was agreed that he could go to Canada and try to enter the RCAF to become a fighter pilot. If he failed, he would come back and go to college. He never went to college.

Soon after his acceptance by the RCAF, his Canadian colonel unaccountably directed him to take a two weeks, leave. Once at home he learned why. His father and mother met him at the station and told him that his brother, Reginald, an airplane technician, had been torpedoed by the Germans as he sailed to England.

The recklessness and perverse rebelliousness that had handicapped Godfrey in civilian life found an outlet in war, as so often happened, and were mainsprings in the equipment which made him one of the AAF's great pilots. These qualities were tempered with grimness over his brother's death at the hands of the Germans. He painted *Reggie's Reply* on his plane. The "reply" was such that after the war the French government exhibited his plane in Paris under the Eiffel Tower.

Maj. Fred W. Glover, of Asheville, N. C., 336th Squadron. Glover didn't unpack the first night he arrived at Debden because it didn't seem likely that he would still be a member of the 4th Group the next morning. Blakeslee was in the bar with some of the other pilots when Glover was brought in. He had never been to combat and had been a Lightning ferry pilot.

"Hm-m-m, hot Lightning pilot, huh?" Blakeslee jeered.

"Well, I think I can fly a plane as good as anybody else I see around here—SIR," Glover snapped, looking Blakeslee square in the eyes.

"Have a drink," Blakeslee snarled. It was an order, a sort of smile-when-you-say-that.

"I've had a drink," demurred Glover in his husky voice.

Afterwards they became intimates when Blakeslee found that Glover was one of the few who loved fighting the Germans as much as he did.

Glover had played professional baseball and had been farmed out by the Cardinals, but since he would never talk about it much, one was left to conclude that his success was modest. Once he saw a pilot of the Flying Tigers return home to receive acclaim and adulation. Glover never forgot this. He set his compass by what he saw and it helped him on to become a great pilot himself.

Glover was touchy and bellicose, which was self-doubt flying in the inverted position. Glover, accompanied by several pilot-cronies, appeared at Ft.

141

McPherson, Ga. one day to enlist in the AAF for cadet training and was told, "The army can't use you." To which Glover replied, "Well, to hell with you, friend!"

Glover came to England as a pilot in the RCAF, but was assigned to ferrying planes instead of combat. Glover stormed and fretted. He wanted to be a fighter pilot. They wouldn't hear him, so he took an Oxford transport up and power-dived it. He didn't get killed and the scheme worked. That is, when Glover taxied up to the control tower, canvas and wires were dragging the runway like a bridal train and they got rid of Glover by sending him to combat with the 4th.

Glover roomed with Maj. Louis (Red Dog) Norley, of Conrad, Mont. Red Dog, a tireless clown and one of the most intelligent of the pilots, was red-headed but his nickname was derived from his matchless capacity to lose money at Red Dog poker. Red Dog called Glover "No-Nose." One of Red Dog's friends was named Rose and she was not offended by the name Rose Dog.

In later days No-Nose Glover and Red Dog Norley were both squadron commanders and the very best of friends except for certain interludes after a beat-up of enemy airdromes or dogfight, when the intelligence sections would try to get the squadron scores straight. They would all be on a conference phone. No-Nose and Red Dog then became competitors and no epithet was too strong to hurl.

"How many did your squadron get, Red Dog?" the group intelligence officer would ask.

"We got six in the air," Red Dog would say.

"I'll be damn if you did, Red Dog!" No-Nose would cut in. "You got 5½. You got to share one of those with us."

"Are you kidding, partner?" Red Dog would rasp.

"Now listen here, goddamnit, Fredericks bounced that character just as he dipped in that cloud and got strikes," Glover would come back. The pilots of each would be crowding around as the smoke started coming off the phones.

"Now looka here, No-Nose, you know damn well that Jerry wasn't hurt and we're not sharing a goddamn thing."

Each would pause to take another shot of "operational" whiskey, each pilot being entitled to two ounces of medicinal whiskey after every mission as it calmed the nerves and helped intelligence officers get the entire story.

"Now listen to me, Red Dog, just hold on, don't panic, don't panic . . ."

"Nobody's going to panic but my No. 2 was the one who clobbered that Jerry and . . ."

"Now listen to me, Red Dog . . .."

Etc.

They were immensely fond of each other, but they would fall out in about the same way that two hunters, the best of friends, get murder in their eyes on a dove field in an argument over which one really hit the bird that fell between their two stands. The rivalry between squadrons was one of the things that stimulated the pilots to take such a keen edge of rapacious aggression.

Glover never got enough of combat and lived the game like a Dodger fan. On the wall before his bed was a map of the Continent and he spent long hours gazing at it, until he knew every railway crossing and Luftwaffe drome in Germany. He was a great natural pilot and in combat inspired the admiration of those in his squadron for the animal cunning and craft with which he stalked Huns.

The Cowboy . . . Capt. Nicholas Megura, 24, of Ansonia, Conn., 334th Squadron. Some called him Twitcher and the name would probably have stuck had not Cowboy been used first. The president of Phillips University probably had another name for Megura. In his freshman year at the university some roistering

143

sophomores came to the dormitory and doused the freshmen with water. Retaliating with a fire extinguisher, one of the freshmen scattered the sophomores.

The authorities said the freshman would have to clean up the damage as a matter of discipline. The freshman rebelled and was expelled. Megura then wrote home for some money and with another excommunicated scholar, purchased a Model "A" and began touring the States. They hit 46 States and returned to Ansonia.

Things might have quieted down had not Megura acquired a motorcycle. His mother said the motorcycle was dangerous, that he would have to get rid of it. Upshot of her insistence was that she chased Megura off "that dangerous thing" into the cockpit of a warplane, for Megura left home and went to work for Vought-Sikorski in the blueprint division and began flying on the side. September, 1941 found him in England, an RAF instructor. He was on the point of being sent to India when the AAF began accepting transferees from the RAF.

Megura moved about like a jack-in-the-box with St. Vitus Dance. He talked fast, jerkily and in such disjointed fashion as to be incoherent when excited. His intelligence officer could rarely get the picture from him. The only way a war correspondent could keep him still long enough for an interview was to put his leg on the arm of his chair and block his fidgety path.

When his crew chief saw him coming from a mission he started getting out a new set of spark plugs because it was invariable that Megura bellowed, "Get a new set of plugs in that goddamn kite—are you trying to get me killed?"

On the day he was presented America's second highest award for valor, the D. S. C., he also was fined $10.00 for bawling out a major in headquarters of the 65th Fighter Wing. In the end, the Cowboy, too erratic to be shot down by a Jerry, was clobbered by a

144

Lightning pilot who mistook his Mustang for a 109. Megura tried to bail out of his plane over Germany, but the canopy would not come off and he glided to neutral Sweden. That was wonderful good luck, but when Megura returned to Debden months later he raised hell with his engineering officer because the canopy wouldn't jettison. But of all this, more later.

The Deacon . . . Maj. Howard W. Hively, of Athens and Columbus, Ohio, also Norman, Oklahoma, 334th Squadron. The Deacon doubtless got his scientific bent from his father, a West Virginia physician and political figure. He was after an engineering degree at the University of Oklahoma when *geo-morphology* entered his life.

"I was sitting up in Dr. Melton's class in economic geology," Deacon related, "when he mentioned flying. This woke me up. Now geology is the newest of sciences, and his specialty was *geo-morphology*, the very newest part of the newest science. It is derived from *geo*, meaning earth, and *morphology*, meaning form—earth-form. Get it?

"Well, Dr. Melton believed that a great deal could be learned about the possibility of oil deposits by studying earth form and contour in aerial photographs. So to get these photographs from the air, he paid the rental on the planes and I flew 'em. We covered the whole state in Piper Cubs, Stinsons, Cessnas.

"He and I formed a course in *geo-morphology* in 1939, one of those short courses, but I can't say we made too much money. So I got to fooling around with oil leases and tried to form an aeroexploration firm. But nobody would listen."

In the Baker's Hotel in Dallas the Deacon saw a poster inviting Americans to join the RAF's Eagle Squadrons. He fetched his log book from his car and asked, "Can you use me?" They could, and that's when Deacon began to live.

Deacon and a half dozen others were dispatched to Baker's Field, Calif, for fighter pilot training. The Deacon fell in with the Hollywood set, among them, Willis Hunt, a rich yacht broker who at the time was wed to actress Carole Landis. Hunt loved speed so much that he used to fill in as a motorcycle cop in Hollywood. Hunt parties in the swank Sunset Tower Apartments were memorable.

At Baker's Field the RAF maintained civilian instructors and five AT-6 trainer planes for the Americans who had volunteered to fight in England, which activity seemed very remote to Deacon as he, Willis and Carole flashed around Beverly Hills in a Lincoln-Continental.

The nice thing about the RAF's AT-6s was they had no markings on them and hence there was no way to identify them in flight. They were two-seater planes and just the things to give the girl friend a ride in. Thus Californians would often see a flight of five AT-6s cruising up and down the state at night. What they couldn't see was that the rear seat carried a girl in evening dress, being squired by air to some distant pleasure resort by RAF cadets.

One night Deacon was up giving Lt. Hank Ayers some instrument time. Flying back from Los Angeles, they thought of their favorite haunt, the Ritz Bar at Baker's Field, and of the buxom pianist, Millie, a young woman of many excellences.

"Let's buzz Millie," said Deacon over the intercom.

"Why not?" agreed Ayers.

They turned on the navigation and landing lights to blind anyone who might try to look up at them and came down on the Ritz full throttle. The glasses jumped about on the table as on a Ouija board.

"Pretty low, huh?" asked Deacon.

"Damn low," replied Ayers.

"Er, how low, Hank?"

"Well, as we pulled up, I counted the lights in the

146

hotel. We were four stories high."

Bill Seaton, civilian commander of the RAF field, was already on the phone to his operations officer:

"Find out what sonofabitch is flying that AT-6. I live on the fifth floor of this hotel and I had to look *down* to see it!"

Attired in civilian clothes, Deacon arrived in England Sept. 1, 1941. Like most everyone, he sauntered down to Piccadilly Circus, got drunk and went to the dance at Covent Gardens. A clerical error soon had him taking a Commando course, but after a time he got back to flying.

The Boards missed a great bet in Deacon and his act, *The Red Ace*. At Debden dances Deacon always put it on at the interval (Limey for intermission). You could rarely see it because the people were too tightly packed about him, but you could hear the whine of a diving, climbing, twisting, turning fighter plane on the microphone, punctuated by machine gun bursts. The Red Ace, God rest his torque, was the sum total of all the untoward things that could happen to a pilot. He personified the fall guy. His motor stalled when he took off. He was doused by his own glycol. He was attacked by friendly aircraft, he was clobbered by Huns. His parachute didn't open, nor his dinghy inflate. He almost clobbered a Jerry once, but someone yelled "break" and took the victory from him. The Red Ace earned but one decoration, the Purple Heart.

Deacon was the last of the Eagle Squadron pilots to leave Debden. It was something about a fist-fight in front of the Officers' Club with a lieutenant colonel. But again, that's getting ahead of the story.

Mac . . . Pierce W. McKennon, 24, of Forth Smith, Ark., 335th Squadron. Mac, who logically and appropriately roomed with Deacon, was the son of a venerable Fort Smith doctor. Up to and including high school days, it was plain as a pikestaff that Mac would become a sawbones and inherit his father's practice, or that he would become a concert pianist. Dr. McKennon naturally cherished, as a father will, the hope that his manchild would choose medicine and assume his mantle. As might be expected of a doting mother, Mrs. McKennon hoped that Pierce would choose music and guilefully gave him a Baby Grand on his 16th birthday to foster the choice.

Both parental aspirations were warranted as Mac was a restrained, dutiful boy who, in a tri-state contest, had won first prize with his sensational renditions of *Staccato Etude* (Rubenstein) and *La Campenella* (Paganni-Lizt). And with the *Prelude in G-Sharp Minor,* Mac won third place in the contest. Which performances earned him a music scholarship at the University of Arkansas.

But after three weeks of music study at the University, some gremlin invaded Mac and he had a seizure of chronic, incurable howdy-howdy-hi addiction. It was down with Beethoven and Mozart—up with Calloway and Goodman. Mac told the professor there was a suitable recess in which to file DeBussy's works and deserted to the campus swing band. He hung a cigaret on his underlip and took the veil as a boogie-woogie virtuoso. His talents came to full fruition at Debden, where he arrived via the RCAF after the AAF had washed him out of primary training as unfit. The paint on the piano slowly peeled off as if exposed to a blow torch. Mrs. McKennon would not have been surprised to hear that her son compelled the admiration of all with his renditions of the classics, but she wouldn't have been thinking of a repertoire whose *pièce de résistance* was *Slow Train Through Arkansas,* and next to that, *That Hypothetical, Theoretical Son-of-a-Bitch Columbo.*

Nor would it have brought aught but a gratified smile to the face of Dr. McKennon to learn that his

eldest, despite the stern stresses of gladiatorial encounters with the wily Hun, was still a voracious student, that, as a matter of fact, he read with such concentration and devotion as to require a nudge when
briefings started. At least two pilots swore they had
seen Mac reading in his cockpit over the Zuider Zee
one day. Reviewing the Oath of Hippocrates or delv-
ing into the precepts of Osler, no doubt. Well, not exactly, Dr. McKennon—*Riders of the Purple Sage,
Singing Guns,* and such like. For Mac's money, cattle
rustlers, the marshal and the lone prairie were more
exciting than Huns, Allied pilots and the skies over
Europe (although it might be said that he found the
blonde from Baldock more exciting than Calamity
Jane). Anyway, when Mac wasn't engaged in some of
the more sensational combat encounters of the war, or
hunting rabbits on the flying field with jeep and
flashlight, he was stretched in the semi-supine soaking up Western thrillers, eyes popping, cigaret burning fingers.

Mac was tall and well proportioned, fast and agile.
He had an acute sense of mimicry and gift for
slapstick. Every movement was a rhythm. At the
piano in the lounge during the periods of bad weather,
Mac was a one-man morale section. Deacon would
take the Red Ace aloft and make him bail out in the
Channel and then Mac would take over the howdy-
howdy-hi console. His performances were blent of the
dance of Indians and the whirl of dervishes, Lennox
Ave. and the whistles of trains in the night and the
dead pan of Ned Sparks. A cigaret would hang on the
starboard underlip; a beer mug would ring the piano
at 10 o'clock to his flailing, nimble fingers ... *The
Slow Train Through Arkansas* was picking up speed
on a piney-wood grade ... What chance did a fellow
like Beethoven have at Debden?

149

Seven League Boots

One day in the spring of 1944 the German radio, in a propaganda broadcast, sent a message to Debden: "We know what kind of aircraft you Eagle Squadron boys are flying now."

The P-51 Mustang.

The 4th Group had swapped its Thunderbolts for Mustangs. True, many of the misgivings about the Thunderbolt had faded, and Col. Zemke's Wolfpack was proving it to be an adequate fighter craft (later models were much improved with paddle-bladed props and water injections). But to the ex-Eagles the Thunderbolt was a lumbering, over-rated crate that wouldn't climb, wouldn't turn, and whose cockpit had a way of gathering smoke from burning oil, often unnerving the pilot. Contrarily, the Mustang was in the manner of a Spitfire, fragile and waspish beside the massive Thunderbolt, but wicked looking with its clipped wings and razor back.

The pilots had craved Mustangs since 1943. In a personal interview, Col. Peterson had entreated Gen. Arnold, AAF chief, to order grand-scale production. In the autumn of 1943 it appeared that the 4th might be equipped with Mustangs. But priority on the then slender production went to the Ninth AF, which was building up as the tactical air force for D-Day.

So for a time the 4th went moodily on, flying Thunderbolts. It was a lack-lustre period for the 4th. They were saying the Thunderbolt was not fit for combat, but at the same time the Zemke Wolfpack was racking up impressive combat records. For a time the pilots were not supposed to go below 18,000 feet as the plane was sluggish below that. There were orders that the primary job was protecting bombers and tangling with Hun fighters was secondary. But all the time the Wolfpack was knocking Huns down 10 to 15 a mission, increasing its lead in planes destroyed.

The 4th Group, living in glory echoing from RAF Eagle Squadron days, accepted the fine performance of the Wolfpack with churlish ill grace. The 4th had destroyed 150 enemy aircraft, while the 56th had a bag of 300. The ex-Eagles moulted and sulked and explained to the satisfaction of none, "They boogar off and don't protect the bombers like we do," or, "Oh, they're just getting a lot of that easy-meat twin-engined stuff." Again, they pointed out—factually—that the Wolfpack's base at Halesworth was on the coast and gave them 15 or 20 minutes more scouting time over Germany.

But the ground crews at Debden were getting fed up with gassing and overhauling fighter planes whose guns were fired with relative infrequency. These ground crews, who led a wretched life in the cold and fog, didn't feel like putting out, just like a fine bird dog that trots home if he keeps flushing quail and the hunter misses them. There were ill-humored grunts when the first of the new armor-piercing incendiaries went to the Wolfpack. Blakeslee took it differently: "No, they've been doing the fighting lately, they rate 'em. Just wait."

In December, 1943, the 354th Mustang outfit, "The Pioneer Group" of the Ninth AF, arrived in England. They were a great bunch of pilots, as they afterwards proved, but they needed someone to lead them on their first few missions to show them around. Blakeslee was the natural choice.

He went over to the 354th base and led the group on several missions. But each night Blakeslee flew back to Debden, pearl of the E.T.O., explaining that he couldn't bear the 354th's primitive Nissen Hut station. But probably Blakeslee derived a malicious pleasure in seeing his pilots crowd about his borrowed Mustang, mouths watering, agog and enraptured with his enthusiastic account of the Mustang's combat capabilities.

"It's the ship," Blakeslee said.

"It's the ship," they repeated after him.

Bended knee is not a military posture, but a little later Blakeslee was virtually genuflecting as he implored Maj. Gen. Kepner, VIII Fighter Command Chief, to provide the 4th with Mustangs. Gen. Kepner was sympathetic, but insisted that since a great air offensive was in progress, the time couldn't be spared to change from P-47s to 51s. It would take days of practice flying just to get the pilots accustomed to the new craft, and longer for mechanics to learn maintenance procedure on the 51's liquid-cooled engine.

"No, sir, General." Blakeslee said. "Most of these boys flew liquid-cooled types in the RAF. It won't take them long. As for the mechanics, don't forget they worked on Spitfires when the group first started to operate. Don't worry about them."

Blakeslee, a favorite of this general (though not of certain others), could see Kepner weakening. Blakeslee implored:

"General, give me those Mustangs and I give you my word—I'll have 'em in combat in 24 hours. I promise—24 hours."

A few days later, Gen. Kepner came through. McKennon the Ridgerunner was taxiing his Thunderbolt to a hardstand. He glimpsed the Mustangs lined up and became so excited he went off the perimeter track onto the sodden green grass.

There were high whistles when Blakeslee said, "All ours." But there were low whistles when he told them of his pledge of 24-hour service to Gen. Kepner.

"You can learn to fly 'em." Blakeslee soothed, "on

the way to the target."

But the pilots were so jubilant over getting Mustangs that they didn't reflect much on the size hunk Blakeslee had bitten for them to chew. They felt that they were getting off a mule and mounting a steed with the rocking-chair gait of a Tennessee walking horse, the speed of Man o' War and the sure-footed maneuverability of a—mustang.

You couldn't tell the enlisted men from pilots that raw night of Feb. 27, 1944, for they were both doing the same thing—washing, gassing and slipping the snaky belts of 50-cal. armor-piercing incendiaries into the wing guns.

"Now, by God, we'll show 'em," they said. "We'll show those jokers at Halesworth, the clueless bastards . . . Sonofabitch, listen to the way that motor sounds . . . That's really wizard . . ."

Pilots usually have at least 200 hours of flying time in a Mustang before they are sent overseas to combat. Fourth Group pilots averaged a bare 40 minutes when they undertook the first mission.

Unfamiliarity with the plane and engine failures, chiefly overheating through coolant leaks, caused some pilots to be lost over enemy territory or to have narrow squeaks in emergency landings. But Blakeslee had willed it and the fact was he was right up there with them taking precisely the same risks. Otherwise, some probably would have refused to go.

By early 1944 the Eighth AF had embarked on an offensive to destroy the German fighter strength in the air and on the line. The fighters—more than 1,000 now—were picking fights with the Luftwaffe while the bombers—more than 2,000—were destroying aircraft factories to prevent replacements. German fighter strength had reached alarming, peak proportions and it had to be knocked out before an invasion of the Continent could be undertaken.

When the 4th flew the Thunderbolts on its first missions a year before, the range was about 175 miles, which took in such places as Brussels, Cambrai and Paris. Belly tanks extended the reach to such places as Keil, Hanover, Stuttgart and Vichy. All the time, however, German fighters were adroitly withdrawing east, waiting to attack the bombers until after the fighters had reached the limit of their range.

But the P-51 Mustang was Seven League Boots: the Luftwaffe was presently to find that there was no such thing as recoiling beyond American fighter range anymore. The Mustang had a relatively low fuel consumption and engineering resource had packed it with extraordinary capacity in the wings and fuselage. In addition, it carried not only one belly tank, but two wing tanks which were jettisonable. It was, moreover, a fighter which fought at both high and low altitudes. No other air force had anything comparable with the Mustang.

One thousand American fighters were after the German fighters. There were many stellar performances. But the cruelest hook in the side of the Luftwaffe was to become the three squadrons of the 4th. In Mustangs, the group had been reborn. March and April, 1944 were to become the Great Days, the meridian of the famous air battles over Europe.

"All pilots report to the briefing room at 0900 hours. Repeat . . ."

The order came over the public address system, or "blower." The ground crews were busy arming and gassing the Mustangs parked on the sodden green field. The pilots piled into the weapons carrier trucks and sped to the briefing room. It was cold and gray, or England in the winter.

Lt. Philip "Pappy" Dunn, once manager of the floor furnishing department of Montgomery Ward in Vancouver, Wash., huddled in his leather flying jacket and scratched his balding head as he wondered why he should be going to the briefing. Pappy was already

154

signed out for a 48-hour pass. Joyce Lawson, a British WREN (our WAVE), was coming down for a three-day visit.

Pappy saw what the show was—Berlin, or big "B." Fighter planes were going to accompany the Big Friends all the way to Berlin in the first daylight attack.

"Jesus, fellas," said Pappy. "I don't know what to do. I got this sharp little WREN coming down here, but I don't want to miss this."

The ever-ready Red Dog said, "I'm on pass, too, but damn if I'll miss this one. London has had me for today."

"You just know it brother," said Lt. Vermont Garrison. He was a grave, dignified pilot. He had been a rural school teacher at Mt. Victory, Ky. He and Beeson were the deadliest marksmen in the group.

Pappy looked at the briefing map, whose cellophane gloss shimmered under the neon light, and picked out the "Base" space. It had 3:30 P.M. crayoned in. That meant he could go on the show, bathe, shave, and meet WREN Lawson in Saffron Walden by 5 o'clock, the appointed time. They could go out to Meade Hall, open a bottle and talk about the first Big "B" do.

"Hey, Goody," said Pappy, "put me up, will you? I'm going."

"The customer," Goodson replied, "is always right. You're in, Flinn." Goodson turned to the others, who were getting into their flying gear: "All right, you guys better get the show on the road. We press in 20 minutes."

Thus, on March 3, 1944, Pappy, the Mustangs of the 4th and a bomber fleet were advancing on Berlin in daylight through the worst kind of weather. Goering had said earlier that if ever a bomb fell on Berlin, they could call him Meyer. But his name didn't change March 3: The weather went from bad to impossible and the ground controller, on orders from Pinetree, ordered them to abort and set course for home.

155

Squalls and dense cloud layers made it impossible for Blakeslee to keep the three squadrons together in the widely dispersed (300 yards and more between planes) battle formation. Nine of the pilots found themselves alone between Berlin and Hamburg at 23,000 feet. They were Maj. Halsey, Capt. Gentile, Lts. Millikan, Carlson, Herter, Godfrey, Garrison, Barnes and Pappy.

Vapor trails began to appear off to the right. Their gestures were vicious like a spider hanging his web. Six vapor trails started from 2 o'clock and coursed on around behind. Ten more trails appeared below the sun coming up behind the other six trails. They had obviously been scrambled to hit the bombers, which had turned back.

"Cobweb section to Horseback," Millikan said. "Bandits all about. Are you receiving me, Horseback?"

No reply from Blakeslee.

The pilots went into a gentle starboard turn. They could see at least 60 vapor trails converging on them. Some of the pilots could remember Swope, the weather man, saying at the briefing: "Non-persistent at 10,000 feet to persistent at 15,000 to 30,000." The pilots turned into the attacking Huns. You couldn't turn your tails to Huns even if there were 60-plus of them and only 9 of you. Turning into them was the only defense.

The Huns saw the Americans, "Indianers", they called them. They looked each other over as they raced at each other's noses. Each dropped wing tanks, like two boxers shedding robes at the sound of the gong.

The 190s were long-nosed and painted black with long white or gray bands around their noses. "Heavy and fierce" was the way they looked to Millikan. There were 60 to 80. They enveloped the nine Mustangs in a trap and queued up to pick them off.

Several pairs of the 190s split-essed and a couple of

the Mustangs went after them. This was the way the Jerries had planned it, for other 190s charged down on the tail of the diving Mustangs. Herter, a Detroit boy, was killed.

In the melee that followed the eight remaining pilots were scattered among the Huns, JU 88s, 190s, 109s, 110s. It looked like sure death for all. Gentile managed to escape the jaws of the trap, but hearing the others screaming and bawling for help, flew back into the tempest to help Millikan get the flock back together.

A group of 110s, Dornier 217s and JU 88s passed underneath. Gentile rolled starboard and started down. He was attacked by 10 190s, but Millikan turned into them and they broke off. Gentile got positioned to clobber a 110, but his canopy frosted up in the witch-tit cold and when it cleared he saw another 110 firing on him from short range. Gentile reefed it in and opened fire on a Dornier 217. He got strikes around the wing roots, but before he could polish it off, his gunsights went out. Two 190s flashed past on either side of Gentile, so close the wash made his ship wallow. Call signs were forgotten and names were used on the R/T.

"Are you with me, Millie?" shouted Gentile.

"Hell, no, I've got 10 190s chasing me all over the damn sky!" Millikan shouted back.

"Okay, Millie. Don here. Calling all Mustangs, Form up on me by those vapor trails from that big gaggle and let's give Millie some help."

Garrison had knocked down one. Then, with all guns on the blink except one, he picked off another with a deflection burst as it whizzed in front of him in sitting-duck position. He should have aborted before the fight as his high blower would not cut in, and with no supercharger, he had had to rev it up high to hold his place in formation, thus using so much gas it was doubtful he could make it back to Debden. But now, in the middle of this Jerry swarm with no guns, he

157

had more immediate worries than gas.

Four 190s came screaming down out of the sun on Gentile. He didn't fire back because some of his guns weren't feeding on account of the violent maneuvers and he obviously was going to need all his remaining firepower. Two more came head-on. Then eight more came tearing down upon him, their wings lighting up like Christmas trees. In one way or the other Gentile maneuvered himself away from them. He went down to bounce a twin-engined craft, but over-shot it and pulled up sharply—right into three other twin-engined planes which got him in a cross-fire. Gentile continued to climb. The plane got a rocket surge as the high stage blower cut in and he was in range of the 190. He began squirting without a gunsight. The 190 flamed. Gentile looked to see three 190s on the tail of a Mustang already pouring smoke.

"Break! Break! Break!" screamed Gentile.

The Mustang did a quick snap roll and went straight down.

Gentile saw "Gunner" Halsey and Pappy below and told them to join up as two 190s began closing on Gunner. Gentile saw eight 190s positioning to come down on him through the heavy, dirty, cloud billows, but he coolly calculated that he could get the two off Gunner's tail before the eight could reach him.

"Break, Gunner, break!"

If somebody else had been hogging the radio channel, Gentile could not have warned Gunner. That's why Blakeslee was always making earphones vibrate with, "That'll be just about enough of that goddamn R/T chatter." Thus warned, Gunner saved himself with three violent snap rolls. Gentile met Gunner's assailants in a front quarter attack, but neither fired. The eight 190s all the time were getting within range. Gentile pulled up sharply to meet them, and they passed on to reform.

The eight pilots had more or less abandoned hope of surviving the attacks and it had become a game to just see how long they could elude their adversaries. The Swede and three others encountered a gaggle of 110s, presumably rocket-carriers. To defend themselves, the relatively slow 110s started circling in a lufbery, all the time craftily losing altitude to reach the haven of some clouds below. Carlson failed to work in behind them. Every time he approached the circle, the 110's rear gunners squirted at him. So Carlson started going around the other way. A 110 pulled out of the ring and started for him. Carlson fired his port engine and the 110 crashed. Carlson climbed and joined up with Garrison and they started for another 110. A third Mustang beat them to the 110 and blew it apart. It was Millikan.

"That goddamn Mustang is cutting us out!" screeched Carlson.

"My motor," Carlson said, "is running plenty rough."

"Okay," said Millikan, "we'll head back."

Pappy was also having engine trouble. In the fight he had probably destroyed a 210, but couldn't be sure as a 190 had begun to shoot him up and he had to take his eyes from the smoking 210. Pappy tried to turn too tightly in eluding the attacking 190 and his ship spun out, his canopy picking up a dense frost coating. Pappy climbed back up again and joined with Gentile and Halsey.

"Hey, fellas," said Pappy with a crestfallen manner, "I guess I'll have to fall out. I'm only indicating 160."

It hurt the feelings of the others to think of the lovable, happy-go-lucky Pappy falling out and being forced down in Germany. Pappy couldn't bear to be left behind at Debden, and sure as hell he didn't want to be left behind in Germany.

Gentile said: "Okay, Pappy, we'll just orbit and wait for you to catch up."

"Okay, fellas," said Pappy gratefully, "I'm going on 240°."

A bomber pilot, hidden somewhere in the towering cloud banks, cut in to say: "No, Little Friend, best you fly 270°."

They were all lost to each other and shaken.

Elsewhere in the soup, Millikan, Garrison and Carlson were racing line-breast for England. Millikan saw 15 bandits at 3 o'clock and ordered an attack. But the Jerries scooted into a cloud bank. Millikan's engine began cutting out.

"Millie here. Don't think I can make it back."

By now they were flying on across Germany, carefully skirting all towns to avoid the flak batteries, of which there were many in any town large enough to have a mayor. They missed them all and were approaching the Channel coast when a great cloud loomed up in front of them. Its base was about 4,000 feet and its top at 12,000. It was in the shape of an ice cream cone. They remembered Swope's briefing injunction: "Heavy rime icing all the way." They dived to go under the cloud. Churning along full bore, the three pulled up over a hill—and found themselves smack over a town.

Their formation had been radar-plotted by the Germans and the gunners all along the way were alerted for them. The orange golf balls began criss-crossing their course.

The heavy flak went *whomp, whomp*. The light stuff, 20 and 40-mm., approached a plane slowly at first and then appeared to accelerate as it passed. It didn't hit you like this, though it appeared to be coming at you like the baseballs in a three-dimensional movie. But when the golf balls looked like they were *corkscrewing* towards you, that meant a hit.

The three were over the middle of the town and it looked like every villager was holding a Roman candle. Carlson saw an orange ball and the corkscrew. The slug ripped into his cockpit.

"We'd better get out of here," observed the grave Kentucky schoolmaster. The golf balls came closer and closer as the Mustangs raced over the town at 300 m.p.h. In a moment Garrison said softly:.

"That's me, boys."

He jettisoned the canopy, felt the rush of the air and jumped. The German flak gunners could congratulate themselves on having brought down one of the 4th's most gifted pilots. With 10 planes shot down, many bets were on him to win the ace race.

Millikan hunched forward in the cockpit to expose himself as little as possible and gave it full bore down one street of the town, with Carlson on another. The streets led to the harbor and the harbor to the Channel. Millikan landed at an advance base in England at Manston with five gallons of gas left.

Carlson was so exhausted that as he taxied down the strip he didn't even try to dodge another plane on the runway. He staggered out of the cockpit. His knees trembled as he bent them to get from the wing to the ground. He got on his knees and pounded the earth, and probably would have eaten some had there been something with which to chase it.

An RAF squadron leader asked Millikan how long he had been airborne.

"Six hours, sir."

The Briton looked at the Mustang and said, *"How long, leftenant?"*

"Six hours".

"Six hours? Hm-m, yes, quite, quite." He was too polite to call Millikan a damn-liar Yank.

There wasn't enough beer even in the mess' reserve tanks to wash away the tension of an encounter like this. Nine Mustangs had met 60-plus German planes and had destroyed six for the loss of only one. But it had been a severe ordeal which none had expected to survive. Their eyes were bright and glassy. They didn't eat.

Carlson demanded a handful of sleeping pills from the medic.

Outwardly, Gentile had the calm and repose of one

of Mme. Tussaude's figures. He followed the nightly ritual of tying the string truss about his cap to maintain the operational creases, and, as always on a cold night, went to bed with his khaki shirt on. The Greek said Gentile kicked and writhed in his sleep as the 109s attacked again.

Mrs. Millikan reported that the lord of their thatched-roof cottage waked the baby with his tossing and mumbling of, "Flak's wicked, wicked!"

In the later afternoon WREN Lawson was pacing the station at Saffron Walden. This wasn't a bit like Pappy. Wherever was he? and, blimey, what a spot of bother standing in the cold twilight.

"I don't know how much longer I shall be able to wait," said the cab driver. "I'm booked up y'know for this next train. Regular customers, actually."

Both would have been more forebearing had they known what was befalling Pappy.

After losing Gentile and Halsey in the storm, Pappy had continued on his course of 270° and found himself over the Brest Peninsula. His radio wouldn't work, so he was afraid to chance crossing the Channel to England. For without a radio, he couldn't have given a May Day fix on his position had he been forced down.

Pappy decided that his only chance was to try for Spain. He would be interned, but that beat being a German prisoner.

Eight miles from the Spanish border Pappy emerged from a cloud to find himself sitting on the tail of a Heinkel bomber. Instinctively he flipped on his gun switch, aimed and blasted the Heinkel. He then circled to watch the bomber crash into the storm-lashed trees.

The circling exhausted the gasoline which would have been enough to take him to Spanish territory, but a fighter pilot would rather be a prisoner of war than miss the sight of an enemy plane falling to his guns. So just eight miles from sanctuary in Spain, at St. Peel, France, Pappy cursed and jettisoned his canopy. It flew back and knocked an egg on his head. Rain splattered on his helmet and goggles, and then his balding head when he threw them over-side. He jumped and his pants were ripped by the tail fin.

The chute blossomed and jerked his head. Pappy floated to earth under the blackening skies, the rain stinging his face. He wiped the water out of his eye and looked at his watch. It was 3:50 o'clock. That also happened to be the precise time at which the group was scheduled to hit the circuit over Debden.

Pappy thought of WREN Lawson. He could see her pouting in the station, dressed in one of those natty blue uniforms of the Royal Nivey and holding an imitation leather bag.

Pappy hit the soggy ground, freed himself of his chute and crouched in the underbush. The first two German soldiers missed him, but the next one stuck a gun muzzle in his face.

WREN Lawson to grandchildren: "Yes, my dears, I knew some of the Yank air force types. Right lively blokes, actually, but so unreliable. There was a leftenant—hm-m—Duncan or Dunn I think it was, who . . ."

Mustangs as snapped over East Anglia from the door of a Flying Fortress.

Physical training for the war already won.
Belly tanks.

BABY DELIVERY

A paper droptank is slung to P-51 to give the extra range that won the air war for the AAF.

Armor-piercing Incendia

Loading armor-piercing incendiaries into the wings of a Mustang. It may have been winter, because there is snow—but that doesn't prove it in England.

No. 78 (Kid Hofer) in front of 334th Dispersal after his one-man show to Munich. Capt. Vic France, later killed, on extreme left. Capt. Ben Ezzell, intelligence officer who later returned to England to take a bride, in doorway. Hofer: "Gee, the Alps were pretty!"

Maj. John T. Godfrey telling Debden mechanics how it feels not to be a German prisoner.

Maj. Willard Millikan (extreme left), just landed after one of the war's great air battles, says: "The huns chased me all over the damn sky!" They're speculating whether the others will make it back to Debden.

BIG "B"

Linemen at 335th Dispersal sweat out first mission to Berlin, March 4, 1944. It was inconceivable that fighters could fly to Berlin, engage and return. It still is.

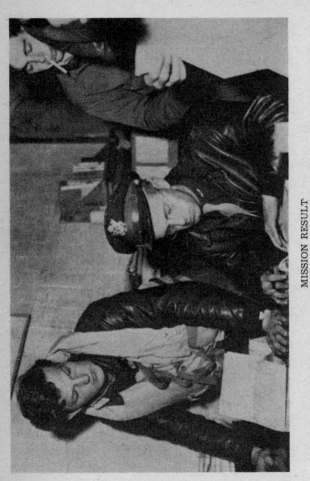

MISSION RESULT

Kid Hofer (left) gives a mission how and where to intelligence officer, Capt. Charles Ashcraft.

Blue Section—Capt. Carl Payne, San Antonio; Lt. Gordon Denson,
Rockville, Conn.; Lt. Arthur Bowers, Tiskilwa, Ill.; Capt. Thomas Bell,
Shawboro, N. C.
Lt. Col. Beeson, the Author and Lt. "Chuck" Carr, Raymond, Nebr.

KILLED IN ACTION

Maj. Mike Sobanski (upper), of Warsaw and New York; Lt. Glenn Herter, Detroit (lower left); Capt. Albert Schlegel, Cleveland, Ohio.

KILLED IN ACTION

Capt. Robert Hobert (upper left), Woodland, Wash.; Lt. Clemens Fiedler (right), Fredericksburg, Tex.; Capt. "Buzz" Riedel (lower left), Ault, Colo.; Lt. Joseph W. Sullivan, New York.

KILLED IN ACTION

Capt. Donald Emerson (upper left), Pembina, N. D.; Capt. Frank Jones, Jr. (right), Montclair, N. J.; Capt. Vic France (lower left), Dallas; Capt. Frank Boyles, Denver. Jones is returning from Russia with teddy bear talisman in right hand; he always flew with it.

KILLED IN ACTION

Capt. Charles F. Anderson (upper left), Gary, Ind.
Capt. Bernard J. McGrattan (upper right), Utica, N. Y., who was
packed to go home but decided to fly one D-Day mission.
Capt. Joseph L. Lang (lower left), Hyde Park, Mass., who flew with his
baby's shoes. Lt. Pete Lehman, son of the former governor of New
York.

It was on March 4, 1944 that Reichmarshal Goering decided that Germany had lost the war. Forty-eight scarlet-nosed Mustangs of the 4th Fighter Group helped Goering decide.

After the war Maj. Alexander Seversky asked Goering at what particular point he realized the war was lost for Germany. Goering, according to the *Daily Express* of London, replied:

"The first time your bombers came over Hanover, escorted by fighters, I began to be worried.

"When they came with fighter escort over Berlin—I knew the jig was up."

The first such fighter over Berlin was marked with "WDC", the Mustang flown by Col. Blakeslee. He had promised months before that he was to have the honor of leading the first fighters over Berlin.

If the 4th had gotten Mustangs by the time of the first Big "B", then he would be assigned to lead another Mustang group. But the 4th, through Blakeslee's ruthless and perhaps vainglorious pledge to have them in combat 24 hours after receiving them, had gotten the Mustangs and the honor of spearheading the first attack.

By International News Service
LONDON, March 4.—Escorted U.S. Fortresses, plowing through clouds nearly six miles high, staged history's first American bombing attack on the Berlin metropolitan district today. ... Fourteen of the Fortresses and tentatively

26 of their escorting fighters are missing from the operations, carried out in 56-below-zero cold and covering 1,500-mile round-trip distances.

"All pilots report to the briefing room immediately. Repeat . . ."

Debden personnel had heard the bombers going out a long time before and knew that there was a show on. Fighters had it soft compared with the bomber boys. Bomber crews, living in Nissen Hut squalor around pot-bellied stoves, had been roused long before dawn, or at about the same time some fighter pilots were leaving the bar to hit the sack. The bomber briefing was necessarily much more elaborate, an hour perhaps compared to Blakeslee's laconic five minutes (or, as on one occasion: "Okay, not much time boys. Form up at 3,000 feet and follow me"). Sometimes bomber crews would return to the sack, but they couldn't sleep because their bellies jumped with the thought of the cold, the flak, the bandits.

The Forts, the lumbering but majestic Forts, began taxiing out in the dawn gloom. For my money, the Forts were the proudest craft in the skies. They always sent them on the tough shows in preference to the Liberators. The Libs were bigger, faster and carried more bombs. But the Libs, with their cumbersome controls, couldn't fly tight formations like the Forts. The Forts could pack in wing-to-wing and thus present a more bristling defense against the fighters. They were more maneuverable and could thus evade flak better. The worst the Germans could throw at them never once turned them back from a target. The Forts kept their dignity. The gunners just blazed away at attacking fighters and, though the pilot might close his eyes, he held it on the bomb run until he heard the "bombs away." The fighter boys could always break off, climb or dive. But the bombers had to keep wading through the death hail until the eggs were dropped. It was like being trapped in a submarine on the ocean floor. Sometimes it brought tears to a fighter pilot's eyes to see a swarm of Huns queueing up on a straggler like a bunch of buzzards and explode it before a single chute blossomed. Where the much faster fighters stayed up five or six hours, the Fort crews froze for 10 hours. Fighter piloting was a piece of cake beside bomber work. When the bomber crews said, "It's rough in the E.T.O." it meant something. But however badly they were shot up and regardless of how many of the crew lay dead inside, when you saw them from the ground returning to base in the gloomy salmon-streaked winter twilight, they looked majestic, unflinching—serene.

So on this March 4 morning the Forts had already taken off, disappearing into the soup at 30-second intervals. They had a hard time getting into the formation; one bomber C. O. rode herd on his bombers in a Thunderbolt. Then they coursed out over Debden, from which the Mustang pilots would take off, catch up and shepherd them to Berlin.

Duke the dog and the pilots alighted from the weapons carriers in front of the dingy group intelligence building behind the control tower. On this day they didn't stop to get coffee or glance at the *Stars & Stripes*. They clogged the door to the briefing room as they stopped to look at the red crayon course on the glistening map. That meaningful red extended from Debden to Berlin. Mac put *Riders of the Purple Sage* back in his hip pocket.

"Rough, brother, rough," you heard them say.

The chatter stopped suddenly, the same as the shrill cacophony of sparrows in a magnolia tree suddenly subsides at the sound of a BB shot perforating a leaf. It was Blakeslee. The pilots popped to.

Blakeslee strode up the aisle as if it wasn't long till press time. He turned around to face the pilots.

He said: "Okay." At Debden that meant at ease.

You couldn't rightly tell whether Blakeslee had a glint or twinkle in those pale blue eyes, and whether it

180

was excitement or a March bluster that flushed his face.

As always, he wore the beaten-up, clay-colored leather jacket he had drawn when he first came to Debden and the one in which he said he would finish the war. He was champing gum. He held a cigaret in his right hand. The cigaret was a reliable herald of what was known as a shaky do.

"Well," Blakeslee began in his vibrant baritone voice, "you've seen what the show is. We're going to Berlin."

He paused. That sentence had a lot of punch. He continued:

"We're going to Berlin. The weather is not too good. Swope will give you the gen on that in a minute. We'll be with the bombers over the target on the bomb run. And we've been chosen to lead the first box in over Berlin. Any questions?"

Blakeslee went on: "Oh, yes—you can keep your wing tanks until you reach this point on the map, but if you drop 'em back here you'll still have plenty of gas to make the show. There'll be another group of Mustangs with the second box of bombers and coming out we'll see Thunderbolts back around this point, so watch out what you bounce. They may be friends. Okay, Swope, can you tell us anything about the weather?"

Swope walked to the map and conveyed the bad news, which really wasn't news at all because he said the weather was bad.

"All right," resumed Blakeslee, "a time check . . . In 15 seconds it will be ten hundred hours . . . 10 . . . 5, 4, 3, 2, 1—zero . . . ten hundred hours. Okay, let's go."

The pilots rode out to the dispersal huts to don flying gear. Blakeslee slipped his on in group intelligence and walked into the sanctum sanctorum of the I.D.s. He half reclined on a cot on top of a gray English blanket. The air was charged and all spoke quietly and as little as possible. Blakeslee looked at his watch, then down at his black flying boots. They looked like Cossack boots, with his flying pants tucked in. It was hard to make conversation.

Blakeslee said reflectively: "We'll miss lunch, won't we?" He kept his voice low so as to muffle the tremor. He chewed his gum as though to tide himself over until dinner.

Somehow he wasn't the commanding officer of the station now, object of twang pop-tos and vacuum producing salutes. Now he was just another boy about to undertake a mission from which chances were good he'd never return. You could discern this change in Toy's action. Toy was a surly, sallow-faced captain in the operations section who had been a G. I. in the Regular Army. He was entrusted with keeping Blakeslee's log book so too much time wouldn't show. Toy went over to Blakeslee, leaned over him with a familiarity which would have been unthinkable any other time, and slapped Blakeslee on his rump. Blakeslee, who would presently be all fire and flame in the midst of battle, looked up shyly like a girl and smiled softly and self-consciously.

Blakeslee looked at his watch, arose and got into his khaki Ford sedan and sped to Narvik dispersal where he always parked his kite.

"Here comes the Chief Cook," said S/Sgt. Harry East, of Omaha, Nebr., who crewed WDC. It was Chief Cook because of the "C" on the plane and the chicken on the shoulder.

Blakeslee got out of the Ford into the Mustang's cramped cockpit. He looked quizzically at the faces about him. They looked curiously at him. They wanted to say something, but they were too shy or couldn't think of the right thing.

East pulled the battery cart up and connected the wire with the kite. The Mustang was cranked off. Blakeslee listened to the motor. The right bank of cylinders always ran rough and nothing East could do

182

would remedy it. Blakeslee could have had another ship, but he preferred to take his chances with a spit-and-fuss right bank than give up the only Mustang at Debden which at the time had a balloon canopy for better vision. That was Blakeslee: galloping to Berlin in a Mustang with a trick knee.

The mechanics, shivering in their greasy green overalls and leather jackets, stood atop the revetment to see their motors off on the historic mission. The wind was so icy it was hard to remember that the mechanics had been burned brown there in the summer before. Each speculated whether his plane would make it back.

Blakeslee taxied out on the east-west runway and made a radio check with the tower. The other 47 planes taxied up behind, weaving left and right in order to see ahead. In a way it made you think of the taxi fleets at Pennsylvania Station. Bundled in heavy flying clothes, their faces obscured by helmets and oxygen masks, the pilots appeared stripped of their individuality and personality. Through the glass canopies they looked like shapeless brown sacks. When they moved you couldn't recognize them, save for the plane numbers.

Locking the wheels, Blakeslee gunned his motor and the plane pranced. He released the brakes and the craft moved forward, somewhat sluggishly at first because of the heavy babies under each wing. He and his No. 2 were clocking 100 m.p.h. by the time they reached the hump in the runway. The flagman beside the runway, a pilot thus disciplined for breaking R/T silence on a previous mission, waved the next two off.

They circled about the field where the blue ribbon beets once grew until the group was in combat array. All 48 Mustangs, plus two spares, were airborne in eight minutes. The ones and twos were joined by the threes and fours, making a section of four. A flight of eight joined another flight to make a squadron.

Then the squadrons, led by Blakeslee with 336th, joined and the group was formed. Blakeslee got over the control tower and set his compass for Berlin. They pointed their noses up for the climb across the Channel. At the French coast they reached an altitude of about four miles and leveled off.

The Forts were already far ahead, escorted by Thunderbolts whose range at that time was not sufficient to take them all the way to Berlin. They would turn back when the 4th arrived at the rendezvous.

"Shirtblue Red 2 to Horseback," said Lt. Woodrow Sooman, of Republic, Wash., just after they passed over Dummer Lake. "Oxygen failing. Over."

"Horseback to Shirtblue Red 2," Blakeslee came back. "Let down and return to base. Off."

Sooman banked out of the formation and started back for Debden at 10,000 feet, below which oxygen was not needed. "Red Dog" Norley moved up on to take Sooman's place on Blakeslee's wing.

Others called up for permission to abort on account of this kind of engine trouble and that. Soon Blakeslee and Red Dog were the only ones left of Shirtblue (336th) Squadron. Lt. Charles Anderson, a sallow, black-haired ace from Gary, Ind., flying with 335th Squadron, called Blakeslee:

"Greenbelt Blue 4 to Horseback. Rough engine. Don't think I can make it to target. Over."

"Horseback here," responded Blakeslee. "Okay, Blue 4, return to base."

The rest continued on towards the rendezvous with the bombers. They were tense and uneasy, but even so, flying in the rarified atmosphere five miles up left them drowsy and listless. But flak bursts prevented any from nodding.

Sooman felt lonesome as he scooted back alone over the heart of Germany. He sighted a JU 52 (transport) at 1,500 feet. Sooman worked himself upsun and attacked the transport from the side.

As he was about to break off, pieces from the

splintered transport flew off and bounced off the metal side of his Mustang. The transport spiralled down in such fashion as to suggest that Sooman's burst had killed the pilot.

Meanwhile, Anderson was fretfully cruising towards Debden. The show of shows, the first attack on Berlin, story enough for a hundred grandchildren— and he was going in the opposite direction. His hankering to see Berlin was keen, especially where the RAF had plastered it. His motor sounded a little better now. Why not try it? Anderson kicked the rudder, completed a port turn and resumed the vector leading to Berlin.

Shortly after noon, at the appointed time, Blakeslee caught sight of the five combat wings of B-17s. He took his place some distance in front of the first bomber box to sweep away any Huns in the path of the bombing run. Weaving back and forth with high speed skids, Blakeslee scanned the dirty billows for specks that would grow into 190s and 109s.

The specks were spotted just before the Forts discharged their bombs, single and double contrails appearing in all directions. Fifteen-plus 109s and 190s came in for a frontal attack on the bombers. Green flares, fired two at a time, rainbowed out of the Forts to signal for fighter intervention.

"Horseback here. There they are. Stick together and clear your tails . . . Here we go!"

The pilots caught the eagerness and zest in Blakeslee's voice. For a moment he rammed the throttle forward and spurted ahead of his squadrons, jinking his craft from side to side to clear himself. Blakeslee always did that before attacking. Millikan used to say: "That's why he's been here so long."

Blakeslee whipped his plane over to initiate the split-ess, diving down on the Huns in a violent bounce. All Blakeslee's bounces were violent. He was heavy with the reins and spurs in racking his Mustang about. The air speed needle popped the whip towards the red line, which line was the factory's means of saying that the wings might or might not stay on beyond this speed.

Blakeslee positioned himself astern one of the 109s and flew right up his slipstream for some of his garden hose shooting. The 109 racked it this way and that, but he couldn't shake Blakeslee. Red Dog was following on his right wing, rigid and excited. Red Dog fidgeted in his cockpit and shouted, "Let 'im have it, Colonel, let 'im have it!"

Blakeslee flipped the gun switch on and trimmed his kite up to get set for the kill. He pressed the red tit on the stick to water the flowers. Nothing happened. He got the 109 in the ring again and pressed down. Red Dog kept watching the leading edge of Blakeslee's wing to see the orange powder puffs. But Blakeslee's guns wouldn't fire. He was a hornet without a stinger.

"Goddamn sad sack!" roared Blakeslee. The Hun was flat out, wondering why the American hadn't fired. In angry frustration, Blakeslee pushed the throttle to the firewall and pulled up abreast of the 109. He looked over the Hun. He waved with mocking sweetness. The Hun didn't remember anything in the book about this, but what did he have to lose? He acknowledged Blakeslee's wave with a waggle of his wings.

About this time, Anderson, the sightseer who had to see Berlin regardless of the inconvenience of a sputtering motor, reached the outskirts. He peered down through a hole in the clouds. "Looks a lot like Paris," he thought. Further reflections were interrupted by the attack of six 190s. Anderson skidded into a cloud to hide, but when he emerged, the 190 sextet was waiting. Anderson popped back in the cloud. Again, the 190s were waiting for him when he came out of it. So Anderson dipped back into the cloud cover and burrowed through it until he was halfway across the

English Channel.

In the tangle about the bombers, Lt. Paul S. Riley, of York, Pa., lost his section leader when his windscreen frosted up and he had to go on instruments. He found himself alone behind the bomber formation. A 109 started in for Riley, but Riley worked himself on the Hun's tail and squirted away as they dived. Pieces flew, smoke plumed.

"Horseback to that Greenbelt kite," said Blakeslee. "Don't follow him down too far."

Riley began pulling out of the dive. He was already past the red line and the Mustang bucked and quivered. The blood went to his feet and Riley lost consciousness. His head cleared as he began climbing, but the glass windscreen gathered more frost in the 56-below cold.

Blakeslee reassembled as many Mustangs as he could, giving them form-up directions like quail bob-whiting to get together for the night in a sedge patch. Below, Berlin was in the shelters, as London had been in 1940.

"Cowboy" Megura, over another part of the capital, made a quick survey to clear his tail and found that he was over an airdrome on the outskirts of Berlin. He spotted a JU 52 in a hangar and zoomed down. He set the transport ablaze and leap-frogged the hangar. That was one thing: nobody said anything about low flying over Jerry dromes.

A few miles away Megura saw a train growing big in his path. He pulled up to a height of 50 feet and opened fire. The train stopped.

Megura set course for home alone. Anderson, with his air speed indicator knocked out, was ahead of him, wondering how he was going to make a landing if he did get back to Debden. Blakeslee was leading the other pilots on the homeward course across Germany in the gathering winter dusk. He kept straining for sight of a familiar landmark. Over the Ruhr Valley an intense barrage from the world's heaviest flak concentration came up. Black puffs were all about.

"Goddamnit, that's what I was waiting for!" ejaculated Blakeslee. There was no other flak like that—he had his bearing now.

Mechanics and intelligence officers were standing about waiting for the pilots to return from the mission. It was too icy to stand outside, but it was too nerve-racking to remain indoors. So they stood outside, on one cold foot and then the other. Jimmy Happel's dog got in a fight with the mechanic's dog, but nobody paid much notice.

Anderson circled the field. He said: "Greenbelt Blue 4 to tower. Coming in for landing without air speed indicator. Over."

"Carmen Control to Blue 4. Continue in circuit. Will send help up. Over."

"Okay, Carmen. Will do. Thanks. Off."

The control tower make a hurried call to Anderson's dispersal across the landing field. Capt. Leighton Read, of Hillsboro, Tex., ran towards his plane. But Millikan, who had been running some fuel tests and was already upstairs, heard Anderson talking to the tower and flew up alongside.

"Okay, Andy, this is Millie. We'll get you down all right. I'll clock you on my speedometer."

"Cheers."

"Okay, Andy, take it easy now . . . You're coming in too fast . . Let's make the circuit again and lose some more speed . . . Okay, let's go in now . . . You're doing 130 . . . Now it's 120 . . . Now it's 110 . . . Chop your throttle . . . You're straight into the wind . . . You shouldn't have any trouble landing now . . . Cheers."

"Cheers, Millie."

Anderson came in low over the road bordering the field, the winding little macadam road that connected Saffron Walden and Thaxted. The Limeys on the road always thought the planes were going to take their heads off. You could look at those red spinners coming right at you and get the feel of being strafed.

Anderson cleared the fence. His wheels touched down and gave off a smoke puff. He was okay.

Later Blakeslee came in with the others. Each crew chief sprinted out to the hardstand where his kite parked and turned his back as the pilot gunned it. Tired and aching, the pilots signed Form 1 and got out of their ships stiffly. Their knees were too stiff to bend. They just sat on the wings and smoked, so numb the icy wind went unnoticed. They looked like football players on the way to the showers, or miners emerging from the shafts at the end of the day.

Blakeslee was a little different. He whammed the canopy back and there was a sulphurous cascade of four-letter words, followed by:

"Can you beat it?

As if the mechanics crowded about his ship could know what he meant.

"Beat what, sir?"

"I'll be a sad sack—my goddamn guns wouldn't fire. Not one of them. There we were—I had the son-of-a-bitch right in my sights and my guns jammed!"

"Jesus, that's tough."

"I pulled right up beside him," Blakeslee went on, "and looked at the dumb sap. He must have thought I was crazy!"

Blakeslee signed Form 1 with a right hook, got out and flailed his legs with his gauntlets as he entered the 335th's interrogation room. He repeated his story. He unloaded his chute pack and let it crumple on the concrete floor. He slumped in a chair and bit a chocolate bar in two as if it were the Jerry's head.

Blakeslee picked up *Esquire* and stared at a Varga cutie, but it was probably the most aloof look the gal ever got. He was still muttering about being a sad sack. Capt. Victor Croxton, a bustling rapid-fire little lawyer from Norman, Oklahoma, turned away to get the gen from Riley on flak concentrations, weather, and on whether the bombers were on course and on time at the rendezvous. For Croxton, the G. I.s' invariable choice for defense counsel when they were being court-martialed, had been around long enough to know that there were times when one just didn't seek to interrogate Blakeslee.

That was the first Berlin show. It was pretty ragged all the way around. The Germans said the bombing was laughable, and probably it was inept; certainly the formations were poor. Motor troubles caused half of the 4th's Mustangs to abort before they reached Dummer Lake. But Goering's name was changed to Meyer; and he decided that Germany had lost the war. Blakeslee had carried out his assignment in Field Order No. 260. He had become the first fighter pilot over Berlin escorting bombers.

The pilots repaired to the Officers' Mess for a 5 P.M. brunch. The waitresses were slow about bringing the food because they were fascinated by the pilots' rehash. The Forts from nearby Bassingbourne were streaming home in the sunset to roost. Blakeslee's picture was being rushed to London to be wirephotoed to America. The O.W.I. would try to get it printed in Spain as part of the propaganda to lure its citizens from the Nazi fold. The desk men at The Thunderer, otherwise *The London Times*, were composing a headline saying that "The Eagles" were at the head of the U.S. fleet.

The mechanics were removing the guns from the wings to clean them. The Officer-of-the-Day was mounting the guard on the parade ground. Blakeslee, Clark and the others had their hindsides in the great log fire, standing underneath a large framed map taken from a JU 88 which three years before had made Mrs. Kettley's swans leave home, but which had been shot down at Thaxted.

"Well, hell, Don," Clark was saying, "I can beat that. I was positioned on *four* Huns and my guns jammed."

Berlin radio was tuned in and it announced that an American force of fighters and bombers had been turned back before they could reach Berlin.

"Those lying bastards!"

"Yellow bellies!" exclaimed the usually reticent Clark. "Can you imagine us not coming up, or turning tail and running if they came over our capital?"

That night CBS phoned to say the London studio was keen to have Blakeslee make a broadcast to the States. Blakeslee was tucking his shirttail in when asked.

". . . So how about it, Colonel?"

"Naw, not me," he demurred.

"This is your big day."

"Naw, can't do it. Sorry."

Then he said. "But I tell you what to do. Go down there and pick out any two of the boys on the show and tell 'em I said get the hell to London and make that broadcast. You can use the Blue Goose."

"All pilots report to the briefing room immediately. Repeat . . ."

They jammed the door again, expecting to see the red crayon line extend to Berlin as it had the day before. You could look at the map, prepared for use by fighters based in England, and discern that the Germans were not alone in failing to foresee the tremendous range of Mustangs. The crayon line went across the Channel in a southeasterly direction and continued over France to the border of the map. The mission then, would take them off their map. The I.O.s explained that they were to escort Liberators to the Bordeaux area across the Pyrenees Mountains from Spain. Before taking off pilots were refreshed on the markings used upon Spanish aircraft. A pregnant incident might have grown out of an over-eager pilot clobbering a Spanish craft.

Near Bordeaux the group was protecting the rear of the Liberators, Beeson at the head of the leading squadron. Someone spotted specks whizzing through the bomber boxes. Two 109s had already started through the box when Beeson's squadron dived upon them. The Jerries observed the attack and turned head-on into Beeson, each firing. Beeson and his section pulled up for another pass and the Jerries repeated their maneuver. Beeson and five others pulled up again and dived on the 109s. Hively, sometime Deacon, and his section sought to join in the attack, but Beeson had marked them for his very own.

The two 109s were diving and being dived upon by Beeson and The Greek. Beeson had apparently hit his 109 in the head-on attacks, for he began to give off a smoke plume. At 150 yards, Beeson, the little man who looked like a boy, gave the 109 a burst. The smoke plume grew into a column. Many pilots throttle back to keep from overshooting a target, but Beeson's technique was to overshoot in order not to slow up and make himself an easier target for whatever might have gotten on his tail.

As Beeson overshot the blasted 109, the pilot bailed. All the while The Greek was blazing away at his 109. The pieces began to fly, but The Greek kept pumping steel jackets into what was left. He was still in pursuit when Beeson pulled out of his dive and directed the squadron to reform on him. During which time Deacon had found two other 109s which Beeson had not marked for his own. Ordinarily Germans kept their planes spotless, but these two were dirty and had two bright orange spinners. Deacon shot one down and got in a good burst on the second. It, too, started diving straight down. But Deacon had seen that trick before and dived after the Jerry. Deacon almost crashed himself following the Hun, who wasn't playing 'possum after all, and went straight into the ground. Deacon remarked later in his report:

"A Mustang can out-turn, out-climb, out-dive and out-run Messerschmitt 109s."

Beeson's squadron passed over an airdrome in the vicinity of Bordeaux and saw some FW 200s

(4-motored coastal patrol bombers in use as Bay of Biscay shipping raiders) and Heinkel IIIs, but recognizing that the flak gunners had been alerted, ordered them to continue on to another drome. The squadron swooped low over the next one at 400 m.p.h. Beeson got strikes on an FW 200 and headed on across the drome with light flak showering up. Near the far end Beeson felt a heavy blow on his kite. It threw him against the side of the cockpit. He wrestled with the stick and rudders to gain control. To get back to base, Beeson had to reduce his speed and nurse his kite along with hard left rudder.

On another drome in the area, Lt. James F. Steele, of Coatesville, Pa., found eight multi-engined Focke-Wulf Kuriers circling for a landing. Steele tagged on to the rear of the formation and blasted at the hindmost. The great bomber shuddered as the barrage swept along the fuselage from rudder to starboard engine. The slugs ripping into the pilot's cabin made it look like a bag of lime being flailed with a hickory stick.

By this time Steele and the bomber were skidding along 50 feet over the trees. The giant crashed and exploded, the concussion blowing the Little David 100 feet upwards.

When Beeson got down and examined his plane with his crew chief, Staff Sgt. Willard Wahl, he had an impulse to take off again so he could bail out. For the flak had shredded his rudder until it looked like a lattice fence. They weren't supposed to come back like that.

The Berlin mission the day before and this day's mission revealed the remarkable versatility of the Mustang. Before now there was general acceptance of the cliche that there could be nonesuch as an *all-*

purpose fighter craft. But here was one that could engage the best in the Nazi arsenal five and six miles above Berlin one day, and then escort bombers to the Spanish border the next to out-perform German craft on the deck. Further, it revealed that the Mustang was actually performing two missions every time it performed one; that is to say, the Mustangs defended the bombers at high altitude en route to the target, then came back at tree-top level to destroy aircraft squatting on German dromes.

By UP

LONDON, March 6.—A 15-mile-long parade of American bombers thundered across the heart of Berlin for 30 minutes today and set great fires in the stricken Nazi capital after smashing through a huge German fighter screen . . .

Nazi fighters swarmed up to challenge the great armada 100 miles west of the capital and fought them all the way into the target, across the city and along the homeward flight.

And the first in the 15-mile-long procession was Blakeslee. Fighter Command had again chosen the 4th to spearhead the attack and protect the bombers during the most crucial part of the operation, the bombing run.

At 4 o'clock that morning, the batmen, most of them Limeys who had fought in the other war and were now pressed into service as orderlies, roused the pilots. The ritual was unvarying and never bowed to fact. The batmen shook the pilot and said:

"Time to get up, sir, nice morning, yes, yes—quite."

It might be raining, snowing and sleeting, but the batmen would always say it was a nice morning.

The pilots were being routed at 4 o'clock because they had to be driven by G. I. truck, suction tunnels for icy winds, to a depot to obtain some new planes. It was the beginning of a long day. The pilots were beginning to understand what Blakeslee had meant when he promised that the next few days would "separate the men from the boys."

The group began climbing to the altitude at which they were to meet the bombers 500 to 600 miles beyond at 10 minutes past noon. Winds aloft, temperature, etc. had been assiduously plotted by the I. O.s so that, traveling at economical cruising speed, the Mustangs would reach the bombers just as the shorter-range 47s left them. If they had to buck an unexpected head wind and were 10 minutes late in reaching the rendezvous, that was 10 minutes in which the Big Friends would be left to the mercies of enemy fighters. Each bomber carried a crew of 10: their life, imprisonment or return to base depended a lot on Blakeslee getting the escort there on time.

The Mustangs reached altitude over France's coastal range in close-packed, wing-to-wing V-formation. Then, with no signal or direction, they spread out in battle formation, which was line abreast, 300 or more yards apart. Each section leader had his own interval preference.

The Mustangs loped across France into Germany, familiar landmarks becoming few and far between. It made a pilot feel alone, especially when clouds would hide the other planes from him. Radio silence was rigid during the penetration; some chatter would have diverted them from their apprehensive speculation on what the Germans had in store for them. Lt. Bernard L. McGrattan, of Chicago and Utica, N.Y., was one whose belly felt empty as he looked down at the strange scenery. A pilot might feel tempted to discover that his blower wasn't working, or that his engine was running rough, and turn back. A few always did. But most of them just looked off the end of their wings at the others and were sustained by the soldier's immemorial spur: the other fellow was carrying on and if he could do it . . .

The Germans were plotting the bomber formations

by radar almost as soon as they took off from their bases. They were studying their track to determine where they would likely attack. Then the fighter tracks showed on their plotting tables, the fighters charging in to hold the Luftwaffe fighters at bay until the Forts could discharge their bombs.

Over Germany the radio sets were receiving the alarms. This was the *Achtung Service*. It would be interesting to know what all the *Achtung* warning interrupted that day: perhaps Goebbels dictating his weekly *Das Reich* column on the futility of Allied bombing; Hitler chucking Eva Braun under the chin, or maybe breakfasting on Oriental rug; Luftwaffe Gen. Hans Stumpff, Kepner's opposite number, mulling over reports on encounters with Mustangs; Frau Meyer, *née* Goering, recalling the little Meyers into Karin Hall; the endless card game of Debden prisoners of war. They would peer into the sky to see if they could catch sight of the 4th's red-nosed Mustangs and curse because they weren't up there too.

"*Achtung! Achtung!* Enemy bomber formations approaching Berlin!"

A great battle was being joined, great even by the scale of land battles. *The New York Times* estimated that the onslaught engaged 600,000 Germans and Americans, which is roughly 40 German infantry divisions. The estimate included 12,000 American and Allied airmen in the bombers and fighters, 1,000 Nazi airmen, 50,000 Allied and 25,000 German ground crewmen, plus 500,000 Germans manning the anti-aircraft guns and rocket-gun emplacements that reached all the way from the continental coast to Berlin.

"To launch such an attack," *The Times* said, "the Americans have to load their planes with 3,000 tons of high-explosive and incendiary bombs, 19,000,000 rounds of machine gun ammunition, 120,000 rounds of cannon ammunition, 3,360,000 gallons of gasoline and 163,000 gallons of oil."

In short, 500,000 Germans were arrayed to prevent 60,000 Americans from discharging 3,000 tons of bombs on Berlin. Three thousand tons of bombs—Napoleon was vanquished at Waterloo for the exchange of but 37 tons of cannonballs; the Boer war consumed but 2,800 tons; the Battle of Jutland required less than 2,000 tons.

Thus, the ground crews at Debden who stayed up most of the night before to handle the 4th's fraction of the 19,000,000 rounds of machine gun bullets to fill the Mustangs with their thimble of the 3,360,000 gallons of gasoline, were engaged against the Nazi G. I.s doing the same thing across the Channel on the airdromes along the bomber lanes to Berlin. A Debden mechanic who didn't give in to his sleepiness and extracted the tubercular carburetor for just one damn last treatment might have won his part of the battle against a German mechanic who let his 109 go up with a dirty carburetor and get shot down by the Mustang with the clean one. Perhaps the American weather officer had the ability to foretell and warn his team against the rime ice at 31,000 feet, while his German counterpart let his *flugzeugfuhrers* go without warning them.

The bombing assault corresponded closely with a great land battle, with relatively few soldiers in the front line and the mass behind it maintaining the system requisite to the planes' operation. The fighters were light cavalry; the bombers, heavy artillery firing vertical salvos.

The Germans, as soon as they saw the armada had committed itself to Berlin, had plenty of time to marshal their interceptors. Before the bombers reached Brandenburg Province, the Germans had scores of German interceptors waiting upsun. They were chiefly Dornier 217s, JU 88s, Me 110s; they carried rockets with which to bombard the bombers. FW 190s and ME 109s, the single-engined fighters, were mixed in the same gaggles to protect them from the

Mustangs while they uncorked their rocket missiles at the bomber boxes. The Germans sighted the approaching bombers. They were each pulling four persistent, flour-thick contrails. Also they could see the Mustangs skidding and skittering above and below them and in front of them—the 4th—like minnows. The fighter vapor trails were wispy, cobweb plumes.

The R/T exploded:

". . . Bandits at 12 o'clock . . . I see 'em at 1 o'clock . . . Good God, here they come! . . . Can't see 'em, where are they to the bombers? . . . Jees, colder'n witch's tit up here today . . . Green 4, for Chrissakes quit lagging and pull up . . . Hey, you, Pectin kite—you still got your starboard baby . . . Whoo, look at 'em coming in . . ."

Then:

"That'll be just about enough of that goddamn chatter!"

Abrupt silence.

It was, of course, Blakeslee. When somebody was transmitting it meant that the channel could not be used by another. A minute of unnecessary flapping of the mandible meant that an attack on a crippled Fort couldn't be reported. One pilot couldn't shout "break" to another with a Hun diving on him.

The 4th swarmed up to the attack. In a moment the R/T was crackling with directions from Blakeslee. He was in fine fettle. The pilots could always tell it in his voice, a blend of boyish enthusiasm and rapacity. Earphones vibrated with orders. Pilots somehow were able to attune their ears to a personal frequency and therefore heard only messages preceded by their own call signs. It was the same as in a hotel lobby—you hear the page only if it is for you. But one word that everybody reacted to: "break".

"Shirtblue Red Section, break up that gaggle of 110s coming in on that Fort box at 4 o'clock to you . . . Red 3, give that 109 some more—he's not burning yet . . . Greenbelt squadron, don't point your dumb noses at those bombers"—bombers took no chances, firing at any fighters coming straight into them as the Jerries were known to be flying some captured U.S. planes—"Those two Mustangs under the first box of bombers—form up on me. Form up, I say . . . I'm orbiting at angles 25 on the port side of the bombers . . . Pectin kite—break, break! . . . Can't you see that Jerry? . . ."

The fight raged over Berlin. After the first mission everyone at Debden had asked how the RAF damage looked. Had they seen the Unter den Linden? Tiergarten? Tempelhof Airdrome?

"Hell, no, I was too damn busy," the pilots had answered petulantly, but they were curious, too. The twin-engined Huns were bringing their murderous rocket fire to bear on the lumbering Forts. Chutes dotted the sky and many of the bombers were giant torches falling on Berlin. Despite the heat and urgency of the battle, McGrattan, like others, was curious about Berlin. He took a furtive look down now and then as he banked. He saw that Berlin didn't appear as large as London. He cleared his tail and took another gander. He was surprised to see that buildings stood in the heart of the city. He thought: "Those lying Limey newspapers." Berlin hadn't been bombed so badly after all. But hold on, what was that? The buildings were there all right, but they didn't cast any shadows—because they weren't buildings anymore, but just blackened shells several feet high that gave a first appearance of undamaged buildings from a plane.

Mc Grattan looked up to spot a JU 88 flying away from the bomber formations, having already lobbed its rockets. He dived down and began firing at 300 yards' range. Pieces of the 88 began flying back, but McGrattan closed too fast and overshot the Hun.

"Greenbelt kite, give 'em some more. He's not through."

McGrattan turned to resume the attack, but the 88

was going down out of control. Pilots liked impeccable claims and McGrattan started down after the 88 to photograph the crash of the plane. At 10,000 feet he passed a chute.

"Greenbelt kite, don't go down any farther. You got him."

Climbing back to rejoin the fray, McGrattan observed a speck attacking a spot. But before McGrattan could reach the speck, the 109 had clobbered the spot. Fire broke out, enveloping the 10 men in the Fort. He counted the chutes. Only four of the men got out. The six others were being seared and consumed by the flames.

The sight made the skin on his head draw tingling tight. His fist whitened on the stick. He roared: "You miserable bastards!"

Whipped into a frenzy, McGrattan pulled up into the 109 full bore. The 109 met the attack with cannon fire and McGrattan felt his kite shudder as the explosive shells gouged the metal hide and insides of his plane.

The elevator cables had been shot away and each of the four prop blades had a cannon hole. McGrattan broke off and set a course for Debden. All the way across Germany and France, McGrattan, called Big Mac because of his powerful frame, had to brace the stick against his rumpside to maintain ball-on-needle flight. The stick was trying to shove him out of the cockpit as though it were alive. McGrattan gritted his teeth to hold his own against the several hundred pounds of pressure exerted on his body by the berserk stick. His muscles began to ache, but not so much that he wasn't wondering how he was going to land without brakes, trims or flaps.

Blakeslee had shot down a 210 by this time, flown by a Hun who thought a 210 could climb with a Mustang. Lt. Edmund Whalen, a red-headed New Yorker who affected dark glasses and canary yellow sweater, had destroyed another, but then had been clobbered himself and bailed out.

"Hey, lookit!" somebody shouted.

Whalen was floating down on Berlin, swinging back and forth in his chute harness—twiddling his thumbs. A little while later he was killed, we don't know how.

Lt. Archie W. Chatterley, a handsome Californian with the best-looking teeth at Debden, chased a JU 88 down at a rate which made his air speed indicator whirl past the red line. It got up around 650 m.p.h. as Chatterley got in position to fire. He was a superb pilot, but never learned to shoot well. However, no firing was necessary on this one. Pieces of the 88 began peeling off, then bigger pieces and it crashed. It couldn't withstand the stress of the dive. That encounter was won in the Mustang factory.

"Pectin leader here," said Maj. Hank Mills, Leonia, N. J. "Form up on me. I'm right above you at 10,000."

Mills was with Capt. K. G. Smith, of Boise, Idaho, and Godfrey. The squadrons were scattered by this time, for each of these three was in a different squadron. Godfrey was bent on becoming an ace (five destroyed) by his 22nd birthday, March 28.

Mills, a classmate of Clark's at Dartmouth, was getting on the ragged edge. One of the ex-Eagles, he had been on combat status a long time during December and January; when the nights were long and bilious and the days unfit for flying, you would see Mills kicking the logs in the great fireplace as if that would dry them. He sat for hours in the half-light reading with a deep scowl. By nature urbane and friendly, Mills got so he would pass friends in the hall without speaking. He was preoccupied and worn looking. One reason was he had not seen his wife, a lovely model girl, in nearly three years, and their baby daughter, never. Mills was one of the Eagles who had joined up out of pure patriotic impulse.

Having completed his 200-hour tour of ops (the tour was elongated later when the fighting became less bit-

201

ter), Mills was free to go home. But he kept getting 25-hour extensions because he couldn't bear to miss the invasion. Finally he decided he would do just 25 hours more of combat and then sail home. He was on his fourth hour of this last extension as he summoned Godfrey, Smith and Chatterley to join up. Four more shows, three or four more Huns, and he'd be back in Leonia.

The four pilots were setting course for home when a 109 met them head-on. All four jammed throttles forward to reach the meat first. The 190 started a shallow climb, which gave the four Mustangs time to gain.

"Pectin leader, this is Godfrey, are we going to queue up on him and take turns?"

"Hell, no!" answered Mills resoundingly. The words thudded in the earphones. "First one there gets him!"

Mills got there first and clobbered the 109. The 190 spun out of control.

Mills, ordinarily calm and self-possessed, screamed: "I got the pilot, I got the pilot!"

Continuing across Germany towards Debden, Godfrey's black eyes were able to pick out a train on the horizon which the others couldn't see.

"Cover my tail while I go down on that train," said Godfrey.

Godfrey sprayed the train with machine gun fire. They climbed back up and resumed the homeward course. Godfrey saw an airdrome and charged down to perforate two JU 88s on the runway. This time they remained at roof-top level and in a few minutes Godfrey and Chatterley saw a second train coming straight down the track to meet them. The headlight of the German locomotive and the noses of the Mustang were at the same level. Godfrey and Chatterley concentrated their eight machine guns on the locomotive until they had to pull up to avoid flying into the boiler. A few minutes later a 109 pounced upon Chatterley from above, concerning which he

202

wrote in his official combat report:

"... I was just beginning to relieve myself
when tracers passed on each side of me, converging in front. I could hear the firing and I thought
my guns were running away. Godfrey called me
to break, which I did without putting any of the
relief equipment back in place."

The 109 made three head-on attacks upon Godfrey,
who had but one gun firing. Godfrey maneuvered onto
the 109's tail and chased him down to the trees. Godfrey put the gun tit in his navel and managed to pull
up. One wing of the 109 failed to clear the tree and
Godfrey saw his adversary cartwheel through the
foliage.

The last boxes of Forts were still making their
bombing runs over Berlin. It was sickeningly cold
four and five miles above Berlin. Relief tubes were
frozen; some used their pants as diapers and the pants
froze. Their feet were numb and their hands purple
under fur-lined gloves, but at the same time some, like
McGrattan, were bathed in fright-sweat. McKennon
fidgeted and kicked the floor of the cockpit and beat
his hands together to agitate the blood. He was looking for an opportunity to dive down on a Hun to the
ground in order to warm his hands.

The opportunity came in the form of a silver, long-
nosed 190, a superb hybrid of the 109 and 190.
McKennon followed the 190 down as it dived. A short
burst brought those flashing puffs from the cockpit
and around the wing roots. Oil from the silver ship
sprayed McKennon's windscreen as the Hun led him
right over Tempelhof Airdrome on the outskirts of
Berlin.

As McKennon pulled up he looked over the side at
the great drome and saw dozens of planes preparing
to take off from the snow-blanketed field. They had
fired their rockets at the bombers and were going

aloft to launch another barrage. McKennon pulled up into a 109 whose camouflage was excellent and blended with the treetops like a bird's nest. McKennon's windscreen had a film of oil on it and he kept losing the wary 109 as it skittered across the trees. McKennon would honk his Mustang up in order to look down on it and then swoop back down. He felt like ramming his fist through the oil-coated windscreen. Finally he lost the Jerry and set course for home.

The Cowboy was it again. Until the first Berlin show two days before, Megura had never made a kill. But he had gotten doubles on the first Berlin do, and with blood on his spurs, hadn't come off on this mission for the six-hour ride. He gave his kite the gun to make for three rocket-bearing Me 110s which were sidling up to a bomber formation.

Seeing Megura boring in at them, the 110 trinity began diving. Megura looked back to clear himself before following after. Which was fortunate, for the single-engined escort of the 110s was bearing down upon him. Megura turned into the single-engined kite, but found it was another Mustang and went after three more 110s which were belching their rockets with fiery breath. Megura raked one, which disappeared and was later claimed as a damaged, rather than a destroyed, and attacked the second of the three.

A Mustang had happened by, sized up the situation and hooked on to guard Megura's tail. The 110 exploded. Megura climbed into the third 110 which was trying to sneak up on the tail-end-Charlie of the bomber box. The 110's port wing snapped off like a piece of peanut brittle as it hit the ground and bounced above its own flames.

By this time Megura was lathered and ready to shoot down the remainder of the Luftwaffe. He drew a bead on the belly tank of a 190. One slug in the tank meant one of those combat films in which you saw an incandescent flash enveloped in sable smoke and brought a spontaneous chorus of, "Kee-rist, good show, good show!" Megura steadied the ship, drew the bead again and pressed the red tit.

Nothing happened. No bucking, no orange powder puffs on the wings. A train came around the bend. Megura used it to testfire. He pressed again. Same result. He headed home.

In singles, pairs and larger formations the pilots streaked across Germany at varying altitudes. They all flew fast, either from cold, hunger, fright or exhilaration. McGrattan was an exception. He was in no hurry to land because he hadn't figured out how he was going to make a landing without brakes, trims and flaps.

McKennon was flat-out on the deck, which he preferred to altitude anyway. The oil was clearing from his windscreen and he was taking in some of the German countryside, still and unfamiliar, an exciting place at that time. The ground crews would want all the details. When he reached the coast he would light a cigaret. Germans on the ground did not take cover at the sight of the fighter whizzing across the hills and dales because it never occurred to them that it could be aught but a German fighter rushing to England.

In the distance loomed an icepond on which swarms of German children skated. McKennon dived on the lake. The tiny skate blades flashed in the sinking sun as the Hansels and Gretels scooted to flee the roaring thunderbird with the red nose and white star. That is, they all fled save one little Nazi—he stood his ice and shook his chubby fist in angry defiance. "You little gorilla," McKennon chuckled in his oxygen mask.

By now Mills had joined up with Blakeslee and the rest. They heard Mills say:

"Pectin leader here. Gotta get out." His voice rose: "Tell Jim to write my wife I'm okay."

"Don here," Blakeslee cut in. "What's wrong, Hank?"

"Sorry to blab so much over the R/T, Colonel . . . So long . . ."

They saw Mill's chute blossom. Had his luck held out for 19 hours more of ops, Mills would have gotten home to see his baby. But his motor had failed him, and he was beginning the long wait in prison camp for the liberating armies.

Megura, whose mother didn't think he'd be safe on a motorcycle, and Big Mac reached Debden about the same time. They circled the field and honked it up in a sharp peel-off to lose speed for landing. Megura got clearance from the tower to land west-to-east. He let his flaps down and felt the drag reduce his speed. McGrattan, wobbly from his long struggle with the berserk stick, had no control over his flaps and didn't lose much speed. If he had to crash, he thought, he might as well do it before dusk.

"Greenbelt kite to tower," he said. "Get the crash truck ready. I'm coming in without brakes, trims or flaps."

Without flaps, McGrattan couldn't reduce his speed below 150 m.p.h. The tires gave off a puff of smoke as they smacked the asphalt runway; it looked as though the landing gear would buckle under the impact.

McGrattan shot down the runway wondering when, if ever, the craft was going to begin to slow down. He loathed ball bearings. Megura's kite was dead ahead. McGrattan gave it a hard right rudder and gunned it, averting a side swipe. McGrattan swerved around a second aircraft and ploughed into a hedgegrowth. The crash truck, painted with black and white checkers, charged out. McGrattan looked through the cannon holes in his prop blades and shook his head. The driver of the crash truck saw him alight, and thought whatever thoughts they think when the crash doesn't occur after all.

"Aha," said Lt. Col. Ben Lyon, star of World War I's *Hell's Angels*, and in World War II, director of radio news coverage for the Eighth AF. He had his sound recording truck with him. In a few moments McGrattan, standing beside his plane, made a recording disc which was on the ether waves to America that night.

Non-flying personnel who had been sweating them out for six hours sprinted to the kites as they taxied to their parking places, like fans running to the players after a football game. They held their hats as the March bluster became a blast in the switching-off gunning of the motors. Even the intelligence officers abandoned their blase posturing and ran to the planes.

The face of James R. MacDonald flamed as he stood in front of 335th's dispersal hut, which looked like the entrance to a tube station. The wind whipped grit across the green bleakness of the landing ground. *The New York Times* had become aware of the 4th Group and had dispatched this amiable Scotsman, elderly but spirited enough to fly on night raids with the RAF, to Debden to obtain such news as was fit to print.

The pilots, stiff and worn as a frozen dish-rag, were helped off their Mustangs. However, McKennon's excitement overwhelmed his exhaustion and he danced across the greensward, incoherently blubbering the story of the second attack on Big "B." His rendition of the story and his gestures carried him atop the revetment. Mr. MacDonald pursued after.

"I say, young man," Mr. MacDonald opened, "did I hear you say you encountered German fighters today?"

"Mill-yuns, boy! Mill-yuns!" responded McKennon with a howdy-howdy-hi roll of his brown eyes.

"I say, is that so?" said Mr. MacDonald, stalling to digest the import of this disclosure.

But before the correspondent could complete the interview, McKennon was taking jack-rabbit strides ino the dispersal for his slug of operational whiskey.

Meanwhile, Mr. MacDonald hooked on to another

lead. A portion of *The Times* account next day said:

"... One flier returned to base growling with disappointment. He was Lt. Peter G. Lehman, son of the former governor of New York. Pete ... had to turn back when he reached Hanover on account of engine trouble. He was very disgruntled because he wanted 'to see the big city'."

Pete, big, good-natured and unassuming, had married and was the father of two when the flying bug bit. He was holding down a desk in Lehman Bros., investment bankers, but he was leaving the desk often enough to take flying lessons at Roosevelt Field in 1940, nor took the trouble to inform the boss. But one day the Governor of New York summoned his heir and assign. On his desk lay the noon edition of *The Sun*, carrying a story that Pete had won his pilot's license.

"What's this, Pete?" intoned the Governor.

"Yes, sir," gulped Pete. But by the time Pete had won his wings in the RCAF the elder Lehman had relented. In fact, he brought his father's pride to Ottawa and himself pinned the wings on.

By the time Pete reached Debden his father had declined to run for governor again and had followed his two sons (the second was a captain in the tank corps) into war service, as director of United Nations Rehabilitation and Relief Administration. Pete was too modest ever to talk much about his distinguished father, but one night in the station cinema the newsreel showed him and everybody roared as Pete involuntarily shouted, "That's my papa!" Pete had participated in 57 bomber escort missions but had destroyed no Huns as yet. However, the Huns had almost destroyed him: "Once over Emden, Millie saved my life by shooting a Hun off my tail. I didn't see him. Another one got on me over Bremen. I didn't know that until 1 saw the tracers."

But by now Pete had served his apprenticeship and meant to get some Jerries himself. He confided the hope that he could win a DFC in time to send his father for his 70th birthday on March 28.

The pilots rubbed the aching areas as they made their reports, which were flashed to Widewing to the war planners, and devoured chocolate to sustain them until they could reach the Mess. Blakeslee ordered the Free Beer sign on the bar mirror. The beer foamed and frothed. But no more so than The Birdmen.

Out on the line in the winter twilight, however, the day's work was just beginning. During the change-over period from Thunderbolts to Mustangs many of the crewmen worked 24-hour stretches. One night they were routed off their biscuits at 2 o'clock to change spark plugs in all the kites. There were kinks to iron out for the next day's mission. One pilot's radio had a high-pitched whine to it, or at least he thought it had. One's gunsight bulb had burned out. Another's high blower wouldn't cut in properly. The pilots were worn out, and in their reports of performance deficiencies it was often a case of hearing music the band wasn't playing. But the mechanics would check anyway. A mechanic didn't want to sit on the ground for six hours during the next day's mission wondering if his engine was giving trouble over Germany.

In the Mess lounge McKennon was ordering another head on his pint before pouring the coal to *Slow Train Through Arkansas*. Mr. MacDonald was bent on hearing him expand his testimony. He thought for a moment and tapped his shoulder. Would the gentleman be so good as to estimate the number of German fighters encountered over the capital of the Third Reich?

"Boy, I'm telling you—mill-yuns of 'em, simply mill-yuns!"

Mr. MacDonald repaired to his scotch-stocked suite

in the Savoy Hotel. The testimony of McKennon went through the pasteurization process of the ladylike *Times* copy desk and emerged in next morning's edition:

By JAMES MACDONALD
By Cable to The New York Times

A UNITED STATES FIGHTER BASE, IN ENGLAND, March 6.—Physically weary but undauntedly cheerful, American fighter pilots jumped out of their Mustangs here late this afternoon . . . and almost unanimously described the day's activities as the "best hunting" they had ever had.

The Officer-of-the-Day started out to the dispersal area for his first inspection of the guard. The field manual and army custom required the O.D. to inspect the guard once before midnight and once after midnight, but at Debden it was also required that the inspections be made four hours apart. Behind Hangar No. 2, constructed on the bed of the meadow lake where Mr. Kettley had fished 10 years before, the O. D. pricked up his ears. Out of the darkness came the roar of a Mustang motor. Assuming that enemy agents had picked the night on which he was O. D. to steal a Mustang, the officer crept up with a truculent, "What goes on here?" The annoyed mechanic, called from his motor-tuning in the darkness, identified himself. The O. D. mumbled something about being a "good show" and departed quickly.

In some rooms in the officers' quarters squadron execs were going through the effects of M.I.A.s (missing in action), preparing them for shipment home. The squadron I. O.s were phoning their intelligence reports to group intelligence for teletyping to higher headquarters. The group had destroyed 17.

The I.O. on night duty watch kept a weather eye on the teletype for tomorrow's order. Some time after midnight only the telephone orderly and the cooks were left in the Officers' Mess.

Out in the darkness about the parked Mustangs the guards huddled in their leather pants and coats, wishing the O. D. would hurry up, ask them if they knew their General Orders and get the hell back. There was a barrage of pistol-like explosions. The guards saw a dark shape in a clump of brush.

The guards got on their bellies and crawled over the frost-crusted grass to within 15 yards of the shape.

"Who goes there?" said a guard with hoarse nervousness.

"Eisenhower," replied the shape.

"I SAID—who goes there?"

"Why Eisenhower, old boy."

"Eisenhower, hell! I'm getting ready to blast you!"

The shape quickly surrendered: a British soldier on night maneuvers. Password: *Eisenhower*.

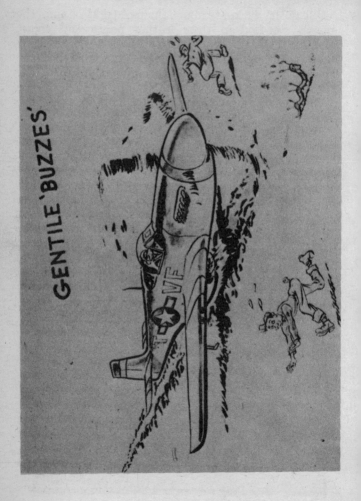

GENTILE 'BUZZES'

GENTILE

"... I got three. How many did Beeson get?"

Prepare for inspection!
Open ranks - harch!

DEBDEN VISIT

Gen. Eisenhower; Gen. Carl (Tooey) Spaatz, commander of USAAFE; Gen. James Doolittle, commander, 8th Air Force; Maj. Gen. Wm. Kepner, commander, VIII Fighter Command; Col. Don Blakeslee, commander, 4th Fighter Group.

SUPER GONG SHOW

General of the Army Eisenhower pins D.S.C.s on the "One Man Air Force" and Col. Blakeslee. Said Eisenhower: "I feel a sense of humility being among a group of fighting men like this."

Taxiing out for Take-off

D-Day Take-off

Col. Blakeslee briefing for first Britain-to-Russia mission, which the 4th was chosen to spearhead. Picture was highly secret at one time. The Deacon back from Russia and sporting the belt of a Russian general.

The Birdmen leaving briefing in Group Ops building for the take-off on the Britain-to-Russia shuttle mission.

Lt. Col. Oscar Coen (left, facing camera), Maj. Gen. Kepner, Lt. Col. Jim Clark, Mr. Banks (standing), Gen. Eisenhower, Col. Blakeslee, Gen. Spaatz, Maj. Gentile, Brig. Gen. Auton. Capt. Joe Lang, Col. Fallows (left, nearest camera), Brig. Gen. Curtis, Maj. Good-son, Lt. Gen. Doolittle, Capt. Bob Johnson, Commander Harry Butcher, Capt. Alfred Markel, Lt. Rowles.

The Deacon delivering the gen on the Britain-to-Russia to the squadron surgeon, Dr. Cecil Blackburn, Birmingham, Ala. McKennon is just back from the first American attack on Berlin. "Huns? Millyuns, pal, millyuns!"

A SHORT SHORT

1. *Gentile comes in low.*
2. *Too low.*

NO. 1 AND NO. 2

Maj. John Godfrey, Gov. Dwight Green of Illinois, and Maj. Don S. Gentile. Godfrey and Gentile were the greatest fighter pilot team in the history of the American Air Force. Both, as you will see over their hearts, received some recognition.

"RED DOG"

Maj. Louis Norley, Conrad, Mont., a latter-day commander of 334th Squadron, highest scoring of the three. He was the second fighter pilot over Berlin.

Map. Fred Glover, Asheville, N. C., one of the C.O.s of 336th Squadron. He had great natural cunning and craft as a fighter pilot. He loved every day of it.

MAJ. JOHN T. GODFREY
His may have been the keenest eyes in the U. S. Air Corps.

11
The Cowboy Rides Herd

John Godfrey, the gangling, shuffling, black-eyed boy from Woonsocket, R. I., who hated classrooms and ran away from home, had, as we said, the keenest eyes in the group. His vision was superb to start with and he sharpened it by a discipline in which he strained to sight distant objects as he practice-flew about Debden. Vision was 50 per cent of becoming a high-scoring ace. It meant that you could bounce a Jerry before he got set and that you got to him ahead of competing pilots. Godfrey also had an eye for the ladies as you could see by the lavish gallery of pin-ups in his room and his constant attentions to an army nurse, Lt. Charlotte Frederick, of Rochester, Pa.

Charlotte, Godfrey, Lt. Rob Richards, of Walden, N. Y., and Lucky, a poodle dog imbued with more personality than most people, had become a quartet. On leave in London, Godfrey and Richards had left base pay, subsistence and flying pay at the Embassy Club, to whose greedy gouging Americans submitted because it was about the only club which remained open after midnight in wartime London. They had left a green railroad ticket to Debden and 10 shillings.

With this last 10 shillings they bought the poodle and named him Lucky. A few days later Richards, who had destroyed three Huns and gave promise of becoming an outstanding pilot, was killed as he crash-landed in England on his return from the first Berlin mission. It was Godfrey's first brush with the reality of a killing war. Seeing a buddy killed for the first time was the usual rude awakening of pilots. Godfrey's grief was sharp. He was so shaken that the 336th's flight surgeon decided to drug him.

"Take these, Johnnie," the flight surgeon said. "Put you right to sleep."

Godfrey popped the pills in his mouth and washed them down with the whiskey he was drinking.

"See you in the morning, Johnnie. Cheers."

"Cheers, Doc."

The surgeon dropped back by Godfrey's room later. Instead of being asleep, Godfrey was still staring at the window. His expression didn't change as he took an occasional bite of the whiskey and flushed its fire down his throat.

The surgeon handed Godfrey more pills, thinking to himself, "This is enough to put two horses to sleep."

Godfrey swallowed them, but an hour later Godfrey was still awake. The surgeon said: "Lookit, Johnnie, you gotta get off that booze or the things won't put you to sleep. Alcohol is an antidote."

"Okay, Doc." With that, Godfrey shuffled down to the bar. From there on, there was a new glint of grimness about Godfrey.

When Godfrey first began to fly with the group he displayed a rump-over-teakettle aggressiveness in seeking dog-fights that prompted some of the ex-Eagles, imbued with a Battle of Britain defensive spirit to warn, "You'll get yourself killed." The same rebelliousness and indifference to authority that had handicapped Godfrey at home now served him well.

"Well, we're here to *fight* the war, aren't we?" Godfrey would ask testily. And despite repeated injunctions from the more experienced pilots, Godfrey went right on bouncing Huns and if the rest of the section didn't split-ess with him, then to hell with 'em. And, as it turned out, Godfrey the smartaleck showed the elders up.

When the pilots were briefed for the third Berlin show March 8, Godfrey went about his business as usual. He zippered on his flying clothes and saddled himself with chute and dinghy pack.

"Big 'B' again, huh?" said the crew chief as he polished the windscreen. The target was always a closely guarded secret, known only to the pilots and I. O.s, until after target time. The assumption was that an agent could communicate the target to Jerry and he could, if forewarned, deal deadly with the bombers. But somehow the mechanics on the line always knew what the target was.

Godfrey picked Lucky up by the left hind leg and swung him around. Lucky was imperturbable and didn't mind anything except being ignored. Godfrey licked his finger and patted the cowling of his plane. He had picked the habit up during training days in Canada when, as a starry-eyed cadet, he used to look at his glistening trainer plane and say to himself, "Gosh, you beautiful kite, I'd kiss you if nobody was looking."

The three squadrons taxied around behind Blakeslee and took off two at a time, circling the field until all were airborne and in squadron formation. Godfrey made a wider orbit than the others because he always flew by the Newport Hospital two miles from Debden to let Charlotte know he was taking off on a mission.

The field hospital, set up to receive the wounded from the impending invasion, was a collection of large canvas tents in an oak grove. Hospital personnel knew what it meant when a silver, red-nosed Mustang buzzed over so low the canvas tent tops rippled like wheat in the wind. Surgeons looked up from their appendectomies with a shake of the head, night duty nurses were awakened and all hands wished Godfrey would carry on his courtship on a higher level.

Godfrey gave three throttle blasts. That was their signal, a signal being needed because other pilots were wont to buzz the hospital, especially in the sun-bathing season. Sometimes Charlotte ran out and waved, while other times she was handing a scalpel to a surgeon. On his return Godfrey would buzz again with three throttle razzles to signal a safe return.

Godfrey took his place on Gentile's wing over Debden and Blakeslee led them towards Germany in tightly packed V-formation.

By UNITED PRESS

LONDON, March 8.— American warplanes, 1,500 to 2,000 strong, made the greatest fire raid in history on Berlin today... Hundreds of Fortresses and Liberators, shielded by more hundreds of fighter planes, smashed through Hitler's most powerful defenses to lash Berlin... Desperate German Air Force fighters struggled in vain to fend the blow...

German interceptors began to attack as the lead box of bombers reached the outskirts of Berlin, 20-plus ripping into the box head-on. Gentile and Godfrey met five 109s. Gentile was one of the few to whom Godfrey would listen. Godfrey had flown his first mission on Gentile's wing; he had fired his guns for the first time while flying on his wing. Godfrey on other occasions had gone to attack Jerries only to find that others had not taken the bounce with him, but Gentile was all fight and skill. Godfrey acknowledged Gentile as the masestro and willingly flew No. 2 to him.

Gentile and Godfrey singled out two of the five 109s and made six or seven turns with them, sparring and feeling them out. Godfrey maneuvered onto the tail of one.

"Okay, I'll cover you," Gentile said.

Godfrey gave the 109 a few short bursts and got strikes. The veteran Gentile pressed the transmitter button and said into his mask mike:

"Give 'im more . . . More!" The 109 rolled over and Godfrey clobbered him. He watched the German bail out.

Lt. Raymond Paul Clotfelter, Hillsboro, Ill., had hooked on behind Gentile and Godfrey, turning and twisting behind as he awaited his chance to fire. The turns were so violent that Gentile was having trouble making them without using flaps. Clotfelter found it harder and harder to keep step with Gentile and Godfrey in the maneuvers.

Gentile clobbered a 109 from 75 yards line astern.

"Gimme cover, Johnny, while I go after that 109 at 2 o'clock to us," Gentile said.

"I'm with you," Godfrey came back.

Using combat flaps for tighter turns, Gentile, with Godfrey guarding his tail and with Clotfelter trying to catch up, gave the 109 a squirt at 100 yards. The Hun's cockpit filled with smoke. He jumped from his plane.

By this time there were 50-plus Jerry fighters going up and down, in and out, in pairs. The bombers sprayed the sky with green flares to signal for help from the fighters. In these first Berlin shows, bomber pilots complained that the fighters, busy keeping their own heads above water, often ignored their distress signals. But they weren't talking about Gentile and Godfrey.

"All right, Johnny, there're two flying abreast at 1 o'clock. See 'em?"

"Yep."

"Okay," Gentile said, looking over at Godfrey, "you take the one on the right and I'll take the one on the left."

"Reet."

Gentile and Godfrey pushed the throttle to the firewall to overtake the two 109s. Clotfelter, still awaiting his chance to do some shooting, put everything forward. He had never seen two pilots keep together like the two in front of him.

The quarry were not the crafty, resolute killers like the 190 pilot who had stalked Gentile down by the railroad track a year before, or like some they were to encounter later. The 109s took no evasive action, maintaining a duck-on-pond formation. It was possible the Jerries knew they were being followed and planned a violent Immelman which would bring them down on the tails of their pursuers. If so, they waited too long to pull the stick. The wings of the two Mustangs flamed as two thumbs pressed down on the red firing tit—the same movement you use on a cigaret lighter.

Gentile's 109 rolled port and went down burning. Godfrey's rolled starboard and went down burning. Shooting them down was like pressing a dynamite detonator and seeing two bridges in the distance blow up.

"Nuts," said Clotfelter to himself, "can't keep up with these two." He went off by himself and bagged a 190.

Gentile and Godfrey had destroyed five Huns between them. They climbed back to 22,000 feet to get close to the bombers. Suddenly Godfrey looked over his right shoulder and saw it.

"Break! Break! One coming in at 4 o'clock to you!"

"Okay, break starboard," said Gentile.

They broke together and the 109 made a head-on pass.

"All right, Johnny," said Gentile, "when he comes back around on the next turn you break right and I'll break left."

They circled and the 109 came boring in for another head-on attack. He looked mean and vicious. He was bold enough to joust with two Mustangs. As the planes bored straight at each other's spinner, Gentile ordered the foxing maneuver:

"Now!"

Gentile broke sharply to the left; Godfrey to the right. They honked their sticks back, climbed and came barreling down on the 109's tail.

Thus trapped, the Jerry reacted fast. He pushed the stick forward and went into a steep dive for the clouds below. The Mustangs followed, firing and peppering the 109. Godfrey finally got in a solid burst as the 109 began pulling out of his dive at 500 feet, after a four-mile chase downward, and it gave off smoke.

"You take him, Don, I'm out of ammo," yelled Godfrey.

The German was weaving across the treetops. Gentile closed in and the next burst punctured the 109's belly tank. The German pulled up to 1,000 feet, jettisoned his canopy and crawled out the right side. He had the distinction of being No. 6 in the series.

"Guess we've had it now," Gentile said, "we'd better go on back."

Godfrey scanned his instrument panel to see if everything was ticking. He was numb and tingly with exultation. A pilot is not likely to do much reflecting for some time after combat like this, but one thought did stab through his numbness: "I made it for my birthday—I got five now." Fact was, Godfrey was an ace with one to spare.

"Hey, Johnnie, you see it?" Godfrey heard Gentile ask.

"No, where?"

"At 9 o'clock to you."

It was a straggling Fort. Gentile spoke of the Fort as *it* because it had to be assumed that the German ground stations were tuned in on AAF radio frequencies. Thus, reference to a straggler, its altitude, direction, etc., might summon a gaggle of Jerries to maul the cripple trying to limp home through the clouds.

There may have been one rump in the skies over the Berlin suburbs that ached more than Gentile's. If so, it was Godfrey's. Both wanted to push the throttle forward, streak home and get the harness off. Taking the Fort under their protection meant slowing down, tiresome weaving back and forth in order not to outdistance the cripple. Further, Godfrey could do no more than bluff enemy fighters as all his ammo was in the smashed 109s behind. Gentile was down to his tracers.

234

But there were 10 prayerful Americans in the limping, but majestic Fort. They were stomach-sick with dread of the gauntlet they would have to run all the way across Germany.

In the infantry, it would be putting a wounded friend over your shoulder in a retreat from mortar fire. In the AAF, it was kicking the rudder and sliding over on the starboard wing of the lame bomber.

"Mustang to Fort," Gentile said. "Okay, we'll take you in."

"Fort to Mustang," the bomber pilot responded. "Thanks, little friend, thanks."

"Woody" Sooman and a few others became separated from the rest of the group after it had charged in to frustrate the attack on the bombers and had arrayed itself on the port side of the bomber box. They had been flying along thus for about five minutes without molestation when Sooman saw a 109 initiate an attack on a lone Fort. Sooman overtook the 109 and with 30 degrees deflection from the port side, fired two short bursts from 700 yards. He closed in to 40 yards and saw a few slugs rip into the cockpit. The bullets probably tore into the cockpit where the armor-plate ended and killed the pilot, for the craft flicked over and went spinning down, its path blazed by a wake of white smoke.

Sooman began hearing the muffled *thump-thump* that meant a 109 firing. He forgot the 109 spinning down and turned to joust with his assailant. The 109 got the best of it. Two explosive 20-mm. cannon shells splattered Sooman's motor; others exploded as they pierced his starboard wing tank and tail assembly. It slapped the Mustang into a spin.

Sooman kicked and pulled and pushed, but he couldn't rein his Mustang in. He had lost control at 24,000 feet. He decided he had to bail or go in with the plane. He unbuckled his safety belt and released the canopy catch, thinking to himself that in jumping from this nose-down position his chances of bashing

235

his skull on the tail fin were good. The canopy should have flown off when he flipped the catch, but it wouldn't budge. The Kroll Opera House was rushing up to meet the nose of his plane. He tugged at the canopy catch until he could feel the metal on his finger bones through his thick gloves. He had spun down two miles and was at 9,000 feet. At 8,000 feet he regained control over the berserk craft and pulled out of the dive. His knees quivered so much, however, that the ball and needle wouldn't stay together.

The pilots were scattered by this time and busy. Lt. Robert Tussey, a taciturn Altoona, Pa. pilot who subsequently perished in the Channel, saw a plane under him near Madeburg going in the same direction. Tussey pulled the throttle back to let the craft forge ahead of him. He dived and came in on its tail. It was only his second combat mission and he wasn't taking any chances on clobbering a friend. But what he saw ahead corresponded with the cardboard silhouettes of a JU 88 on which the I.O.s drilled pilots on "released-for-training" days.

Tussey opened the throttle to close on the twin-engined craft, but misjudged a little and overshot. Tussey chopped his throttle, got back on the 88's tail and opened fire. The rear gunner in the fighter-bomber returned the fire, but the bullets streamed over Tussey's wing.

The 88 pilot started diving on an airdrome, probably his own, in the hope that the ground-gunners would shoot the Mustang off his tail. Tussey blazed away at the hangars as the 88 pulled up out of his gunsight. He gave the Jerry another burst from line astern and a chute blossomed, but only one. The dead tail-gunner crashed with the plane.

Lt. Allen F. Bunte, of Eustis, Fla., a stringy, gaunt man with the mustache of a western desperado and a yearning to become an actor, flew with another squadron attacking five 109s, which broke to the deck. In his excitement, Bunte opened fire at 1,000 yards. But by the time he closed in to 200 yards, his fusillade found the mark. The German spun out and jettisoned his canopy, but Bunte lost sight of him.

A few minutes later Bunte encountered a German trainer plane put-putting along just over the trees.

"Well, whatta you know, Joe?" the pilots heard Bunte growl.

No use in letting the cadet win his wings. Bunte squirted but saw no strikes. He was almost ramming the German cadet's trainer. Bunte pulled the stick slightly and nimbly leap-frogged the cadet, looking back to see him and his trainer in the top of a tree, like a bird's nest.

Lt. James Dye, a Dallas, Tex. oilman, scrutinized a fighter that was flying close on the rear of a Fort box. The craft wasn't firing, and neither were the bombers. Dye passed by and recognized it as a black 109; its landing gear was down for some unaccountable reason. It was just lazing along with the bombers, a stowaway. Dye fired several bursts at short range. As if puncturing a bag of water, Dye's fire peforated the cooling system of the 109 and glycol drenched his windscreen. The 109 went down. Soon after, Dye exploded the baby of a 190.

It was the Cowboy's third trip to Berlin. On the two previous missions, the sallow, erratic, rambunctious Megura had gotten doubles each time, plus planes and trains damaged or probably destroyed. He had blood in his eye on this, his third trip.

Clark ordered the squadron to climb full bore to a cluster of bombers which had called for help. As the Mustangs reached the heavies, five 109s zoomed down out of hiding in the sun. Clark clobbered one and Megura chased one down 33,000 feet to 8,000 feet. The left wing root of the 109 gushed fire. Megura saw another 109 on his tail, but shook him with a few skidding turns.

A mile away some 109s were ganging up on a lone

Fort straggler. Megura chased one down, firing as he skimmed over Berlin. Those white strike puffs came out of the starboard wing as Megura opened up and the engine began vomiting smoke. Megura was close enough to see the pilot throw his glass canopy off and pull the stick back.

But instead of jumping, the Hun stood half-in and half-out the cockpit of his Rubicon. Megura squinted and saw that the pilot was a giant. His flying togs looked black and he had one knee flexed in the cockpit trying to decide whether to jump. He looked at the smoke billowing from his 190, then he looked at the American pilot raging in on his tail.

The Hun was debating: Maybe the engine wouldn't burn up and he could land it ... Would the American break off the attack? ... Would another German force the American to break? ... Would the American machine gun him in his chute?

Megura steadied his swaying machine gun nest and fired a short burst to help the giant decide: jump or no. The ugly sparkling wings of the Mustang made up the Hun's mind—he jumped, tumbling end over end until the chute blossomed and jerked him head-up.

By now Megura was low over an airfield on the outskirts of Berlin and he began trailing a 109 in the field's pattern. The 109 didn't appear to mind his company in the least, nor did the other 109s circling the field to land.

Megura kept circling with them in their own fashion, doing as the Romans did, and was ignored. He saw a 109 coming in low, its flaps and wheels down for landing.

"Hah!" exclaimed Megura, "I'll sandbag this character and they'll think one of his buddies did it."

Megura began stealthily positioning himself on the unsuspecting 190 pilot. But the jig was suddenly up as two 190s came slicing across the field at 3 o'clock to him. They had recognized the Mustang silhouette.

Megura whipped around and broke into them.

Before the Jerries could come around for another head-on pass, Megura was on the first 109 again. Just as the 190's wheels were touching the runway Megura fired, but before he could get more than a few stinging strikes, the 190s came tearing back to deal with the Yankee who had the effrontery to masquerade as one of their own. If not dispatched, an American like this might show up at the mess for dinner and put arsenic, or Spam, in the food.

Megura gave it full throttle to out-distance the Huns, but they were keeping up pretty well and were markedly persistent. Megura could see that they were bent on nailing him, an insolent intruder. Megura glanced at his compass and found he was heading east—straight for Russia—a one-man *Drang nach Osten.* Russia was a friendly country all right, but that wasn't where he had left his toothbrush.

Megura began banking to turn south. But this permitted his pursuers to cut his corner and close the gap a little. So Megura would spurt ahead towards the Russian steppes, then use the gain to turn south for a moment. Finally he lost the 190s by this spurt-and-turn method. On the way back to Berlin he attacked a train, leaving it shrouded in a cloud of steam from its Swiss-cheese boiler.

Soon Megura reached Berlin and flew low over the southern part of the city. West of Berlin on the homeward flight across some mountains, Megura was pounced on by six unidentified craft. By weaving in and out of valleys and flying low over forests, he lost the six and climbed to 14,000 feet on a Debden heading. Megura glanced his watch, looked over the side and reckoned that he was over Happy Valley. He flew along for a few minutes and happened upon a JU 88 at 10,000 feet. Megura rolled it over and gave chase down to the factory tops in the densest flak area on the Continent. With one gun firing, Megura held the tit down and saw the slugs take effect.

Then the tracers started coming, which meant the

end of the roll. No more bullets. Megura pulled up alongside the Jerry like a motorcycle cop accosting a motorist and saw that the starboard engine had been knocked out.

Megura thumbed his nose at the plane and hollered, "You ugly bastard!" One more burst—but there wasn't any more, and he headed home with film to show that he had destroyed another double, damaged two more, and stopped a locomotive. A month later Megura was awarded the Distinguished Service Cross for this action and the one two days before.

Gentile and Godfrey were reaching the coast with the crippled Fort.

"Mustang to Fort," said the weary Gentile, "we'll be leaving you now. Good luck."

The bomber pilot came back fervently: "Thank you very, very much, Little Friend."

Inside the bomber, crew members were bending their trunks in with hands overhead rendering *salaams,* an oriental form of salutation meaning peace.

As the pilots streaked in over East Anglia they began seeking their own landmarks to hit Debden, excellently camouflaged. For many it was a little cluster of white houses at nearby Newport; for others the railroad tunnel on the line to Cambridge.

Godfrey broke off from Gentile to buzz Charlotte at the hospital. Charlotte heard the throttle blast signal and ran outside to see Godfrey victory-rolling over the hospital tents.

At Debden ground crews and I. O.s went outside to receive the pilots. A plane flashed by with a victory roll. It came in too hot to see the marking on it, but when it gave the 336th dispersal a second sandpapering buzz they knew it was Gentile.

"They're all split up," someone said. "Must have had a good mix."

If the group had come back in group formation you

240

knew they hadn't engaged.

You could tell the veteran pilots from the newer ones by their conduct in the circuit. The tyros made long approaches to the landing strips, while the veteran hot-rocks turned into the strip so short you'd swear the left wing was going to brush the ground.

Across the landing ground from Gentile's dispersal in 334th's hut, the squadron I. O., Capt. Charles Ashcraft, suave, foxy Pittsburgh salesman who addressed Southerners as "you Democrats," was engaged in his roughest labor—extracting Megura's combat report. The cowboy's recital gushed out in an incoherent spray. The words stampeded and piled up in his mouth, each word bumping the fender of the one in front.

"How many'd you get?" Ashcraft asked.

"Got two, damaged two and this train," Megura answered, grinding his gum.

"Now where were you when you clobbered this train?"

"Near Berlin—three of my guns jammed and when I was in the circuit this character came tear-ass across the drome, boy, I'm telling you that flak, but the main thing is my kite started cutting out—where is that crew chief?—if he'd just gimme some new spark plugs like I told him ... Jesus—say, Chat, did you see that Fort get clobbered just before the I. P.?"

"Take it easy, Twitcher," laughed Chatterley.

"Now look, Nick," pursued Ashcraft, "where were you when you clobbered that train I was asking about? Here, point to it on the map."

"Listen, can't you jokers do anything but ask questions? Told you—right near Berlin, those goddamn spark plugs ... Say, Ash, if that's all you wanted to know I'm going up to the Mess to eat ..."

Ashcraft decided to continue the interrogation in the morning.

Hofer stood about listening to the others rehashing the mission. He had made none of the Berlin shows because his ops time had accumulated quickly and Beeson, the squadron commander, was giving others opportunity to catch up.

"Gee, fellas," Hofer ruefully bleated, "I'm missing all the fun."

12
"Ain't the Alps Pretty?"

By United Press

LONDON, March 9.—Powerful American bomber fleets skimmed the top of a four-mile-high cloud layer today... and without a challenge from the German Air Force, stoked the great fires they had started in Berlin 24 hours earlier.

German fighters apparently were kept aground by the dense cloud bank over the Continent, unable even to make a pass at the big raiders.

Lt. Millard Jenks, a lanky I. O. from Madison, Wis., who viewed anything connected with wenching, boozing and movies as just another facet of the depravity of *homo boobiens* and airily brushed it aside as "high school stuff," noted that it was time for the pilots to be returning. He walked out in front of the dispersal hut where Blakeslee parked his plane and fingered the shutter on his Kodachrome camera. Jenks might lose his A.G.O. card and he couldn't remember when, if ever, he had a dog tag, but that camera was always moored to his long neck.

"Now if you take some of these characters," Jenks was saying. "All they think about is boozing and wenching. That doesn't take any talent. Those are the pursuits of the *Pithecanthropus Erectus*. Why can't they get interested in elevating their cultural level? Now you take photography . . ."

At this point the group, in close-packed formation, came whipping over Jenks' head. A Berlin show and all of them returning as though they had been on a Balboa?

Jenks pronounced: "Something fishy about this."

Blakeslee was first down. As he reached the revetment, he switched the tail of his kite around with a little more than ordinary violence and gunned a gale of grit into the faces of those ringing his craft. From his vexed expression it was assumed that his guns had failed or that somebody had been hogging the R/T.

"I'll be a sad sack—not a Jerry the whole damn way!" Blakeslee exclaimed. "Not even over Berlin." He shook his head dolefully.

"What you reckon it was, Colonel?" asked Croxton. "Weather?"

"I guess," Then Blakeslee blurted: "All that trip and not a Jerry!"

At that period of the war, it was incredible.

As the other Mustangs taxied past, the crews looked at their guns and saw the tape still covered the muzzles, which meant they hadn't fired either.

The other pilots were browned-off. They had been nervous or frightened when they took off, but now they were vexed and disappointed because no Huns had come up to fight with them. They sulked to their 5 P.M. meal, which others had eaten at noon.

"Is this the lunch or the dinner meal?" asked Goodson. "What does it say on the menu, Emerson? Lunch? Hm-m, pretty good lunch, wasn't it? Say, I just can't figure these characters out."

They began speculating whether it was the overcast which had prevented the Huns from swarming up as they had the day before. The 10/10ths cloud layer would not necessarily prevent planes from taking off, but it might prevent them from landing. Even so, it was incredible that an air fleet could bomb Berlin in daylight without molestation.

"I just can't figure 'em out," Goodson repeated.

"Well," interjected Sooman, "it isn't because we

shot 'em all down yesterday. I'll guarandamntee that!"

"You said it, kid," the Cowboy agreed.

The post mortem was interrupted at the entrance of Brig. Gen. Jesse Auton, of Covington, Ky., commander of the 65th Fighter Wing, of which the 4th was one of the five groups. He walked up to Lt. Col. Blakeslee and said, "Congratulations, Blakeslee." Turning to the others at the table, Gen. Auton, who never appeared to feel quite at ease at Debden, added:

"You boys have got a real old man now. Don's promotion came through today while you were on the show."

Gen. Auton, Blakeslee, the photographer and a few others repaired to Blakeslee's suite upstairs. A pre-war pinch bottle, rare as English sunshine, appeared.

"You'll notice, Don," said the General, "that I brought you two sets of eagles. That is because the heads of both eagles must face forward."

"I'll be damn if I knew that before," Blakeslee said. I noticed he didn't say "sir."

He was frugal in his use of "sir," and downright abstemious with Auton.

The General, looking over his mustache, pinned the eagles on the shoulders of 26-year-old commander. Blakeslee looked over at "Gunner" Halsey, and old Eagle type, and there was a suggestion of flinty twinkle in his eyes. He hadn't forgotten that on his transfer from RAF to AAF, Peterson was started off with a majority and he with railroad tracks. Nowadays he was acknowledged as the daddy of 'em all as E.T.O. fighter pilots went, the commander Pinetree always picked for the big jobs.

Blakeslee called the bar and told Irish to get out the Bon-Ami and write the sign on the mirror:

"FREE BEER TONIGHT (FULL COL. BLAKESLEE)"

Downstairs in the dining room the speculation continued as to why they had found no one home over

Berlin. Hofer beamed.

"Gee," he said, "I'm sorry you fellows didn't have any fun, but at the same time, I'm glad I didn't miss anything."

Time magazine saw the air war situation thus:

This week the Allied air command had sober reason to think they could force the Luftwaffe into a decisive battle with only one result: elimination of Germany's air defenses. They had some reason to think that at least part of that task was already accomplished. Germany's airmen could still fight well—but not every day.

In the overall sense the great air attacks now being launched from England are only the prelude to the unopposed destruction of German war potential and the land invasion that will finally destroy Nazi power. But in the immediate sense, the air campaign is itself a sizeable war, which has inflicted critical damage on the enemy's cities and armed forces.

The Allied air weapon was cutting as a two-edged sword. Air officers welcomed the chance either to dismantle Germany's war industry at trifling cost, or, better still, to whittle down the tiring Luftwaffe squadrons in the process. Last summer, after frantic efforts, the Nazi had lifted their fighter-plane production to an estimated 1,200 ships a month. Then the Allies opened their methodical campaigns against aircraft factories, assembly plants, repair depots. Last week Allied authorities reckoned that the Germans were getting only 25 percent of the new fighters expected by March.

But it was no guess that the Luftwaffe had lost 301 fighters in two daylight air battles over Berlin last week, and it was no guess that when the U.S. bombers came back in force for a third attack within four days, the Luftwaffe planes

246

did not come up to oppose them.

For a precedent military historians looked back to the classic battles of landbound days, and wondered if this might be the stage when the weaker side had committed its reserves and was failing.* Then the stronger would strike the knock-out blow. He would send in his cavalry, ripping through the flagging line, then pour infantry through the breach while his horsemen drove on, carving a decision in the enemy's disorganized rear areas. The days to come would tell whether the parallel would hold good for the U.S. Eighth Air Force's 'heavy cavalry.' But as the most powerful air offensive in history rolled through its third week, the Luftwaffe behaved exactly like a fighter who finds the going too rugged, knows instinctively that he must break off or risk exhaustion and knock-out . . .

Early in the week 800 U.S. bombers and nearly 1,000 fighters had fought a terrific battle to, from and over Berlin; 176 enemy fighters were downed, but the German was still impressive, capable. The U.S. losses were the biggest yet: 68 heavy bombers and 11 fighters. Two days later a slightly smaller attacking force slugged its way in through a thinning overcast and plastered the key Erkner ball-bearing works at Berlin. Their combat was still large scale: 38 bombers and 15 fighters were lost, 125 Nazi planes shot down.

But again next day; a similar bombing force went out, and this time the Eighth cashed in on its recuperative powers. Flying above a heavy overcast the U.S. ships sorted out their Berlin targets with secret instruments, got off their

---

*It was.

bombs. They flew home in peaceful wonderment. Along the entire 1,200-mile route there was nothing to worry about but flak barrages ... American gunners claimed no enemy ships: they had seen none to shoot at.

Even conservative observers wondered whether the week might not have brought an historic turning point to World War II. No Allied airman was so brash as to say the Luftwaffe was not strong enough to go up to fight. Weather, weariness and disorganization from the earlier battles—any or all of these might have influenced the Nazi fighter command's decision. But if the Germans could not defend Berlin, then what could they defend? And if Berlin was no longer worth defending, then what center of German pride and might did not face the same fate?

The Luftwaffe is not yet entirely committed to inaction; it is still believed to have some 1,000 planes assigned to defend North and West Germany. But at week's end it was still on the ground ...

Time's diagnosis and prognosis was to prove strikingly penetrating and accurate. But nobody could be sure then.

The strain of the grueling missions could be detected among the pilots and the ground crews, but the strain was alloyed with a buoyant, exultant spirit stemming from the pilots' stellar performance. The mechanical bugs in the Mustangs, which had caused some losses and held the score down, were extirpated, and the older pilots were sagely recalling that the same thing happened when the group changed from Spits to 'Bolts.

The pilots compared notes, drew conclusions from their combat encounters and decided that there was not the slightest doubt that the Mustang was the world's finest fighter plane. Of course, Thunderbolt

248

and Lightning pilots were convinced that *they* were flying the finest planes, but the important thing was, 4th pilots now believed in what they were flying.

On the days when the mission had to be scrubbed on account of bad weather, many of the pilots would fly to Col. Zemke's base to horse around in the clouds with the Wolfpack's Thunderbolts, showing off their new kites. The Thunderbolts had been greatly improved by this time and some of the pilots would return to Debden to report that they couldn't outdistance some Wolfpack pilot even on the deck. But in the main, as they got the feel of their new planes, they came back to tell how they could turn inside of the Thunderbolts, out-climb them and, in the early stages of a dive, easily keep up with the 7-ton milk bottle.

On March 16 the group accompanied bombers to Munich and shot down 13 Huns for the loss of one. When they hove into sight of the blue-white Alps, Hofer couldn't repress an outburst:

"Gee, ain't the Alps pretty!"

Nobody could swear that Blakeslee's cockpit was filled with smoke, but it sounded like it was on fire:

"That'll be just about enough of that goddamn R/T chatter!"

The pilots tangled with a Hun gaggle and Blakeslee was trying to reform the group.

"Horseback to his No. 2. Pull up line abreast me," Blakeslee said. He liked tight-packed formations.

"Roger," murmured his No. 2, a newcomer to the group.

But Blakeslee couldn't see that his wing man had pulled up any closer and he repeated:

"I said—line abreast."

"Roger," came the faint murmur.

A few minutes later the pilot still hadn't pulled up. Blakeslee rasped:

"Will that WD kite pull up line abreast or won't it?"

Another pilot, trying to join up, interrupted:

"Pectin Green 3 to Horseback. Where are you, Horseback?"

Blakeslee exploded:

"About two miles in front of the bombers with a damnfool for a No. 2!"

On the morning of March 18, Kid Hofer and Duke jumped from the beaten-up weapons carrier in front of the group intelligence building. The police dog's master, "Digger" Williams, of St. Petersburg, Fla., had been shot down,* after which Duke's fur grew coarse for a time and he took to snapping at people. When he saw an officer in the distance, he would run out full tilt and eagerly sniff his knee, always hopeful the scent would prove that of Williams.

Finally he took up with Hofer as a foster master and on this morning both were frolicsome. Hofer was as radiant as a girl with a new party dress because Beeson had put him on the board to go on the show. The pre-briefing tension was relieved by the act Hofer and Duke put on. It consisted of Duke's running through a forest of legs, some trembling, in pursuit of a ball thrown by Hofer. Suddenly everybody popped to. "Down," said Hofer to Duke with a slight motion of his finger. Duke assumed the position with his ears at attention. Blakeslee breezed through the briefing; they were always short and acid. The red crayon line extended from Debden to Munich in southern Germany.

"Okay," said Blakeslee as always, "we haven't got long before it's time to press."

The Wolfpack's way of designating the time for cranking off the motors was S/E—start engines. *Press* was an RAF carryover.

The weapons carriers sped out to the dispersal huts on the far side of the field opposite the three black

---

*He later returned to England and married.

hangars. Duke watched Hofer don his football jersey, blue with a flaming orange "78" on it (signifying nothing). Some pilots removed their rings for a mission because there had been cases of getting the hand hooked to an instrument switch with them, but Hofer never removed the snake ring he wore on his throttle hand.

Hofer gaily pointed his finger at the black and tan animal and admonished. "Now you be a good dog while I'm gone and stay away from the Mess, or Clat will put you in the guardhouse again, and I'm tired of getting you out." That was the law at Debden during the reign of Lt. Col. Walter G. W. Clatanoff, of Easton, Md., able administrative executive officer who loved the paper on which the rules of army discipline were written. Dogs found in the mess were confined in the guardhouse, prison population at the time permitting, until their masters bailed them out. Duke hadn't been to the clink as often as Godfrey's irrepressible poodle, Lucky, but he had a record; and in the expert opinion of Cpl. Clifford Reich, of Cleveland, Ohio, whose melancholy duty it was to arrest dogs on Clatanoff's warrant, Duke would never go straight. Clatanoff held that a dog was guilty of breaking and entering if he got as many as two legs across the threshold. Cpl. Reich was more lenient, abstaining from action until at least three legs were clearly inside. Two legs elicited a warning in Reich's croaking voice, "Move on, ya bum."

Hofer buckled on his parachute pack and said with a wink and smile to Ashcraft, "Two Jerries for me today, Ash."

The group began its laborious climb-out over the Channel. It was a part of a mission's routine that all the pilots abhorred, especially if clouds forced them to climb on instruments. One morning Blakeslee had said, "We won't take off unless I can see the end of the runway," and they didn't break into the blue until they were six miles up.

Hofer was a good deal less susceptible to anxiety and nervousness than most of the pilots. He didn't even take fright at the orange golf balls. Clashing with Jerries was a lark. It was a prize fight in the Golden Gloves Tournament with everybody cheering his K. O. of his opponent in the 5th. Being a champion, he didn't bother to dwell on the other side of it, which was being the guy over whom the referee was counting 10. Hofer had been around long enough to see numerous skilled pilots shot down, but he went about his combat with undiminished gaiety.

Like many others, however, Hofer had a special phobia. And that was climbing to altitude over the Channel on the way to Germany. It made his heart flutter. He didn't know why, but to him there was something sinister about the reflection of the sky in the steely water. It made him dizzy, and sometimes sick enough to vomit.

The group reached altitude, leveled off and spread out in battle formation. Hofer felt better immediately. Coming back over the Channel wasn't so bad because you weren't climbing, and you traveled at high speed. Hofer thought how beautiful the Alps had been the day before and that he would take another good look today (but it was for sure he wouldn't get Col. Don all riled again with any commentary on the R/T!). He was flying No. 4 to Maj. Gerald Montgomery, of Littlefield, Tex.

"Pectin Blue 1 to Blue Section," said Montgomery, "let's go down on those 109s."

Montgomery rolled over and dived down. Hofer hadn't heard a word of his order because his radio wasn't working. This was an entirely acceptable reason for turning back from a mission, but Hofer gleefully followed after and shot down a 109 which fell near an airdrome.

Climbing back up, Hofer attacked another 109 and the pilot bailed out. Hofer bounced a third 109 with a baby, but the 109 picked out his cloud and scurried on to overtake the others. With no radio, he had not heard Blakeslee's order to return to base. So Kid Hofer cruised on towards Munich, a one-man fighter screen for several wings of combat bombers.

Failing to find the rest of the group, Hofer checked his compass to ascertain that he was on the course for Munich. He forgot all about the heading, however, at the sight of two 109s passing above and in front of him. Hofer climbed full bore into their smoke trails and got within 600 yards. At which point his prop began running away; it was giving his kite no more lift than an egg-beater. His air speed fell and the panel recorded a great deal of boost and r.p.m.s. Hofer decided he was going to have to bail. But there was no use taking a chance on German farmers with pitchforks if he could surmount the Alps and land in neutral Switzerland.

Checking the map on his knee, Hofer steered towards the Alps at 6,000 feet. He passed by the German part of Lake Constance and saw the bombers raining destruction on what he took for an assembly plant for aircraft. He saw a Hun clobbering a Mustang of another group, but was helpless to intervene. The Hun beat the American out of the sky and the Mustang began flaking mophandle-sized debris.

Hofer was far from sure that he could get over the Alps with the malfunctioning prop that just wouldn't take a good bite of air. The football jersey began soaking up his sweat and if there was any luck in that snake ring, Hofer wanted it in a lump sum. Below, but not as far below as he wished, were the blue-white Alps, over which Hannibal mahouted the elephants. But Hofer didn't have to see the Alps' rugged peaks and gaping canyons to know he was over the mountains, because over mountains the air is turbulent and a sudden turbulence buffeted his Mustang about like a canoe in a rapids. The prop whirred, but wasn't biting.

253

into it. He went on to circle the drome, but seeing nothing, climbed up again to rejoin the group. But he couldn't see a single Mustang in the sky. Assuming that they had proceeded on the course to Munich, Hofer set his compass for Munich and poured the coal

Hofer's heart, urgently slapping his chest, beat less quickly as he felt the air getting smoother. He knew he had succeeded in nursing his ship over the Alps into Switzerland. That meant he wasn't going to be imprisoned or lynched in Germany and that he wasn't going to splatter himself to cold pulp on the icy crags of the Alps. He had lucked out. He would soon be a guest of the Swiss. He remembered that in Switzerland you could get all the milk and steak you wanted. Or was that Sweden?

Now was the time to bail, for any minute the motor might conk out altogether. But it was a sweet ship, even if the prop wouldn't bite. He flipped the canopy hatch; it bore the red stenciled caps: Emergency. The glass covering was raked off by the powerful air flow and sailed in erratic course over the tail assembly. Hofer shuddered as the icy blast pinned him to his seat.

Hofer decided that he would jump out over the right side the way he had seen the Jerries do it. This wasn't the AAF-approved method of jumping from a fighter, but it always seemed to work for the Jerries.

Hofer yanked the stick back to get all possible altitude for the jump, unfastened the safety belt and began to climb out. But as the nose of the ship went up, the motor came back with a roar. The prop bit big bites of air. Air speed increased. It was almost a mockery of his intention to jump. Hofer couldn't think why the motor had come back as he yanked the stick, but conjectured that the altered altitude of the nose had somewhat restored the proper pitch to the prop.

Hofer sank back in his seat and went into an orbit, debating what to do. The motor sounded all right now and the instruments showed everything was working smoothly, but, then for that matter, it had sounded all right when he took off from Debden. He put the nose down in a shallow dive to see what would happen. The motor roared on. Just the same he'd better jump; that way he knew he would live out the war. But the combat film in the wings of those 109s he had shot down? If he jumped, the film would never be seen. He couldn't bear that.

Hofer was alone in the blue haze around the Alps, yet he felt that a thousand eyes were hard upon him. It was silly, but he felt that he was being watched. He looked down to check his fuel gauges. He wasn't sure there was enough for getting back to England and began doing mental arithmetic on a basis of some gasoline tests he had recently run at Debden. He thought of that combat film again. It decided him: He would have a go.

He would continue on until his gauges showed that exactly half his gasoline was burned. He could then decide whether the remaining half of the gasoline would get him back across the Channel to England. If not—barring a head wind—he would set course on the reciprocal vector and return to Switzerland to finish out the war as an internee.

Hofer thereupon re-crossed the Alps, re-entered Germany and set course. Over the Channel he looked down at his gauge and kicked himself. But he made it to an RAF coastal base and landed with—six gallons of gas.

But also—with his precious combat film.

The others had landed at Debden sometime before. Beeson hung his flying togs in his locker, put his valuables back in his pocket and strode into the small interrogation room. Beeson helped himself to a stick of gum and a cigaret.

"Hofer is N.Y.R.," Ashcraft said. "Afraid he's had it."

"Golly, that's too bad," replied Beeson with his

blinking, perplexed frown. He looked up at the board and saw that Hofer's plane-plate was still up in the No. 4 position to Montgomery.

"You get anything today, Bee?"

"Yeah, a 109," Beeson said matter-of-factly.

Ashcraft wrote it down on the glass-covered map on his desk with a red crayon.

"How'd the other boys do today?" asked Beeson.

Ashcraft knew what this question was aimed at. He said:

"Gentile got a 190."

"Good show," said Beeson breezily.

Gentile was going through the same motions in his dispersal on the other side of the field.

"You get anything today, Gentile?"

"Yeah, a 190," Gentile said with genuine casualness. "How did the other boys do?"

The I. O. knew what this question was aimed at. He said:

"Beeson got a 109."

"Good show," said Gentile.

In 335th Squadron a pilot asked, "How did the others do?" and the I. O. replied:

"Beeson got a 109 and Gentile got a 190. Puts 'em even with 15 each."

"Good show," said the pilot.

Next morning *The New York Times* reported:

LONDON, March 19.—An Eighth Air Force group commanded by Col. Don Blakeslee has destroyed 212½ German planes to become the second U.S. fighter outfit in the European Theater to pass the 200 mark.

The leading group inferentially referred to in *The Times* story was Col. Zemke's Wolfpack, which had been moved from Halesworth to Boxstead. The 4th had destroyed 212½ planes, but the Wolfpack—flying P-47s, which the 4th said were hopeless—had shot past the 300-mark.

Stars & Stripes carried a chronic feature story on how and why the Wolfpack was the "hottest" in the E.T.O. As the oldest group in the theater, as the aristocratic descendants of the old Eagle Squadrons, Debden pilots were testy and morose in their second fiddle status.

Undisputed as was the leadership of the Wolfpack, Debden connected the evergreen coronations and annointments of their rival in *Stars & Stripes* with things other than sound newspaper practice, such as Col. Peterson's bad manners at the press conference. *Stars & Stripes* became popular at Debden like Li'l Abner during his tenure as inside man at the skonk woiks.

But it all added up to good effect. Zemke was a brilliant commander of a brilliant team. It is indisputable that the Wolfpack set the pace for all groups in early 1944 by seeking combat with the Jerries. Between the 4th and the Wolfpack there was jealousy and hostility. But it was the basis of a rivalry, a sort of Hun-killing tournament, that sparked and stimulated the aggressiveness of all the other outfits in VIII Fighter Command. It was a bomber boon.

The 4th was in the process of regeneration. At first the pilots made snarling, graceless alibis to rationalize the Wolfpack's leadership; then they began grudgingly to acknowledge that the Wolfpack had taught them a lesson. It left them frantic to rack up a bigger and bigger score.

The new combat ardor, however, was nourished by things other than rebelliousness at the Wolfpack's eminence, and the most potent of these was the rivalry between Gentile and Beeson for top-scoring honors. Many of the older, defensive-minded pilots had retired from the lists, leaving such ones as Godfrey to their own combat devices. Beeson and Gentile, and to some extent Garrison, deserve a great deal of credit for inspiring the others to go after big scores, for their boldness and skill had demonstrated that it could be done.

A third factor was the P-51 Mustang. The pilots had unqualified confidence in it. They were getting the bugs out of the 51s and there had been enough combat in them to reveal what it could and could not do against the 109 and 190.

A partial answer to malfunctioning guns had been found. At first the machine guns in the wings were slanted, or turned sidewise, and in a steep bank at combat speeds, the tremendous pull of gravity would prevent the .50-cal. bullets from feeding. A second difficulty was that at the 50-below temperatures, oil in the guns would congeal. This was remedied in the North American factory probably by some maligned 4-F civilian—with the installation of an electrical gun-heater to keep the oil fluid.

A pilot could usually tell whether it was sluggish oil or the pull of gravity which prevented his guns from firing. If it were the gravity, the malfunctioning guns would fail on one wing or the other, depending on whether the turn had been port or starboard. The recoil of guns firing on only one wing caused the ship to skid and, at critical altitudes, might even cause the craft to spin out.

Each Mustang carried a cine camera in the wings to record combat action. When the guns were fired, the camera ground automatically. It was on the basis of this film that planes most often were officially confirmed or disallowed.

But in these first days of Mustang combat the camera lens would frost up, resulting in a blurred film that might prevent a pilot from obtaining confirmation of his claim. This was corrected by punching holes in the camera orifice to make the temperature of the air the same on the inside as the outside.

At first the oxygen tanks were not large enough and there was a limit on the time a pilot could remain above 10,000 feet without passing out. Larger tanks were installed.

So the 4th, revitalized by inner and outer rivalry and superbly equipped with the Mustang, was primed for a supreme performance. The Wolfpack was far ahead in planes destroyed, but the surging comeback of the characters over at Debden made the head that wore the crown rest uneasy. Other groups delighted in dismissing the 4th as a raunchy bunch of has-beens who couldn't make the team in the AAF, but the Wolfpack paid them the compliment of curses every time they got a bag of Huns.

The Wolfpack was constitutionally allergic to the 4th. When the baseball and football teams of the two groups met, the betting and bitching were fierce (the 4th won more than it lost, regardless of whose referees were used). Once when Zemke couldn't land his squadron at Boxtead on account of fog, he found an emergency field and had his wheels down to land when he saw the big white letters in front of the tower—"DB."

That "DB" were the initials of Don Blakeslee was simply an appropriate coincidence, for they really were the code letters for Debden Airdrome.

The Wolfpack, as Blakeslee was fond of relating, refused to land.

Dinghy drill in Saffron-Walden swimming pool. Boats were carried in parachute pack. Sometimes used to fish from.

Capt. K. G. Smith (dark glasses), Boise, Idaho, has been liberated by Patton's tanks and relates prison experiences.

Left to right: Lt. James E. Halligan, Jr., Capt. Oliver B. Bucher, Jr., Lt. Henry A. Lee, Lt. Charles B. Greenlese, Lt. Wade F. Underwood, Lt. George D. Green, Lt. Thomas H. Elffner, Lt. Enoch Jungling, Capt. Smith, Maj. McKennon, Capt. Grover C. Hall, Jr. (rear view).

"THE SWEDE"

Capt. Kendall E. Carlson, Red Bluff, Calif., who fought the Germans even after he was shot down. He bawled, yelled and clobbered in some of the great air battles of the war.

"MAC"

Maj. Pierce W. McKennon, who, you can tell by the painting, had bailed out twice and hailed from Arkansas (Ft. Smith).

COL. EVERETT W. STEWART

Stewart, the 4th's last C.O., hailed from Eisenhower's hometown, Abilene, Kans. If a man had to be in the army, it was best to be in Stewart's command. He had a fine gift for picking the right man for the right job.

13
Blakeslee's Prediction

By mid-March there was no novelty in a Berlin show. The early ones had been like blazing a Northwest Passage, but the later ones got to be just well-regulated Big Business. McKennon started bringing *Singing Guns* to briefings. He would look up at the red crayon line from Debden to Berlin and say, a little self-consciously but genuinely, "Oh, hell, the milk run again." It was still a dangerous, rugged mission, but it had become routine; the unknown had become familiar. Every pilot knew the outlines of Dummer Lake like those of his D.F.C.

March 9th was not the last time the 4th and other outfits used Berlin for a parade ground. But it was still incredible to them when no Jerries came up. One day after the pilots had swaggered up and down the Unter den Linden for 10 or 15 minutes without incident, an anonymous pilot murmured a spontaneous "Ho-hum." The murmur made a box insert on most U. S. front pages next day.

But there was no doubt that the Germans still had a formidable fighter force and it had to be destroyed before the ground forces, over whose training maneuvers the pilots flew often, could hit Omaha and Utah. So, if Jerry wouldn't come up to be shot down, then AAF fighters would go down and destroy him in his hole.

On March 21 the group, led by Lt. Col. Clark, the shy, aloof New Yorker, churned up and down France for more than four hours at treetop level, spewing armor-piercing incendiaries at German planes on the ground and at those landing and taking off. Swooping down on German airdromes from the Pyrenees Mountains bordering Spain, to the Paris area, at speeds ranging from 400 to 500 m.p.h., the Mustangs destroyed 21 planes. In addition, the four-hour spray damaged other craft, rattled and killed German soldiers.

The pilots saw scores of French peasants at their spring plowing and sowing. Their horses cavorted, but the Frenchmen looked up impassively as the Americans whipped over the furrows low enough to suck up dust. The pilots waggled wings at the farmers, but few waved back. The fourth harvest under German bayonets had left them wondering whether deliverance was coming at all.

As the hot rake was drawn across the German dromes on a zigzag track 1,200 miles long, ground fire belched up, luminous and accurate. The orange golf balls sliced and hooked before windscreens. Sometimes the missiles caused glycol leaks and the pilots had several minutes in which to bail before the motor overheated and caught fire. The Germans scurried across the perimeter tracks to take shelter or to man the gun posts.

Lt. "Roger the Lodger" Braley, of Pasadena, Calif., crouched low and charged a blister hangar. These Germans apparently had not been alerted and were sitting about in the gold-bricking attitude common to all armies. Braley, pointing his kite's snout at the mouth of the hangar, opened fire. The slugs kicked up a path in the dirt right up to the hangar entrance. The soldiers scattered as Braley held his fire upon them. A horse, hitched to a wagon, loped out of the hangar into the path of Braley's fire. Godfrey came in hard behind Braley. The ground gunners missed Braley, as they usually did miss the first plane, but they were ready for Godfrey. A flak burst struck the fuselage just behind him. His cockpit filled with smoke.

Braley was white and drawn when he landed. The

I.O. asked him: "What's the matter, Roger?"

"I'm afraid," Braley gravely answered, "I killed him—a horse. I didn't mind the Germans . . . but that horse."

Godfrey laughed and said: "Don't worry, Roger, you didn't kill the horse. I came in behind you and I saw him galloping off behind the building, pulling a wagon with one wheel missing."

But Braley wasn't satisfied until he saw his combat film run off in the Photo Lab. It showed the horse alive and kicking.

"Hell's bells! What happened to your kite, lieutenant?" a crew chief on the other side of the field was asking Lt. Vasseure (Georgia) Wynn,* of Dalton, Ga.

Georgia stooped and looked at the belly of his Mustang. It had a long, gaping rent in it. Georgia shook his head: "Rough!"

"That ship won't fly anymore, lieutenant."

"No, it's had it," Georgia agreed. A former page in the U. S. House of Representatives, Georgia had also worked for the F.B.I., quitting to enlist in the RCAF. In July, 1942, with 13 hours of practice-flying in Spits, Georgia took off from the deck of an aircraft carrier in the Mediterranean and landed at Malta. The Blitz was at its meridian and on the third day after his arrival, Georgia got 15 cannon holes in his Spit and another one in his leg. He applied a tourniquet and made ready to hobble off to the sick bay. Instead, he was told to get into another Spit and go up to intercept a second wave of bombers headed for the island. Georgia fought on through the celebrated Blitz and got three kills and three probables before Jerry decided the RAF had made it too expensive to carry on the bombing of Malta. Georgia didn't think Jerry was as tough as his brothers over Malta two years before, but he could look at the ripped belly of his

---

*I saw Georgia in early 1946. He married while stationed at Craig Field.

Mustang and see that Germany was still no place for a lady.

"If I'd known my kite was like that," Georgia said, "I wouldn't have tried to make it back. I was beating up this drome when I saw this building and some sort of pole by it. I pulled back hard as I could leap-frog it. But I see what happened now—I scraped the belly of the ship on that pole."

"Yes, and you're lucky as hell," the mechanic observed.

"Yeah?"

"Well, your prop hasn't got a scratch on it. It was your good luck that the blades didn't hit that pole. It just happened that the turn of the blades synchronized to let the top of the pole pass through its orbit."

In short, had Georgia started his engine earlier or later when he took off, the prop blades might well have been splintered.

Jim Dye, the Texas oil speculator, was on the way to Debden. Deep in France Dye had been attacked by several 190s at low altitude. Dye dived, turned and twisted to keep from presenting a deflection target to the Huns. But he saw oranges on the wings of a 190 and his plane shuddered as a cannon shell smacked the right side of his cockpit. Dye jerked his right leg from the rudder, feeling a red-hot poker against his leg. Looking down, Dye saw his green coveralls turning dark red. Then he felt his leg getting wet.

Dye eluded the 190s and set course for Debden, wondering if it were vein or artery which was soaking his leg. Feeling faint, Dye tied a handkerchief about his leg. But the blood still oozed. Dye then managed to get his belt off in the cramped cockpit and to keep the ball on the needle. The belt laced tight about his leg staunched the blood-jet.

Dye was thankful when he spotted the railroad tunnel near Audley, Eng. Over Debden he wondered how he was going to land since he couldn't use his right leg on the rudder. He made a long, slow approach to the strip. The Mustang veered sharply to port in a cross-wind. Forgetting that his leg was useless, Dye kicked the right rudder and came down almost three-point.

A mechanic helped him out of the ship. Dye wouldn't go to the hospital until he had limped into the dispersal for a long, hot shot of whiskey. His nerves were hurting more than the cannon wound. Sweat drops fell in his whiskey pony. Dye pulled his tongue and sleeve across his mouth and said huskily, "Okay, where's the meat wagon?"

Clark walked into group intelligence to report to Blakeslee. He sat by a radio over which he had followed part of the show by listening to the R/T chatter.

"How was it, Jim?" Blakeslee asked.

"Okay, I guess, Don," Clark answered. "Got seven N.Y.R.s, though."

"Seven?" asked Blakeslee.

"Yeah, the light stuff was plenty wicked."

"Seven men—I don't know how much of that we can stand," mused Blakeslee. "Anyway it was a damn good show, Jim."

As soon as Clark left, Blakeslee directed that a citation awarding Clark the Silver Star, third-highest decoration for valor, be written up and forwarded to higher headquarters. Weeks later the Silver Star was approved. The citation read:

". . . For gallantry in action over enemy occupied Europe on 21 March 1944. Knowing of a concentration of enemy aircraft deep in occupied France, Col. Clark asked for and received permission to lead a fighter group against this heavily defended military installation. He personally planned the entire mission and selected the routes and targets on the *longest sweep into enemy territory* yet made by American fighter aircraft from bases in England . . ."

In short, if the Germans wouldn't send their planes up, then the Americans would seek them out and demolish them on the ground. The AAF was out to nullify Luftwaffe strength. So the infantry could invade.

Months later the 4th destroyed five times this many planes in a strafing attack, but this was a pioneering job. Fighter Command held it up to show other groups what could be done.

The mission might be described as a mass rhubarb (nobody was sure why a low-level attack was a "rhubarb" unless it was the obvious connotation of brushing the rhubarb tops). It sharply contrasted with the two-ship missions Clark and Goodson had flown two years before.

Goering had evidently decided to let the bombing targets take it on the chin and hoard his fighter strength for D-Day. He could disperse the craft on the ground and obtain some measure of protection from bombs, but dispersal didn't thwart zig-zagging fighters. And there was some poetic justice in the strafing tactic, for the Germans had invented it 30 years before; in fact, *strafen* is a German verb meaning to punish.

Here is the way the London *Daily Express* viewed the beat-ups:

The strafing of airfields across Europe to Berlin and the Baltic is about the most dangerous job that thousands of young American and Allied fighter pilots are doing these days ... To shoot up enemy planes on these distant fields, Thunderbolts, Mustangs and Lightnings fly through hundreds of miles of enemy territory and run the gauntlet of hundreds of guns. Some of these guns shoot as high as 40,000 feet, others are set to cross-fire above the growing fields of corn, and even rifles and tommy guns are now aimed at the strafers.

The strafer zooms down and across at speeds ranging up to 450 miles an hour. He flies, perhaps, only 10 feet above the ground. He must keep his eyes skinned for obstructions on the airfield, buildings that rim it, and other planes of his squadron knifing through the dust, smoke and fire.

This perilous game of strafing has seen the loss of more aces of the U. S. 8th and 9th Air Forces than any other form of flying.

Terrific speed protects the strafer in the early stages of his attack. As long as he stays low, using the shelter of trees and hills, he is a difficult target. To check his position on the map as he turns homeward, the strafer pilot must often climb high enough to pick out a string of landmarks. The moment he sticks his nose up, like a prizefighter coming out of a crouch, he becomes vulnerable. While he climbs, his speed naturally falls. His evasive action—the bag of tricks that makes him a tough target—becomes restricted and he may feel what he is—a clay pigeon for flak batteries . . .

The low-level onslaughts on German craft, which were likely to be 190s, 109s, 88s, Do. 217s, He. 117s and even seaplanes, were costly. Pilots frankly dreaded the missions. It gave them a feeling of helplessness. It wasn't the American's snap roll against the German's; it was offering himself as a target without power to parry.

"Just like you walk out in the street and get run over by a car," the pilots epitomized.

The thought of a hot pilot brought down by a ground-gunner was hateful. When Maj. Walter Beckhan, of DeFuniak Springs, Fla., at the time the leading ace, was brought down, Beeson fumed:

"Think of it! A great pilot like that shot down by a *ground type*. That's a helluva end for a great pilot!"

The beat-ups were interspersed with escort missions. The toll of Jerry fighters mounted and with it, individual scores. High scorers were Gentile and Beeson with 15 each. Top scorer for the E.T.O., however, was Capt. Bob Johnson, Lawton, Okla., a member of the Wolfpack, with 22 destroyed.

On March 23 the group took the heavies to Brunswick, which the Germans undertook to defend even when they let Berlin take it. Gentile and Godfrey put on their sister act again. It was, "Okay, Johnnie, you take that one while I cover you . . . Now give me cover while I bounce this one."

The rivalry between Gentile and Beeson was frank, though approximately friendly, and it was multiplied by every pilot and G. I. in their respective squadrons. A day previously when Beeson had a one-Jerry lead over Gentile, he had gone to London to appear in a "Salute the Soldier" program. He returned to find that Gentile had tied his score during his absence. Beeson was good-natured but serious that night in the mess when he said, "Boy, those people in London have had me. I'm not going to miss another damn show!"

He was standing before the fireplace, looking down at the impassive Gentile slouched in a big leather chair, cigar going. Beeson, so boyish looking as to appear a little ridiculous smoking a cigar, pulled a cheroot from his impeccable blouse, removed the band and threw it at Gentile.

"Damn you, Don!" Beeson grinned.

A grin cracked Gentile's waxy countenance.

On the way to Brunswick Beeson's engine had given some warning coughs and he decided that he would have to return to base. But the thought of leaving Gentile up there knocking down more Huns made him take a chance. When the fighters arrived at the rendezvous the Huns were swarming through the bomber boxes.

Beeson positioned himself on a 190 and braced his elbows against the cockpit sides, holding both hands on the stick. His left thumb pressed down and the 190 exploded. Then Beeson skidded over to tangle with a 109. It was one of the most vicious combats Beeson had had with a Hun, the latter being brave and skillful.

But finally Beeson made the Hun's foot slip and he was forced to crash-land in a meadow. Beeson barreled down after him to get confirmation of the kill in his camera. As he flew over the 109 the pilot opened the hatch, vaulted out of the cockpit and began sprinting across the savannah before Beeson's guns.

Beeson thought, "He's a fine pilot. If I let him go, he'll get another plane and be up again tomorrow. He might explode a bomber with 10 Americans in it, or maybe shoot me down next time."

As the fleeing Hun reached a hedge, Beeson opened fire. Last he saw of the Hun he was huddled in the hedge, whether dead or hiding none can say.

Beeson spotted another 109 above him with his wheels down, but he dipped into a cloud before Beeson could attack. Beeson sprayed a locomotive and made for Debden.

Hofer bagged a 190 and damaged another, while the Cowboy rode a wild Mustang all over the sky. His engine had also been running rough and he had turned to leave the area. But seeing a lively tangle, Megura recklessly forgot his engine trouble and horned in. He was chasing four Huns when his engine sprang a glycol leak, which meant sizzling piston walls in a short time.

Megura turned for Debden again but on the way saw a 190 clobbering a Mustang. Once again he interrupted his homeward race against the glycol leak to close with the Hun. The 109 pilot bailed out and as Megura passed so close as almost to collapse his chute, the German waved to him.

But the Germans were making headway with their attacks on the bombers and the sky, with its scores of chutes, looked like an orchard of apple blossoms. The other side of it was, the bombers were causing great destruction on the target.

Lt. Tommy Biel, a St. Paul pilot who was later killed, followed a 109 down and was led right over the target area. Near the ground a Fort *whooshed* past in flames. Suddenly Biel looked up to see the bombs showering down about him. Flak from below, bombs from above—Biel broke off his attack and climbed upstairs.

That night the bar mirror said, "10 TO 0—FREE BEER." Next day the group destroyed 26 near Bordeaux. Then they revisited Brunswick. Gentile came back with a spirited buzz of the field. As he taxied up, his teeth could be seen through the canopy.

"How many?"

Gentile held up three fingers. Then he asked:

"How many did Beeson get today?"

"None."

Godfrey signed the crew chief's form and walked over to sit on the wing of Gentile's plane.

"How'd you get yours, Don?" Gentile was asked.

"I saw a string of them down in a spiral dive and bounced what I thought was the last one in the string. I didn't know then that some others were hidden under my left wing. So instead of bouncing the end man, I flew right into the middle of the string. I was a piece of cake for those behind me, but at first they didn't bother me. I got two of the 190s and then found a 109 shooting hell out of me. I got away from him and a little later I got this 109. Godfrey went on down after those that were left in the string. How many did you get, Godfrey?"

"Two," answered Godfrey. "I followed the string down to the deck and started hedge-hopping along behind one. He blew up. Then I got another one. It seemed like I fired for about five minutes. I just sat there cursing him because he wouldn't bail out. But I took one more squirt, and his wheels came down and he crashed in some trees."

273

"Here comes Goody," said Gentile. "Hey, Goody what did you get?"

"Boy, it was really lovely," Goodson said dryly, precisely. "There were some 190s clobbering the Forts. We went down to clobber these characters, but my windscreen iced up so I couldn't see to shoot. I scratched away the ice with my fingers and found myself down low over a drome. A JU 88 was coming in to land. I got him. Another was in the circuit to land. I shot him down and went back and strafed him to be perfectly sure I had dispatched him. As I say, it was lovely, lovely."

With the day's triple kill, Gentile had run his score up to 21, swept past Beeson and stood just one behind Johnson of the Wolfpack. The group total for the day was 24 planes destroyed.

Gen. Eisenhower's headquarters issued press release No. 8548:

During March the Mustang group commanded by Col. Donald J. M. Blakeslee, Fairport Harbor, Ohio, established a new Eighth AF record by destroying 156 enemy aircraft, probably destroying 8, and damaging 52. This was the largest number of enemy aircraft destroyed by one group in any one month . . .

But these spectacular records were not being racked up without pilot loss. The Gentiles and Beesons were the exceptions whose luck held out long enough for them to run up impressive totals. Nor were their exploits more than incidents to the prime job: protecting the bombers from the bitter costly attacks of Hun interceptors.

Take Black Snake, otherwise Capt. Kenneth D. Peterson, 29, of Mesa, Ariz., who, incidently, had never been one of the high scorers, but a reliable, competent flyer. Following is an official combat report written by Staff Sgt. Edgar M. Johnson of the 306th

Bombardment Group after the war:

"On 29 March, 1944 I was flying as left waist gunner on a 1st Division B-17 raid to Brunswick. Between Brunswick and Hanover, our formation was attacked by about 60 Focke-Wulf 190s and Me. 109s. All members of the crew up forward were killed. We went into a dive and dropped out of formation.

"Twelve 190s were continuing their attacks as I bailed out. I opened my chute too soon, at 23,000 feet, and saw the ensuing action. The 190s were still firing at our plane when I saw a red-nosed P-51 (Peterson) dive over the tail of the Fort, close to point blank range on a 190 and cause it to blow up. He then pulled up and got on the tail of another 190 and caused it to blow up immediately. The plane caught fire and the left wing came off. The 190 pilot did not get out.

"At this time there were still several members of my crew trying to bail out. They owe their lives to the fierceness of Capt. Peterson's attack.

"Immediately after Capt. Peterson shot down his second 190, I saw a third 190 fire at him at a range of 100 yards. This lucky shot must have put out the controls, for I saw the P-51 shudder and wallow badly ... Capt. Peterson bailed out ... That night I was put in jail in Hildesheim along with Capt. Peterson ...

"Capt. Peterson's action saved the three men besides myself who bailed out successfully ... He attacked 12 enemy aircraft alone, with full knowledge that his chance of survival was very small."

That illustrates what fighter planes were for. And also why the red-nosed Mustangs were well known to bomber crews.

Clotfelter, the ebullient championship half-miler from Hillsboro, Ill., went down without any of the spine-chilling sensations which ordinarily attend such episodes. In fact, all Clotfelter knew about how he was shot down (he related after the war) was that on the night of March 27 he entered the blond mahogany bar at Debden for a few vesper libations and remained for the regular service afterwards.

Somewhere around 10 o'clock that night alcoholic amnesia took dominion over Clotfelter's mental apparatus. He knows nothing of what happened from the commencement of that felicitous state in Essex County, England, until he waked up next day in the back of a German staff car in the heart of the Third Reich.

This was by no means an unusual experience for bomber crewmen, as it was possible that the C. Q. would just throw them in a gun blister, connect the oxygen and let them sleep it off until the flak began bursting. With a fighter pilot it was obviously different, for he was the only man in the plane. At any rate, there was a short briefing for a long-range strafing mission in Germany. Not that Clotfelter heard, but Blakeslee said, "Keep weaving—that's all, let's go." How Clotfelter went through the motions necessary to dress, brief, take off, form up in the right position in Greenbelt squadron, continue over Germany on instruments in the cloud banks—well, that must have been a new kind of booze.

Next afternoon Clotfelter opened his eyes and tasted the taste in his mouth. It was pretty dark in the winter twilight, which helped Clotfelter think it was dawn at Debden, time to get the show on the road and why th' hell hadn't his batman awakened him? He reached over in the "chair" for his pants and felt a leg. He shook his head and sat up straight.

Clotfelter saw, though it was later before he believed it, that he was sitting in the back of a German sedan. A Kraut sat on his left. In the front seat beside the driver, he saw his chute.

"Funny," mused Clotfelter, closing his eyes to go back to sleep, "how realistic dreams can be sometimes."

The German opened the car door and the frigid

wind waked Clotfelter. No dream about it, he decided. He discovered that he had bruises and cuts as though he had been dragged along the ground. Inside the building, the Germans were playing cards. They must have received many U.S. airmen, for they scarcely looked up when Clotfelter was led in.

With jocular self-possession, Clotfelter walked over to the card game and tapped one of the Germans on the shoulder. The German looked up. Clotfelter shook his head by way of reproof.

"Not *that* card, you silly joker—*this* one." With that Clotfelter snatched the card from the fan and slapped it on the table. Eyes popped. The Germans stood up. Clotfelter motioned them to sit back down, and continued to kibitz.

The Germans thought Clotfelter crazy. So did Clotfelter.

He shuffled over and put his arms about a stove, reflecting, "So I'm a prisoner of war. Cheers." A major came in and spouted a guttural roar because the non-coms hadn't locked the prisoner up. In his cell Clotfelter was visited by a flak gunner who stayed around for two days, mooning and staring with an inscrutable fascination. Clotfelter learned that he was the first airman the Germans had brought down. He was oafishly proud.

In the latter part of March the Wolfpack still led the Blakesleewaffe by approximately 100 planes destroyed. But the fact that the group had established a new month's record of 156 evoked jubilation and speculation.

One night Blakeslee was asked a purely academic question:

"Colonel, do you suppose it's possible this group will ever pass Col. Zemke's group?"

"What do you mean, *possible?* Hell yes, man."

He let that sink in, then added, "I'll either have the best damn group in England or there won't be anybody left but me!"

The pilots standing about him exchanged knowing looks and shook their heads. They thought: "Rough!"

Ol' Man River, he jes keeps rollin' along . . . For three years German pilots and ground-gunners had been shooting at Blakeslee, but a miss was as good as a mile with him. One day he looked at a flak rent in his kite and said in wonderment, "Boy I'll be surprised as hell if I'm around for Christmas." But always the next day found him rampaging over Europe, radiating zest that took the form of hell-raising about the R/T chatter and No. 2s that wouldn't do right. He was confident that he could survive another three years of uninterrupted combat operations. "Hell, with the invasion coming," he said, "the fun is just starting."

So when the Colonel looked at you, slapped you on the chest with the back of his hand and said, "Hell yes, man!" you believed that was the way it was going to be. Blakeslee was never one for making a systematic, careful plan to accomplish a thing. He just up and did it, improvising as he went.

Next day I was phoning a news release to Maj. Farley Manning, of Southbridge, Mass., who was P.R.O. for VIII Fighter Command:

"Farley, I think the 4th may pass Zemke."

Manning laughed. He had been proclaiming the glory of the Wolfpack for so long he couldn't imagine it.

"Boy, you're a real chamber of commerce," he said.

"Naw, no kidding," I responded defensively, "the group's had a change of life. Blakeslee is monkey glands."

"Okay, we'll see," Manning rejoined tactfully. "What I want to ask you about is getting Gentile up to London to make a broadcast. CBS wants him for tomorrow night for a network spot. Think he'll do it?"

"Don't much think so, Farley. He and Beeson didn't want to miss any shows now, but I'll ask him."

It was put up to Gentile. He asked: "Think I'd better go?" Then he answered himself: "I'd like to, but not right now."

He added with a laugh: "That is, not unless you get Bee to go along to London with me."

The ace race was in the stretch and Gentile was taking no chances on Beeson regaining the lead. America would have to wait.

Next day, April Fool, Blakeslee led the group on an escort to Mannheim, Germany. No more than a half dozen Huns were encountered and the group bagged only three. And of these three, Gentile got one and Beeson got one (the third: Kid Hofer). There were 40-odd Mustangs scouring the skies for Jerries, 40 eager, score-happy pilots, but these three beat the others to the draw.

That made it: Gentile, 22 destroyed; Beeson, 21.

The Beeson gallery was waiting for him at his parking place, the same as Gentile's. Gentile taxi-weaved along the perimeter and cut his switch. White smoke spewed from the right bank like steam from a kettle.

"It's overheated," said Gentile blandly.

There was nothing theatrical about the casual utterance. Gentile wasn't clever that way. Simply, the motor was spewing smoke and that was what he had said. To those on the ground it brought home vividly the odds against survival over Europe. A pilot wouldn't see it that way because he was mindful of the dozen times each mission when his survival was balanced on a razor's edge. The smoke was just one evidence. He might be remembering how close he came to colliding with his No. 2 in a cumulus bank, how he just managed to pull out of a spin, what would have happened if he had fish-tailed right instead of left when that flak came up.

His crew chief, Sgt. John Ferra, deftly removed the plate from the right bank and extracted a mushroomed cannon shell. The Jerry had pulled deflection on Gentile. Ferra handed the hot mushroom to Gentile with his expert opinion: "Sir, one inch lower and the shell would have punctured your glycol pump."

"Boy, I had a close call today," Gentile said characteristically. "Twenty-two. That puts me even with Johnson, doesn't it?"

Suddenly Gentile looked my way and said reproachfully, "You see what would have happened if I had gone to London?"

The 4th's score was now 300. But the Wolfpack had nearly 400.

14
The Bitter and The Sweet

That night Ira Wolfert, his drawl and his paunch showed up. "I wanted," said the distinguished correspondent, "to do some fill-in stories while I'm waiting around for the invasion."

"Welcome and twice welcome, Mr. Wolfert." The Wolfpack had just been glorified in the *Saturday Evening Post*. Wolfert would even things up.

An aroma wafted from the kitchen, through the dining room to Wolfert's nostrils.

"Steak?"

"Steak."

"I was all set to go up to the Zemke outfit," Wolfert said, "But I heard that I'd better come to this place instead. I hear you have a couple of boys who are pushing the 26 mark."

"That's right," I said. "Gentile and Beeson. They'll be in soon for dinner."

"No hurry," said Wolfert. "Where's the bar?"

"This way. You can meet some of the pilots."

"Any of 'em getting around the 26 mark with Gentile and Beeson?" Wolfert asked.

"No." I told him. "Nobody else seems to be able to get up around 20 before the flak gets 'em."

"Say," I went on, "I sure liked that book you wrote, *Guadalcanal Diary*."

"A very good book," replied Wolfert blandly. "You ought to tell Richard Tregaskis that."

"Why?"

"He wrote it," said Wolfert silkily.

"Ouch! I'm sorry, I—"

"It's okay. Mine was *Battle for the Solomons*."

The pilots were taking sidewise looks at Wolfert. They were always self-conscious and withdrawn around a correspondent. They stood about like chorus girls in the presence of a producer, eager inside, hard-to-get outside.

"Say," asked Wolfert, "what's this I heard about Gov. Lehman's son being killed?"

March 28 had come and gone, No D.F.C. for the Governor's birthday. And on March 31, while practice-flying near Debden with too much gasoline in the fuselage tank for violent maneuvers, Pete spun out and was killed. Some days later he was awarded the D.F.C. The order, happily and sadly, was dated March 28.

Wolfert was introduced to Gentile and Beeson. "It looks like you boys are trying to shoot up the whole Luftwaffe," said Wolfert. "Looks like you might pass the 26-mark together."

Twenty-six was a mystical number for fighter pilots in the spring of '44. Twenty-six was supposed to be the number of German planes shot down by Capt. Eddie Rickenbacker in World War I, and nobody since had bagged more than 22. Truth was, Rickenbacker's official score was not 26, but 21 planes and 4 balloons.*

There were scores of topflight newspapermen in London waiting to chronicle the supreme act in the history of warfare—D-Day. The saga of the air war with respect to bombers had been written dry, but the story of the fighters was virgin. Quite suddenly, as the ace race shaped, U.S. papers developed a ravenous appetite for stories on fighter aces. Swarms of reporters, marking time until D-Day, began shooting the works on fighters.

Whoever cracked the baseless, mystical 26-mark

*AAF, official AAF almanac.

was going to become a national celebrity and invest himself with an enduring reputation. The sandlot rivalry between Beeson and Gentile consequently developed in a contest for high personal stakes. Both were ambitious and they were running a dead heat. Already the race for 26 was receiving national attention in the U. S. America was ready to gather another hero to its breast in the form of a fighter pilot. Excitement among the officers and men at Debden, who always strove so mightily to appear blasé, ran high.

The essence of the excitement was not that a pilot could shoot down 26 planes, but wonderment that he might succeed, where others had failed, to survive long enough to do so.

On April 5 the group swept deep into the Continent, raising blisters on German dromes where planes were parked. Then U.S. papers carried this:

> BOISE, Idaho, April 20—(UP)—Maj. Duane W. Beeson, 22, who, with 21* planes to his credit, was the third-ranking American ace in the European theater, has been missing in action since April 5, his father reported today.

It was a ground-gunner. Beeson was too good for German fighter pilots, but his skill was unavailing before flak-gunners. He zoomed down low over the parked planes and the German gunners sent up a spray of golf balls. Sending this superb aerial duelist over a flak-studded drome would be like riding the winner of the Kentucky Derby through a snake swamp.

The flak punctured Beeson's cooling system and the plane began overheating. Beeson kept flying in the hope that he might make it back to friendly territory. He kept his eyes on the engine temperature needle

---

*Official: 25.

and watched it rise. Then his eyes shifted to a brightly lacquered ornament swinging from his gunsight. It was a bee. "Bud" Care and his English fiancee, in whose wedding Beeson was to have been the best man in a few days, had given it to him the day before in Cambridge. It was to serve as a luck charm. Beeson looked back at the temperature: 150°. He looked up at the talisman again and shrugged. It was no use. Beeson said over the R/T:

"Got to bail out . . . Tell Bud his bee didn't work so well."

Beeson, the highstrung, ruthless boy killer, floated down in his chute. He had come a long way since Eagle Squadron days when his fretful eagerness to pick fights with Jerries had caused fellow-flyers to view him as a pest, since those days when the RAF had sent him to test-fire his Spitfire cannon and he had flown across the Channel to test-fire at German gun emplacements because, after all, they hadn't said *where* to fire, had they?

Beeson hit the ground and looked up to see the Mustangs streaking back to Debden. He freed himself of his chute. He thought then, in the smothering loneliness that oppressed pilots when first shot down in enemy territory, of Gentile. He was bitter when he thought of what had been snatched from his grasp—by a ground-gunner. Four other 4th Group pilots were already awaiting their turn at interrogation when the German guards herded Beeson in. Prisoners were not supposed to let on if they knew each other, but the four unzippered grins when Beeson added his misery to their company. He couldn't help grinning back. It didn't make much difference: the Germans had a dossier on each one.

Bunte, the stringy, clownish Floridian, flying in Beeson's squadron, thought it was flak that caused his plane to begin heating up as he pulled off a smoking drome. Not until after the war did he learn from

"Monty" Montgomery, who was flying behind him, that the damage was caused when his plane hit a high-tension wire.

Fire gushed from the Mustang. Bunte, who once ended an official combat report with, "I claim one Me. 109 destroyed and one hell of a lot of intrepidity", was on the point of burning up in his cockpit when he saw the lake near Potsdam, on the outskirts of Berlin. Bunte dived the plane into the lake and fellow-flyers saw the red nose of the Mustang plummet into the water, carrying Bunte. The tail section disappeared.

"God, he's had it!" a pilot gasped.

The impact of the plane on the water knocked Bunte unconscious. Strapped in the cockpit, Bunte sank with the craft. Under the water Bunte struggled with his daze. He tugged and pulled to get out of his chute harness instead of undoing the safety belt, which was what held him prisoner in the water. Bunte passed out again and somehow—he never knew exactly—he floated to the surface.

Sputtering, his long black hair glistening with blood, Bunte pulled the string to inflate the rubber dinghy. He got one side inflated, but there wasn't enough strength left in his stringy arms to inflate the other side.

But there was a tree growing in the water a few yards away. "Old J. C. himself must have put that tree there for me to grab," Bunte advised me after the war.

He staggered to the beach and collapsed. He wearily lifted his throbbing head to see some German civilians approaching. But even in his fright of them, Bunte was too exhausted to do more than pant.

To his surprise, the Germans wrapped him in a blanket, gave him a precious cigaret, placed him in a wagon and delivered him to a Luftwaffe airdrome.

But those who did make it back to Debden were able to report a triumph for the group: 50 destroyed and 38 damaged. Goodson alone got six and with the gunners putting up a murderous carpet of flak, coolly zig-zagged in and out of the henna-tinged coils of black smoke arising from the burning planes to count 25 on one field.

"It was really lovely, the way those kites burned," Goodson exulted.

Gentile, unlike Beeson, had survived the strafing gamble and destroyed five on the ground. That brought his score to 27 (five on the ground).

"Don," somebody said, "that makes you the American who has destroyed more planes than any other pilot in two wars."

But Gentile didn't beam as usual. He was looking in the mirror; that is, thinking about Beeson. Both had flown more than enough hours entitling them to a leave in the States, but they had stayed on because the rivalry was so keen and because they each thought they could beat the game. Gentile recognized Beeson as a great pilot. But Beeson hadn't beat the game. Gentile thought also of the big things that awaited him in the States.

His reverie was interrupted when Goodson said:

"Okay, who is going with me to look for Hobert?"

Capt. Robert R. Hobert, of Woodland, Wash., had been flakked-up in the attacks on the drome. He had almost limped home, but was forced to bail out over the Channel and was floating somewhere in it awaiting rescue. They would now fly back, despite aching weariness, to patrol the sea for Hobert. The code called for it.

Goodson quickly mustered three others and Gentile watched them jog out to their planes to take off. He thought how easily it could have happened that it was he, instead of Hobert, riding a bucking dinghy in the cold sea . . . They found Hobert, but he was dead by midnight of exposure.

Wolfert moved into the room with Gentile, occupying the bed The Greek had used until he was forced

286

down in France. Gentile had agreed to do a series of articles with Wolfert for North American Newspaper Alliance and Wolfert was probing for material. As a novelist as well as reporter, Wolfert was not content to limn the bare acrobatics of Gentile's sensational exploits, but sought to explain the inner Gentile as an American representative of the new Air Age.

Wolfert watched Gentile binding his cap up for the night, brushing his teeth and climbing into bed. Wolfert sank into The Greek's bed and doused the light. The radio on the table between their beds was giving off music from America.

"Shall I turn it off now?" Wolfert asked.

"If you don't mind," Gentile said, "leave it on. That's the way I put myself to sleep when I'm keyed up."

"Now that you've got 27, have you thought of taking a rest? You've used up a lot of your luck."

"Yeah, I know," said Gentile. "I've been thinking about Beeson. But this war is my chance. I don't want to go back after the war and pilot an airliner between New York and Cincinnati. I want to come out of it with more planes destroyed than anybody else. That's been my plan for some time. That's the reason I don't go to London and save my money. Rickenbacker got his chance that way in the other war."

"You've had some close calls lately," Wolfert pursued.

"Yeah, but unless the flak gets me, I can make it. I'm gonna make a couple more shows and take a rest," Gentile said.

"You don't really believe a German pilot could shoot you down, do you?"

"Well, I—not hardly."

But the strain of the inner debate was perceptible in Gentile's face. He was weighing every angle: How much longer could he beat the game? He was tired physically and his brain was addled, and that made him sag physically.

"What should I do?" he asked me often. What he was wondering was how far open the door to future opportunity had been opened by his exploits to date.

"I don't know that, Gentile. All I can say is, you'd better do whatever you're going to do before D-Day. After that a pilot with 80 planes won't be worth two lines of agate type." I told him.

Other pilots in Gentile's squadron recognized his fatigue and as he dressed for the next mission, the emotional, combative "Swede" Carlson put his arms about Gentile's shoulder and blurted, "Forget it, old buddy, the whole damn squadron will be your No. 2 today."

_____

LONDON, April 8.—(AP)— Great fleets of American bombers and fighters thundered back into Germany today, blasting aircraft industries in Brunswick ... and provoking the German Air Force into the first major air battle this month ... Berlin broadcasts described great air battles extending from the German borders on into the Reich ...

Gentile's knee could be seen to tremble from tautness as he stepped from tire to wing to enter the cockpit. He didn't look about and wink as usual when the crewmen crowded about to see him off. He just looked straight ahead and rather listlessly, it seemed, hooked up his oxygen mask and pressed. Those watching him were equally nervous. How much longer could he tempt the Fates?

His motor was ragged as he taxied off. It kept cutting out and wouldn't take hold. But Sgt. Ferra, flint in his small black eyes, snapped: "Nothing wrong with that motor. He just primed it too much. You don't think I'd let him go with a bad motor, do you?"

The group soared off towards Brunswick, Gentile leading Shirt-blue squadron in the absence of Good-

288

son, who had been sent to Italy to break in a new Mustang group.

The ensuing encounter with the German fighters was one of the fiercest; any bomber or fighter pilot will tell you that the Brunswick Huns were the toughest of all. It appeared that fighters would rise to defend Brunswick when they would defend nothing else, though I never heard a convincing explanation. The Huns at the head of these Brunswick formations were especially vicious and skilled. It was to be the first battle in which Millikan couldn't keep his wad of gum wet.

As the group came up on the starboard side of the Liberators for the rendezvous, Blakeslee snapped:

"Horseback to all Horseback aircraft. 100-plus approaching bombers at 11 o'clock."

Eyes darted and rolled, then settled on the Hun horde. Gentile and Millikan, leading four-men sections of the squadron, were still three to four miles from the bombers, but there were so many Huns that it was easy to spot their formation. The Huns had evidently been vectored to the bomber fleet and were waiting upsun.

From out of the brilliant April sun the Huns hurled themselves down through the Lib boxes in power dives. Millikan thought: "Like locusts in the *Good Earth.*" They swarmed down through the formation of bombers like angry insects, wings aglow with cannon and machine gun fire. They came firing in unison.

And as they came the Lib gunners threw countless ribbons of machine gun fire at them. The tops, sides, noses, tails and bellies of the Libs flashed fire. It was as if the lights in a dark factory building had been turned on by a master switch. As the Huns flashed through the Libs, six of them plummeted out of the formation in flames. But some of the attackers spun down with them. Millikan champed his wad of gum.

Gentile led his squadron into the attack as some 30 of the interceptors came out of their dive underneath

289

the bombers and climbed up to swarm down for a second attack. Gentile, Millikan and Red Dog selected their meat and went after it. Millikan pulled a 20° deflection shot on a 109 at 300 yards; it spun down and splattered. Red Dog saw a 190 about 2,000 feet below him and chased it down to 3,000 feet, where the 190 did a very tight climbing turn to port. Red Dog dumped his flaps 20° to brake his speed and out-turned the 190. The 190 rolled over and began a steep dive. On top of his tail, Red Dog fired two short bursts and the Hun jumped from his plane. Oil from the 190 splashed Red Dog as he pulled out of the dive.

As Red Dog climbed upward the oil cleared from his windscreen and he saw another 190 diving down and got on his tail by turning into him. After chasing him towards earth for more than a mile, Red Dog pressed the tit, the 190's canopy came off and the German somersaulted into the clouds. Red Dog began climbing a second time and saw a third 190 coming down about a mile above him. This 190 appeared to be gliding and Red Dog calculated he had been hit while rough-housing down through the bombers' lead ribbons. But when the Hun saw Red Dog climbing into him, he showed plenty of life.

They did a complete circle and Red Dog maneuvered onto his tail, but overshot; he did a wing-over and met the Jerry head-on. The 190 split-essed at 2,000 feet and headed straight for the deck, Red Dog hard after him. Red Dog blacked-out completely (the improved G-suits were not in use at this time) as he pulled the Mustang out of the dive. He came to at 4,000 feet, expecting to see the 190 on his tail. But the 190 was smouldering on the ground. Which made a triple kill for Red Dog.

When Gentile's squadron first challenged the 30 FWs and 109s some boogared off while others remained to duel. Gentile selected a 190 and was on the point of clobbering it when three 190s forced him to break off the attack. He selected another and sent it spinning down from 16,000 feet.

"Okay," said Gentile, "let's go after that one at 2 o'clock." It was a 190 clobbering a Mustang. Gentile had everything forward but he couldn't intervene in time to save the Mustang, which torched down. Gentile and the 190 duelled from 22,000 to 8,000 feet. The German would suddenly throttle back and Gentile would sail over him. Then he would get on Gentile's tail. Gentile would turn inside his line of fire and then they would go 'round and 'round in head-on tilts. Finally Gentile clobbered the 190 in a turn and the pilot jumped. Gentile followed him down in a power dive but abstained from turning his guns on the German when his chute blossomed. He blacked-out in pulling up.

Quivering with combat lust, Gentile went after a third 190. The German was good and they tore around on the deck among the trees and ravines for 10 minutes, which is 10 years in combat. Gentile overshot the 190 and McKennon blazed away at it, McKennon missed. Gentile pulled the throttle back to slow down, got on the tail of the 190 and squirted. The 190 crashed, carrying the pilot. That made three for Gentile—and his 23rd kill in aerial combat.

Millikan had destroyed one and now intervened in a tangle between a Mustang and a 109. He put his forehead to his gunsight (the K-14 was not yet in use), laid off three rings of deflection and fired. The 109 crashed in a forest like a stone. Tussey and Lt. Oscar F. La Jeunesse, who had been a fireman in Worcester, Mass., formed up on Millikan for another go. As they climbed back up they found a Mustang having a hard time with a darting swishing, swooshing 109 with a baby.

This 109 was swinging around shooting at everybody with no apparent regard for the guy on his tail. The Mustang could not get in position to shoot, but managed to stay with the 109. Millikan attacked, but had so much speed that he couldn't match the 109's turns. The 109 broke into Millikan's attacks as well as those of the other Mustangs, and then broke away and down full bore on Brunswick, where there was a tremendous pall of black smoke and haze.

Millikan followed behind the other Mustang and when the 109 would shake the 51 pilot, Millikan would spurt in and fire. Millikan got a few strikes on a deflection shot—everything was deflection because the Hun was timing his breaks artfully. Then the other Mustang got a few strikes, but the Hun fought back with unflagging ardor and fine skill. His identity was never established, but there is no doubt but what he was an outstanding German ace.

All through these tempestuous acrobatics Tussey and La Jeunesse remained glued to Millikan's wing, leaving him free to concentrate on his shooting.

The 109 turned to the right with the Mustang, the pilot of which was unknown to Millikan. Millikan thereupon did a tight turn in the opposite direction and dropped down on the 109's tail. The 109 quickly reversed his turn, pulled up and around towards Millikan.

Millikan champed his gum. He had kept it juicy until now. It was getting dry for the first time in his combat career. This kind of aerial combat was unreal in a way. At 9 o'clock that morning Millikan had been parked on a sofa at Debden, sipping coffee by the fire and contemplating *Jane's* latest degree of undress in the *Daily Mirror*. Now, a few hours later, he was over the heart of Germany panting and struggling to dodge the 20-mm. cannon shell that might have his number on it, that might blow a hole in his belly and send him spinning out of the sky, unseen and unmissed until noses were counted back at Debden.

Millikan wasn't rationalizing. He wasn't wondering what kind of a man it was behind the flashing guns of the 109. The German was just an impression of some character up there stunting around. The tracers came closer and Millikan shook himself. Somebody was going to win and somebody was going to lose. Millikan had watched the 109 challenging and flailing at every Mustang on the lot and he had joined in the melee by instinct. Millikan felt professional admiration for the German's courage and finesse; he was almost hypnotized by the exhibition.

Although Millikan and the Hun had exchanged fire, Millikan still felt, because of the other Mustang, like a spectator gripped by the conflict between a bull and matadors. Then the bull ignored the red flags and charged the front row of spectators—the 109 was making straight for Millikan. He thought: "That German is now going to try to kill me, and he's good enough to do it." His gum got rubbery.

Tracers from the Hun's cannon came close to Millikan's tail. They went into another turn and as the 109 streaked head-on at Millikan, he could see the big black ace of spades insignia painted on the spinner. It looked sinister. The chewing gum was now powder dry.

Then another flaps-down turn. The Hun reefed it in, tighter and tighter. Likewise Millikan. Millikan was getting inside. The Hun reefed it tighter. Too tight. His foot had finally slipped: his plane spun out of the turn.

Millikan acted with swift reflex action to capitalize his opportunity. He swooped down low on the 109. Before the Hun could regain control over his 109, Millikan lined him up for a 90° deflection shot (at right angles to the target). He pressed the tit as if to grind it into the stick. Flames gushed from the 109. Millikan gave the rudder a savage kick to dodge the debris.

Tussey saw the Hun bail at 800 feet, and the chute opened just in time to save the Hun. Which was too bad, because this German probably took off next day in another 109 and engaged an American who lacked Millikan's skill and endurance.

"Damn glad to see that," they said when Gentile rattled the window panes in the dispersal hut. The roughness of his motor at the take-off that morning and his reckless determination to run his score up induced apprehension.

He did some rolls over the hangars and came over the dispersal at something like 100 feet. You could see the red and white checkerboard that he and Godfrey had painted on their cowling to facilitate recognition in combat.

Gentile was radiant as he climbed out on the wing. He said in a high-pitched, jubilant voice: "I got three."

He had destroyed 18 planes in less than a month.

But the group as a whole had turned in a championship performance: 31 Huns shot down. This was a new E.T.O. record and it stood for some time. More, it had been made, as we learned later, against one of the outstanding outfits in the Luftwaffe. About 45 Mustangs had attacked from 60 to 90 German planes. The Mustangs shot down 31 of the Germans, but lost only four.*

Thirty-one Jerries for the loss of four. It was a decisive victory, and significant. A lot of 4th Group pilots, Mustang devotees though they were, would not say that the P-51 was better than a Focke-Wulf 190 or a Messerschmitt 109. Arguments and discussions on the subject were interminable. A few drew unfavorable comparisons, the same as some Tank Corps soldiers groused that the Shermans and Churchills were not as good as the German's Royal Tiger tank, while the generals said that each country built its tanks to fit its own combat techniques. Most pilots believed that the Mustang was the greatest all-

---

*Shot down were Lt. Howard N. Moulton, Jr., Sheffield Mass., who got one before bailing; Lt. Robert Hughes, Houston, Tex.; Lt. Robert P. Claus, Bronx, N.Y.; Capt. Frank Boyles (killed), Denver, Colo.

around fighter plane in the world, but its superiority over German craft was not great.

How, then, to explain the 31-4 battle? The Germans had had every advantage: they were over their own country and they outnumbered the 4th's Mustangs. Without indulging in any alma mater lapse, I submit that the answer is entirely obvious and unquestionable. Simply: the American pilots excelled the German pilots in combat prowess.

You couldn't explain this victory, which was typical and not an isolated example, by "weight of numbers." It was a raw test of courage and skill. Thirty-one to four . . .

The 4th had destroyed 76 aircraft in the first eight days of April. The 4th was at the summit of its power. The Germans knew and talked of the "red-nose boys." The name of the 4th was called blessed by the bomber groups: not infrequently they phoned Blakeslee after a mission to express admiration and gratitude for the way the 4th had stomped on Huns attacking the bombers. The group total stood at 373½. The Wolfpack had 384.

The pilots were too exuberant to bother with dinner, preferring to wait for the 10 o'clock buffet which was spread every night. They frothed over the free beer, hands slicing the air in funeral service gesture for the 31 departed Huns, or to demonstrate the maneuvers which accounted for their survival in the battle.

Millikan usually hurried down to the village to his wife and child after the day's work, but tonight he lingered. He gravely reflected:

"That Hun was shot up and being chased, but he kept attacking. He could have bailed out. I would have."

The lid on Blakeslee's silver beer stein flapped open and shut like a pelican's mandible. He jubilated:

"We're going to bring it up to 500 destroyed by the

end of this month."

He let that sink in, then added:

"Let's see now. We're having a party April 16 to celebrate 400 destroyed. Right? Okay then, I want arrangements made for a dance on the night of April 30 to celebrate 500 destroyed."

He held up his stein saying, "Cheers."

"Cheers", all chorused.

In such fashion was sentence pronounced upon 127 planes still at the disposal of the Luftwaffe across the moat.

Debden, due to the exploits of Gentile and the group as a whole, had become a focus of international news and interest. Sounds high flown, but that's the way it was. Newspapers, wire services, and radio networks were broadcasting the saga of the Blakeslee-waffe. Scores of correspondents, with gear sorted and packed for the D-Day lunge across the Channel, went to town on the ace race.

The climactic and biggest story would be that of a pilot cracking the 26 mark. Gentile had done so with his total of 30. But Gen. Doolittle's headquarters had directed me, the Debden public relations officer, to delay the announcement. Seven of Gentile's 30 were destroyed on the ground. At the time there was a burgeoning controversy and confusion over whether parked aircraft should be counted the same as those bagged in aerial combat, though everybody recognized that ground-strafing was far more hazardous than air-fighting. Doolittle's headquarters, whose P.R.O. section was commendably conscientious, did not want to make the distinction between ground and air kills. It wanted to let the newspapers themselves decide how to treat the difference. It was decided that a simple communique would be made to the effect that Gentile had destroyed so many in the air and so many on the ground.

Accordingly, I got directions from on high to abstain from any form of disclosure that 26 had been cracked for the two or three days it would require to get Gentile's claims up to the Claims Board for assessment and official confirmation. This done, I was to detonate.

Correspondent Wolfert, living in the room with Gentile, naturally knew all about the circumstance. He agreed to sit on the story until it was released. Then Gladwin Hill of the *Associated Press*, accompanied by a photographer named Irwin, who was subsequently killed in Normandy by U.S. bombs, showed up one afternoon to learn Gentile's score. In the presence of Gentile and Wolfert, I gave Gladhill, as he was called, all the facts with a crystal clear "off the record" agreement.

Irwin shot some pictures of Gentile. He and the jaunty, aggressive Gladhill left for London.

Next day the detonator on the Gentile story was pressed.

But not by me.

At midnight Ajax (code for VIII Fighter Command) tried frantically to reach Wolfert and me. Neither was available. Next morning Ajax got me.

"What's the goddamn idea of breaking the Gentile story?" Manning, the P.R.O., screeched.

"What's the goddamn idea of asking *me?*" I countered.

"You didn't do it?"

"Hell, naw I didn't. What story you talking about anyway?"

"Listen". Then Manning read the *Associated Press* lead to me:

LONDON, April 8—(AP)—Capt. Don Gentile's claim of five planes destroyed on the ground April 5 was confirmed today while he was blasting three more Nazi planes out of the sky to run his bag to 30, and the Piqua, Ohio Mustang pilot became the first American ace of this war

297

formally recognized as having broken Capt. Eddie Rickenbacker's World War record.

Gladhill explained. He said that on leaving Debden he had filed the information with his bureau in London purely as background against the time when the story would be released and that he had absolutely no idea of jumping the official release. Somebody in the office, ignorant of the off-the-record agreement, had proceeded to cable the story unbeknownst to him.

Gladhill was very apologetic and said to me:

"You know the *AP's* reputation for respecting release dates."

There was no irony in this assertion at that time, for it was made a long time before that little matter of the Rheims surrender "scoop."

I hung up and thought:

"Alas, Wolfert, you are scooped . . . scooped, Wolfert, by the numbers."

I thought further: "And oh, my aching back, I'm the one who's got to tell you the bad news. Maybe I just ought to goof off on a 48."

Wolfert had been living in the room with Gentile for three weeks. He was prepared to write a much more exhaustive story than anybody else. But he sat upon the story in accordance with the covenant. He had been promised that the story would not leak. And now . . .

I went to his room and regarded him as he lay snoring in the spring sun. It was the sleep of the Just. I shook him. He came to, dazed and bloated from an all-night session with Blakeslee. He was told that he was scooped.

"Jesus," he groaned.

He pulled the cover over his head and said no more. Cheers.

The telephone orderly came in (being in the Air Corps, he didn't knock). He said:

"The *United Press* man is on the phone. Says he's

298

gotta talk to you right away."

It was the usually urbane, polished Walter Cronkite, chief of the London *UP* bureau, who was by no means his usual self.

"What'n hell happened?" Walter demanded.

He went on to fume that the New York *UP* office was blowing its top because there had been no *UP* lead filed on the Gentile story, while the *AP* was getting top play from coast to coast with its story. I learned later that as a result of this contretemps *UP* took on another staffer in order to keep a closer check on the air war story.

Anyway, the fat was now in the fire. Gentile was a national figure. He was hailed throughout the Zone of the Interior as the "Ace of Aces." A four-column picture used throughout the States showed Gentile sitting in his cockpit with Beeson standing on the wing shaking hands. It had been posed in the first place when it appeared certain that both would go over the 26 mark together. But editors now applied a caption explaining that it was Beeson congratulating Gentile. Actually, Beeson, who had Gentile's skill but not his luck, was in solitary confinement in a German prison camp.

The breaks had gone to Gentile. From this morning forward, Gentile was destined to be machine-gunned by photographers, shadowed by newsreel cameramen, bound by reporters and gagged with microphones.

The reaction in Gen. MacArthur's headquarters out in the Pacific was swift, sharp, strident. It issued an announcement almost immediately that Maj. Richard Bong, the Poplar, Wisc. ace, who was later killed testing jets, had destroyed his 27th Jap in aerial combat. Gentile had to move over some on the front pages, but not much. All the circumstances, chiefly that of communications and the concentration of the large number of D-Day correspondents, combined to give the Gentile story a coverage that would have been impossible in any theater other than the E.T.O., and at any other phase of war.

15
Lee, Dear

Cooks in the Officers' Mess were directed in early April to begin excising the tenderloins from the sides of beef and to bank them in the ice box along with those obtained from previous tenderloinectomies.

"Wonder who's coming this time?" asked Woo the cook.

"Must be Mr. Big," ventured Wung.

Meanwhile the celebration of the 4th Group and its star performer, Gentile, proceeded apace. A blonde resident of Saffron Waldon, whom Gentile had dated once or twice to the sly merriment of several enlisted men, read a story in Lord Beaverbrook's *Evening Standard* about top-ranking U.S. airmen, but found no mention of Gentile. She phoned the *Standard's* city editor between editions.

"Sir," she said, "I don't wish to be cheeky, but you left out Capt. Gentile. Ectuelly, he's done more than those you mentioned."

The editor re-plated and the next edition carried three-fourths of a column on Gentile for the edification of his British public, which was really someth'n in view of the British Press' pronounced circumspection about the Eighth AF. The Eighth didn't do things like the RAF did them and was, therefore, according to Fleet Street practice, on probation. Fleet Street finally extended diplomatic recognition to the Eighth AF, as it was rather difficult to ignore the world's mightiest air force, but on the whole, its coverage was as disproportionate and sketchy as the American coverage of the British war effort in the Pacific.

But reverting to the glory that was Gentile's and the grandeur that was the 4th's, *International News Service* cabled this story to U.S. papers:

AN 8TH AAF FIGHTER STATION, ENGLAND, April 10—(INS)—Col. Don Blakeslee's 4th Fighter Group today broke all records for the European Theater of Operations, boosting their score to 403 in a strafing mission over France.

The colorful, hard-flying group swept into first place in the fighter sweep-stakes, gaining the triple-tiered crown for having the highest scoring group, the No. 1 ace, Capt. Don Gentile, and the record for 31 kills in a single mission.

The cooks learned why they were told to hoard the tenderloins. Gen. Eisenhower, Supreme Commander of the Allied Expeditionary Forces, arrived at Debden to decorate two flyers the AAF had once spurned as scrubs.

With Gen. Eisenhower were Gen. Carl. A. Spaatz, commander, U.S. Strategic Air Forces in Europe; Lt. Gen. James A. Doolittle, Eighth AF commander; Maj. Gen. Kepner, commander, VIII Fighter Command; Brig. Gen. Jesse Auton, 65th Fighter Wing commander.

There were 20 to 30 reporters in the Supreme Commander's retinue, but civilian photographers were banned. Army photographers were supposed to be limited to three, but theory wasn't practice. Army Pictorial Service sent a baker's dozen. USSAF didn't stand short and dispatched a complement. They squabbled among themselves as to who was going to do the honors and there was a lot of officious talk about how irritated Gen. Eisenhower got when too many bulbs popped. Photographers of the Debden P.R.O. scowled at the invasion of their bailiwick and regarded the intruders as One-Eyed Connollys.

Blakeslee met Eisenhower at the gate with a sharp salute. They inspected an honor guard of M.P.s and repaired to the briefing room. Some combat film was shown and Blakeslee staged a mock briefing for a Berlin show. Gen. Eisenhower in turn briefed the pilots. From *The N. Y. Times:*

By THE ASSOCIATED PRESS
A UNITED STATES FIGHTER BASE, ENGLAND.—(AP)— Fourth Fighter Group pilots were told today by Gen. Eisenhower that their role in the great three-way invasion of Europe soon would be flying a dawn-to-dusk death express against the German Air Force . . .
Gen. Eisenhower said he had a feeling of great privilege and almost humility in visiting such a group of fighting men as the 4th . . .

Eisenhower listened as a citation for the Distinguished Service Cross, second-highest award for valor, was read. One saw that he was taller and leaner than might have been expected. You looked at his high-domed head and reflected on the magnitude of the secrets reposing therein, including the date of D-Day (56 days away.). His manner exuded a completely relaxed, sunny confidence. If he actually felt that confident, you thought, then that invasion could not fail.

Gen. Kepner said: "Don Blakeslee lives in constant dread that some so-and-so is going to take him off flying status."

Then Eisenhower pinned the D.S.C. on Blakeslee's tunic.

The briefing room was jampacked and the 20 to 30 newspapermen were there. Eighth AF policy called for a high degree of freedom for correspondents, but one thing was always strictly forbidden: reporters could not be admitted to briefings. But here they were leaning against wall diagrams of such top secret things as the new G-suit (worn to prevent black-outs) and the battle order of the Eighth AF. Normally heads would have rolled. I thought: "If anybody has to reply by 1st endorsement hereon for this, there is plenty of two-, three- and four-star brass here to answer."

Then Eisenhower turned to the impassive Gentile. It was the same as if Pershing had stood thus before Rickenbacker in World War I.

Gen. Eisenhower said to Gentile:

"You seem to be a one-man air force."

There was whimsy in this. AAF headquarters had done all things to discourage the idea of individual performance and to encourage the idea of team-work. In a few hours all the cadets in America would be reading that the Supreme Commander had called Gentile a "one-man air force."

Eisenhower, Blakeslee and Gentile and the satellite generals went outside by the control tower to enact the ceremony all over again for the newsreels. Blakeslee fidgeted in taut self-consciousness. Gentile was serene.

Eisenhower inspected an array of combat craft. One was a secret P-38 Lightning equipped with bomb bay and a place in the nose for the bombardier. Eisenhower suddenly decided he wanted to go up in it.

"How about it, Harry?" Eisenhower said to his naval aide, Commander Harry Butcher.

"You can go, General, but you'll have to be back in eight minutes."

The crowd was suddenly silent as Eisenhower climbed into the Lightning. P.R.O. cameras clicked, the generals raised hell because the craft was on the secret list. But it really didn't matter as almost every G.I. at Debden had his own camera going. The reporters became tense and calculating as the Lightning taxied out. It was a hot ship. You wondered if the pilot was nervous because Eisenhower was

303

crouched in the bombardier's seat. As well as I
remember, Eisenhower wore no chute. But you
sweated in any event.

Eisenhower's face was florid when he came down.
The pilot must have racked it around, but you
couldn't tell because of the clouds.

Highballs and wine were served in the Officers'
Mess before lunch. Eisenhower told the pilots they
could have anything they wanted, because Washington was giving him everything he asked for. It was
mentioned that they would prefer their operational
whiskey to be bourbon instead of Scotch. From then
on, it was bourbon or rye (plus the stuff labeled
Spiritous Frumenti, which may have been anything).

Wolfert was licking his wounds after the *AP* scoop
on the Gentile story when more trouble arrived. He
had agreed with Gentile to do a series of first-person
newspaper articles for *North American Newspaper
Alliance*. Gentile was giving every cooperation, working with Wolfert all day long in his room, when onto
the scene came Miss Lee Carson, correspondent for
International News Service. Gentile had been giving
Wolfert every cooperation, but now he felt called upon
to cut his cooperation in half and give half to the
luscious Miss Carson.

Miss Carson came to bid against Wolfert for the
rights to Gentile's life story. Hearst had authorized
her to make a higher bid for the Inner Gentile than
anyone else regardless of the figure.

"That's the way Hearst operates," hissed the usually placid Wolfert. He and Gentile were already at
work, but Miss Carson was a resolute woman, even
for a representative of the Fourth Estate's bump-and-
grind element. Gentile explained that he was giving
his story to Wolfert, but it came to pass that the
things Gentile and Miss Carson talked about in a boy-
meets-girl way were serviceable as disclosures for
anybody desiring to write a sob-sister series on

America's "Ace of Aces." Wolfert groaned, but kept his temper below decks.

The scene changed when Gentile was sent to London to make a broadcast. He felt that he was far enough ahead of the pack now to take a day off from his Hun-blasting.

That night he was reclining on a yellow satin bedcover in the Savoy Hotel, a hotel so austerely aristocratic that never one of Hitler's Blitz bombs ever dared fall on it. At that time Gentile was not worldly enough to comprehend the degree and scope of his fame as an American fighting man, but he sensed it to the extent that he knew things had broken his way as they did for few men. But the dazzle and glitter of his new circumstance did not suffocate the practical in him.

"Say," Gentile said as he lay in the bed which perhaps had been occupied by the Nizam of Hyderabad, "do you think Judge Smith will refund that fine now that he sees I sort of turned out all right?"

He was thinking of that fine years before when he had socked the fellow in Piqua because he rolled him for his girl.

Miss Carson was also in London that night and Gentile phoned her. We all met in the lobby of the Mayfair Hotel. She was accompanied by a certain colonel in Eisenhower's Public Relations Office. He was an erstwhile Hollywood mogul, a dapper little man with big ears and "dynamic" personality of a big operator. He never left Hollywood.

We sat down. The Colonel evidently had been a business acquaintance of Miss Carson's for some time, as it was "Lee, dear" this and "Lee, dear" that. Probably his style called for addressing all friends in this fashion. Lee, Dear had the impression that I had employed my sinister influence against her to cause Gentile to do business with Wolfert. But now she looked at me with catlike purr. I had a good guess who the canary was.

305

Soon it became obvious that Lee, Dear had told the Colonel all about the negotiations, Carson vs. Wolfert.

The subject came up.

Lights, camera, action . . .

The Colonel began urbanely but briskly:

"Now, lieutenant you and I are both public relations officers. Me for Gen. Eisenhower. You for Col. Blakeslee. You savvy?"

"Yes, sir."

"Now, lieutenant," he went on in rapid-fire sentences, "as such, it's our job to see that this fine American boy, our greatest fighter ace, gets the best possible break, you savvy?"

"Yes, sir."

"The question is, lieutenant," said the Colonel, "are we doing our job of acting as his protective agents unless we see that he gets the best possible deal, you savvy?"

"Yes, sir."

Gentile listened languidly to this discussion of the most profitable and expeditious means of committing him to posterity. Heads he won. Tails he won. He carried on a little side chat with a Warrant Officer Fox, a Hollywood Fox. Fox, a fat, mellow little man with fawn eyes and soft oboe voice, had come to England as an enlisted man and put up at Claridge's. Last I heard of him I believe he was a major, but that night he was only a warrant officer. Fox knew his business and was telling Gentile how to guard his film, magazine, radio and advertisement rights.

The Colonel said: "Another drink, Lee, dear? Waiter! And you, lieutenant? Fine, bring the lieutenant two double Scotches. Now, lieutenant, I don't want to be put in the position of influencing Capt. Gentile here to either Lee here or Wolfert, but it's up to you and me to see that this fine American boy gets the best possible break, you savvy?"

"Yes, sir, I understand completely."

Lee, Dear and I exchanged looks.

"It's not too late, lieutenant," the Colonel said, "for the captain to go on and get the best possible deal out of this, providing he hasn't already signed with Wolfert. I don't know what Lee here is prepared to offer, you savvy? But it's up to you to do your best to protect your client, you savvy? Now we realize that you and Wolfert sort of play on the same team, so to speak, but I know you're too fine an officer to let personal considerations influence you against the best interests of your clients."

That did it.

I said: "Colonel, I'd like to ask if it isn't true that if any public relations officer, regardless of rank or echelon, tried to influence the bidding on something like this—that is, for personal reasons—he'd be liable to a court-martial?"

Lee, Dear dropped her eyes as though caught in the shower by the ice-man.

The Colonel said quickly: "Now, lieutenant, if Wolfert and Capt. Gentile here have made an agreement, then, of course, as an officer of the United States Army, he will naturally have to abide by it."

It was now time for Gentile to go to the studio for the broadcast, so the conference adjourned to meet again in the morning. We convened in numerous P.R.O. offices all over Grosvenor Square. Gen. Spaatz's P.R.O., Lt. Col Max Boyd, was called in, and he fumed because all this had gone on over his head. He thereupon rebuked me for not going over the heads of two intermediate commands to tell him about the situation! Cheers.

Lee, Dear had received another cable from the Hearst organization: The Gentile story is still hot—get it. I was wondering how long it would be before I was transferred to duty in Iceland. Lee, Dear sought me out in the sea of Colonels and said with a 180° roll of her goo-goo eyes:

"Lieutenant, yawl sho' does look like yawl needs a blood transfusion."

"I do—*you savvy?*"

In the end, Spaatz's P.R.O., Gentile and I motored back to Debden, for a conference with Wolfert.

Wolfert was sore when he heard the story of the Hollywood colonel's jingoism. He snapped harshly:

"The weight of the eagle, huh?"

He was threatening to go to Eisenhower. But Gentile came to and signed a contract with Wolfert (for $2,000 or $2,500).

Lee, Dear had left a wonderful little Swiss-make portable typewriter in my office and I decided that it was worth everything if she neglected to reclaim it. I didn't hear from her for weeks, but one afternoon I got a call from the control tower.

She said: "I want my typewriter. Bring it to me."

She was waiting with a prissy young flying colonel. He was chauffering her about in a Cessna transport.

Lee, Dear said: "You look better now."

Her aide-de-camp, otherwise the dandified young colonel, took the typewriter with a rather austere gesture, leaving me bereft of all save my memories of Lee Carson, Hearst news-hen.

By now Gentile was willing to go back to the States for a month on condition that he could then return to combat with the group. While Gentile awaited action on the leave application, some army newsreelman arrived. They were to shoot a sequence of a WAC enlistment drive in the U.S. The WACS were to be shot with the smiling, debonair Gentile: Join the WACS and associate with an Ace of Aces.

"Look," said Gentile to the director, a Capt. Reese, former Hollywood ace, "would you mind very much if we postponed our date until later today? They need me to lead the squadron. You could meet me right here at the dispersal when I come back."

Agreed.

Near Schweinfert the group tangled with a Jerry gaggle and Gentile soon maneuvered onto the tail of three flying line abreast, an inviting, easy target. They were green pilots. One buzz-saw burst would bag all three. Gentile trimmed his ship up, got one in the ring and gave a short burst, getting good strikes. He looked about to clear his tail and closed again. It was cold meat.

But down below he saw a 190 clobbering a Mustang. His reflexes in a split second had him diving down to get the 190 off the Mustang. In fighter parlance this went by the name of "sense of duty".

Gentile gave the dispersal the ritualistic buzz job. Pilots loved buzzing because it gave a sense of speed which they could not get when flying at altitude. All the way back from Germany Gentile had been thinking about the newsreel cameras set up in front of the dispersal. Not long before he had seen some newsreel shots of one of his buzz jobs; it was good, but it could have been better. This was to be his last mission for a time. He was in a mood for some extra-special cavorting over Debden. He rifled across the field at low altitude and saw the cameras set up by his hardstand, surrounded by a sizeable crowd.

Gentile thought: "I will now fly right into the lens of that camera."

We saw the red nose of Gentile's Mustang come whipping across the field towards us. He was perhaps 25 feet high. There is a rise in the field. For a moment the plane was lost to view behind it. Then its red nose showed again against the green. The camera ground. He was now low enough to smack the camera over. We thought: "When's he going to pull up?"

"He was coming in low," the *Associated Press* said later, "after a seven-hour flight when his plane lost power."

That was a charitable way to explain it. Truth was, Gentile had not circled enough on the deck to regain his depth perception. The plane mushed. It struck the grass field wheels up about 100 yards in front of the crowd, members of which hit the ground or jumped into ditches. The plane banged the ground and appeared to bounce.

Onlookers gasped as the Mustang leap-frogged over their heads, prop windmilling, the blades bent like lily petals. Blakeslee saw it from a distance and cursed.

Gentile realized he was going to crash, and his reflexes rushed ahead to take charge until his thoughts could catch up. He cut switches right and left to preclude a contact explosion, all the while fastening his safety belt. He saw his air speed falling and picked out the likeliest spot for a crash-landing. He braced his feet and hands to keep from bashing his face as the ship struck just short of a ditch and a high-tension wire.

For a moment those over whose heads he had bounced could not move. They assumed his death and listened for an explosion. Capt. Lloyd Benjamin, a skinny little lawyer from Wellsboro, Pa., who was the squadron I. O., jumped into a jeep with six others. There is always room for one more and Wolfert squeezed his lard into the snorting jeep. He had been scooped by the *AP*, harassed by Miss Carson and now this . . .

"Look at him!" exclaimed the first to sight Gentile. He was sitting on the wing of his Mustang, reflecting gloomily on the destruction of his beautiful ship, which he had thought of taking back home for use in bond-selling. The Mustang had a cracked back; it looked like a shrimp. Gentile only had a bruised shoulder and sore finger.

"You all right?"

"Yeah, I guess so," replied Gentile wearily, eyes glazed.

"Any claims to make?"

"Naw, just a damaged."

The flight surgeon, Capt. Irvin Matzner, of Chicago, who didn't mind being told he resembled Peter Lorre, thought Gentile might have a brain concussion and sent him to the hospital. A sleeping pill carried Gentile off to a place where there were no 190 cannon or crash-landings.

Blakeslee was standing at the bar with his silver beer stein. His pale blue eyes were angry, his voice stormy. He had a rule, the law of the Medes and the Persians which altereth not: he who pranged a kite was automatically expelled from the group.

"I saw him!" blazed Blakeslee. "I was standing there. He was buzzing this field. I've warned him. I don't give a damn if he's got 90 planes destroyed— I'm kicking him out of this group!"

Correspondent A. I. Goldberg of the *AP* was among those listening to the tirade. America's "Ace of Aces" being kicked out of his outfit as a result of a sensational smash-up? Man eats dog!

"Say, er—Col. Blakeslee," Goldberg said, "do you mind if I quote you on that?"

Blakeslee whirled upon Goldberg with such heat that I imagined I could see Goldberg's red fat dissolving under its rays.

"No, goddamnit, you can't quote me on anything! And if I have to be careful what I say on my own damn base I'll have a place roped off for you correspondents! You people have just ruined one good man!"

"All right, all right, okay, okay," murmured the nonplussed correspondent.

Blakeslee and I laughed at the incident many times in the months afterwards. "I guess I was pretty hard on that guy, huh?" he would always say. But Blakeslee would never concede that Goldberg had acted decently in asking permission to quote the outburst, for there was nothing to prevent his doing so without permission. I never had the intrepidity until now, in the 99-point phase of my army career, to tell Blakeslee what the usually amiable Goldberg had said of "boy colonels" in general, Blakeslee in particular.

Next morning Doc Matzner, Wolfert and I went to the hospital over at The Towers. Gentile met us in the hall.

"What the devil are you doing up out of bed?" Matzner asked.

"It's 9 o'clock, Doc. I gotta get back to the base and clean up."

"Oh, no, you don't. You're gonna stay right here until I get those X-rays back from Braintree."

"Aw, Doc."

"Hell, yes. Do you feel dizzy when you stand up?"

"No," lied Gentile. His face was drawn, his eyes weak. He begged:

"Lemme outa here, Doc. No fooling, I'm all right. I'll get sick if I stay in the hospital!"

"Not today, Don," Matzner said.

"Well, where are those WACS, Doc? Tell 'em to come over and see me, hear, Doc."

The truth was, WACS and newsreelmen had been whisked off the station. Everybody knew Gentile had been trying to fly his Mustang into the camera lens. Indeed, the cameramen had got some wonderful shots of the most celebrated buzz job since the Fort pilot gave the World Series a going-over in New York. We all knew that every AAF command from Ajax to the Pentagon was going to be considerably agitated over the fact that the most famous of its fighter pilots had set such a bad example for the cadets. There was no deceiving Gentile that trouble was yeasting.

"Oh, hell," he confided, "the crash didn't shake me—what's got me is wondering what Col. Don is going to say about me pranging that kite."

Matzner kept Gentile in the hospital away from the base until Blakeslee calmed down some. Gentile was relatively composed when discussing his chances of a court-martial, but the color drained from his face when it was suggested that a heavy fine might be imposed.

Operations went on. Near the Dutch coast April 15, Capt. Joe Bennett, of Morton, Tex., who came to Debden from the Wolfpack, was flying formation on instruments through a cloud. Suddenly he found himself flying upside down in his plane. He apparently had been rammed in the dark of the cloud by another Mustang. He was left unconscious, strapped to his seat, swaying back and forth pendulum fashion.

Head and face took a cruel beating. The ship's motion forced him out, breaking his shoulder as he was ripped out of his safety harness. He landed very near the Dutch coast in the Channel and disengaged himself from his chute. Bennett floated in his Mae West, but couldn't find his dinghy. Sighting part of his Mustang in the water, Bennett swam some 35 yards to it with a broken shoulder. Nearby he found his dinghy and climbed in it. Two hours passed and the current was taking him away from the coast. "Guess I'll have to float here until the invasion comes along," he thought. But presently McGrattan and some others circled him and transmitted a fix which brought a Walrus.

The following night the dance celebrating 400 destroyed was in progress. One of the news services called from London for its nightly bulletin on Gentile.

"Strong enough to leave the hospital, did you say? Wish you could see what I'm seeing now," I said.

Gentile was doing a tango all over the ballroom with a titled British blonde Goodson dated when not in Italy.

Jim Dye had recovered sufficiently from his leg wound to hobble to the dance. "Damn glad to see you up, Jim," welcomed Blakeslee. "Feeling all right now?"

"Feeling fine, Colonel. They're getting ready to discharge me now."

Two nights later Dye was in a building with some 30 others when a German bomber came over and dropped a stick. Of the 30, Dye alone was injured. The bomb explosion broke his leg—the same one in which he had been wounded by the 190's cannon shell. Cannon wound having healed, Dye went back to bed to

313

wait for the broken bone to heal.

Near Hamm, Germany April 22, the pilots—pushing themselves to bring the total up to 500 destroyed for the party eight days away—fought a battle of classic neatness and skill. Bombers were in the vicinity and the German Fighter Command scrambled 20 Messerschmitts from a nearby base to intercept them. The 109s had climbed to 4,000 feet and were circling near a lake to form up before receiving a vector which would take them to the bombers. They did not see the Mustangs above them at 15,000 feet. Nor, in fact, did the group see the 109s until the Argus-eyed Godfrey picked them out with his keen, systematic sweeping. Godfrey commenced reporting shrilly over the R/T to Blakeslee:

"Horseback, Horseback!...Below us at about 5,000. There's three...seven...nine... Jesus!—bags of 'em!"

"Where are they, where are they?" bawled Red Dog. "Let's get 'em!"

"All Horseback aircraft," Blakeslee cut in. "Take it easy. Orbit starboard and drop tanks...We'll box 'em in."

All pulled the triggers on the sticks and the babies flew off the wings.

"Okay, here we go!"

Blakeslee spurted out, jinked his craft to clear himself and tore down. But in power-diving though the haze and the clouds, he lost sight of the quarry and began screaming like an eagle. Then he picked them up again.

The leader of the German squadrons looked up to see a pack of Mustangs dropping on him like a falcon on a pigeon. But before he could take any evasive action, he and his squadrons were sealed within a box of Mustangs. He ordered his 109s into a lufberry to port. The 109s went around in a tight circle, nose to tail. An Allied flyer named Lufberry had invented the maneuver in the other war. It was like soldiers joining hands to ford a rapids. To attack the circle, a pilot had to expose himself to the fire of a merry-go-round machine gun battery.

Now and then a 109 would venture out of the protective circle in an attempt to run the blockade. Blakeslee nailed one this way. Likewise Red Dog, Emerson, Carlson. Godfrey got two. Seeing a third 109 turning on the deck, Godfrey peeled off and pounced. The 109 sailed lower and lower over the trees. Godfrey had a difficult time on the 109's tail because its slipstream was a surf bouncing his plane about, making it impossible to fire accurately.

Two guns jammed, but with the other two, Godfrey forced his third 109 to fly into a tree. Starting back to photograph the 109 in the tree, Godfrey looked back and saw a 109 about to blast him. Another Mustang streaked in and shot the 109 off Godfrey's tail. Godfrey was too unnerved by this brush to bother with a picture and climbed to scamper back to Debden.

Blakeslee was in high spirits; the group was flying superbly, the trap was as neat as anything he had seen in three years of combat. He had clobbered one 109 and was raging after another hell-for-leather, hunched forward in the cockpit, calling the Hun a sad sack he was going to kill as a dead duck. The 109 headed for the deck, the Mustang on its tail, bit-in-teeth and snorting. The two planes passed low over the streets of a little town and came to a small hill. The 109 pilot failed to honk his plane up quickly enough and the belly tank banged the summit of the hill, exploding the craft as it somersaulted. Blakeslee's Mustang blew its breath on the hill, but cleared it. He climbed back up to direct the remainder of the 109 liquidation.

Millikan and a new wad of gum were going into action. The sections he had coached so diligently were flying compactly and gracefully. That was Millikan's way. He liked to plan ahead, to practice everything possible, even to the manner in which he would bail.

He had it down so fine that his .45 automatic had been clipped with tracer ammunition: he figured that he might have to spend the night in the Channel and he could fire tracers for flares; or, if after the invasion he were shot down behind the enemy lines, he could raise a lot of hell and he figured the tracers would un-nerve people. Millikan looked the 109s over as they circled in the lufberry. One detached itself, as a skater popping-the-whip, and skidded out of the ring by itself.

"Shirtblue leader to Red Section," Millikan drawled. "Stick together and break port."

The break was sharp, but the section remained in-tact. The Hun turned to come in on the tail of Millikan's No. 4. Millikan opened his throttle and dumped flaps to turn inside of him. He laid off a deflection burst which slapped the 109 out of his turn. Millikan charged at his tail and started shooting. He raked the 109 without the use of his gunsight, for he was skidding so violently that he couldn't hold his forehead to the sight without having it spanked by the apparatus. He kept firing without sights. The Hun bailed and Millikan—the AAF cadet who was washed out of the San Diego school for lack of flying ability—had got No. 1 in a series.

Reforming his section, Millikan made for a 109 which was about to polish off a Mustang. The pilot jinked his craft to avoid Millikan's fire and Millikan lost consciousness in one of the turns. The 109 began smoking and crashed. Millikan—the RAF cadet whose instructor had told him he was fit only for ferry fly-ing—had got No. 2 in a series.

Red Dog, flying No. 3 to Millikan, shot down a 109 which had maneuvered into firing position on Millikan. Millikan pulled up into a third 109 and went into some sharp turns to catch sight of his target. The 109 half-rolled and spun down. Millikan—who couldn't be a hot fighter in the light of the Blakeslee dictum that fighter pilots and women didn't mix—had got No. 3 in a series.

The fighting had been going on between 8,000 feet and the trees and church spires. Planes were burning on the ground, and it seemed to Millikan that he had been turning, twisting, diving and weaving over this little town by the lake most all of his life. He spotted a fourth 109 and raced after it, awed by the German's high-G acrobatics. The Jerry must be at least a double first cousin of the one who had dehydrated his gum over Brunswick a few days before.

The grease in Millikan's guns sizzled and the paint on the wings about the gun orifices blistered as he blazed away. The 109 quivered under the fusillade and half-rolled. As it came out of the roll, Millikan pumped more armor-piercing darts into its side. The 109 went into another roll and Millikan was on the point of following it down when he realized that he was but 1,500 feet above earth. The 109 crashed and burned, scorching its pilot's pulp. Millikan—the painstaking, deliberate Iowa boy with the long arms and awkward gait who had to fly 52 combat missions before he destroyed his first Hun—had got No. 4 in the Messerschmitt series.

Millikan and Gentile were among the few and very few out of the thousands of pilots in the E.T.O. big league who had ever bagged four on one mission.

Millikan laid off a ring of deflection on a fifth 109, but another Mustang came barreling in and blasted it out of his mouth. Millikan orbited port, calling for those in his section to form up on him. The group had destroyed 16 of the 109s, but there were four more in their midst which couldn't be sighted in the haze. Blakeslee had the answer to that one. He said:

"Horseback here. All Mustangs start orbiting starboard. Anything orbiting *port* is a 109—shoot 'em!"

The order was ice on Millikan's back. He was orbiting *port*. He acted fast to change his orbit to starboard.

Gentile had finished dinner; he and Matzner drove

the ambulance out to the dispersal to await the group's return. Godfrey danced on the wing of his kite. Somebody threw Lucky up to him. Lucky sniffed at the cannon rent in the leading edge of the port wing.

Godfrey jubilated: "Bags of Huns, bags of Huns!"

"How many did you get?" asked Gentile, who had just learned that orders had been cut for him to go home for a month.

"Three," said Godfrey.

"How many did you get, Red Dog?" Gentile asked Norley.

"Two, partner, two," said Red Dog.

"How about you, Millie?"

"Four," replied Millikan.

The answers hit Gentile with a thud. You could see him wavering in his wish to go to Stateside even for a month. He began pacing about, unable to keep still. He put his finger to Godfrey's smoked-up guns and gazed at them. A father couldn't touch his baby's face more tenderly.

"Hell!" Gentile said frantically. He bit into his cigar. He drooled to think what he could have done in the fight. He looked at the others and said in all seriousness:

"Gee, save me some, will you, fellas?"

"Don't worry partner," Red Dog shot back, "the way they were fighting today there'll be plenty of 'em around when you get back and that's for sure."

But the edge on Gentile's eagerness to visit home was blunted. He wished there was some way in which he could take the 4th and the Luftwaffe back to Ohio with him so he wouldn't miss anything.

Having promised to fetch everybody a quart of bourbon, Gentile took his leave of Blakeslee. Blakeslee was casual about it. I suspect he was always baffled by Gentile's remarkable exploits. There was no novelty in goodbyes to Blakeslee. He had been saying goodbye to them like this, or when they spun down over enemy territory, for three years.

It was natural that he should have grown callous to partings. He was about the only one of the class of '41 left now . . . Ol' Man River, he jes keeps rollin' along . . .

Godfrey, with Lucky concealed in his luggage, sailed with Gentile. In Piqua citizens had already started a bond-selling drive to buy Citizen No. 1 a new Mustang to replace the one in the field with the cracked back. One noon a few weeks later, Debden pesonnel read in *Stars & Stripes* under the headline, "Ace Don Gentile Comes home, and All Piqua Goes Plain Nuts":

PIQUA, Ohio, May 23—With the city's sirens wide open, practically every one of the 16,000 people in Piqua turned out to welcome home a hero yesterday, and nearly every one of them either touched, kissed, gaped at, or tore a souvenir from the hero . . .

In a plane furnished personally by Gen. Henry H. Arnold, chief of the AAF, Gentile flew from Washington to Columbus . . . he was mobbed.

When he finally arrived at the little white cottage at the edge of town where his parents live, he was minus sections of his uniform, his captain's bars and his hat, and he bore smudges of lipstick.

The War Department was naturally desirous that everything should go smoothly as the conquering hero was hailed. Such acclaim was good for morale. What really shook the War Department, I was subsequently informed by a member of its P.R.O. staff, was the discovery that sometime before the army had placed Patsy's Cafe, operated by Gentile's father, off-limits.

Little old R.I. was likewise all-out to hail Godfrey. From *The Woonsocket Call:*

Special to The Woonsocket Call
WASHINGTON, May 4—Capt. John T. Godfrey, Woonsocket's Ace of Aces, was reported by the *AP* zooming over the broad Atlantic ... homeward bound.

Meanwhile Mayor Dupre ... was prepared to extend official greetings to the hero here and invite him to attend the most elaborate civic reception ever planned in Woonsocket ... mill whistles will shriek ... air raid sirens ... will add to the din ...

By April 28 the pilots counted up and found they had established a new record of 207 enemy aircraft destroyed in one month. To destroy this bag, the group had operated over Poland, the Sudetenland in Czechoslovakia, Paris, Berlin, over Munich near Switzerland and the Pyrenees bordering Spain, and the tulip beds in Holland.

But although they had established the new record of 207 enemy aircraft destroyed, April 29 came and they were still a few short of the 500 required for the party. The cooks were already icing "500" on a big black chocolate cake for the party the next night. Blakeslee was in a stew.

The morning of the party night, Blakeslee briefed them for a beat-up of German dromes in France. He said that if they didn't bring it up to 500 during the morning mission, he would obtain Ajax's permission to run a matinee performance that afternoon. In the course of the morning performance, Sobanski, Capt. Joseph Lang, of Hyde Park, Mass., who always flew with his baby's shoes, and Shel Monroe co-clobbered two Me. 110s between them. Blakeslee and Tommy McDill sank two seaplanes moored in an inlet. Blakeslee returned to Debden under the impression that the group was eight short of 500. Here it was noon, and still no 500.

Blakeslee cycloned up to 335th's dispersal, where he parked his plane. Three days earlier he had been shot up in the Mustang with the chronic sputter in the right bank and had turned it in for a new one. It had been slow-timed and was ready for combat service.

"Another show today, sir?" asked Sgt. East.

"Hell yes," replied Blakeslee with gusto. "Got to get eight more by tonight."

"Will you fly your new kite this afternoon, sir?"

"Naw, I like Jim's. I'll use his again."

But soon Group Operations caught up with Blakeslee and told him he was wrong about the figures—the group's total already stood at 500, with 3½ to spare.

Eisenhower's headquarters announced:

"The . . . group commanded by Col. Don Blakeslee . . . has destroyed . . . a total of more than 500 aircraft . . . the first U.S. group in this theater to achieve this mark . . ."

Ajax messaged:

"You are a scourge to the Hun . . ."

The Wolfpack was seeing the heels of the 4th.

16
Germany Threatens Debden

In May the hard little apples growing on the trees about the officers' quarters began to burnish in the sun and everyone was certain that the invasion could not be many days away, same as they had been in April.

Nobody knew it at the time, but with March and April passed the great days for fighter pilots in England. These two months marked the bitterest and largest scale struggle between U.S. and Luftwaffe fighters. For U.S. pilots it was the grand finale of aerial combat; the German fighter command was then bested and mortally wonded. In these climactic months of the air war, pilots were sure of a challenge almost every time they invaded Germany. But in May German fighter resistance sharply diminished; its efforts were perceptibly enfeebled. Sometimes Jerry came up and savagely, effectively mauled the Big Friends, but the sallies were sporadic. The work of erasing Luftwaffe fighter strength as an invasion prerequisite was largely completed.

But the appetite for combat among 4th Group pilots was growing, stimulated by the sensational exploits of Gentile, who had revealed what a Mustang flown by certain pilots could do to the Luftwaffe, and the stunning personal glory he had earned for himself. Now and again the AAF was censured for a tendency to glorify its pilots, but it was lust after personal glory that animated the star performers of the 4th Group in their brutal assaults on the Luftwaffe.

An actor works to see his name in lights; a cub

reporter pounds the pavement to see his name on the masthead as editor; the pilots flung themselves into the teeth of cannon fire and flak for personal glory, whether it was in the form of esteem among fellow-flyers or write-ups in the hometown paper, or both, as was usual.

Effectively, a decoration was the same as a write-up. Both are modes of expressing a recognition of achievement, a means of distinguishing one pilot from another. A medal on the chest then, was about the same as a clipping in the scrapbook. Usually, however, the pilots regarded it as good form to be coy about newspaper notices. They would buy the P.R.O. a beer and explain: "I don't care anything about this bull—myself, y' understand— but the folks back home get such a big bang out of it."

And if the pilot performed some derring-do and the write-up didn't appear, the "folks back home" were very browned-off. You could see that in the eyes of the pilot.

The 4th was a fount of personal glory, individually and collectively. One day three bomber pilots were riding along the narrow, winding macadam roads amid the summer greenery of Essex County. They had completed 30 missions in bombers and now wanted to do a tour of ops in fighters. They were headed for the 78th Group at Duxford, a Thunderbolt outfit near Debden which produced the first ace in the E.T.O. (Capt. Charles London, Long Beach Calif.), but never got going in the spectacular way common to some other groups. As the three pilots bounced past Debden in a command car, one looked over the hedge at the red-nosed warplanes of the 4th.

"Gee, fellows—Mustangs!" ejaculated one. "Say, let's apply here."

The bomber trinity was escorted to the commanding officer.

"Sir, we'd like to join your group and do a tour in fighters."

Blakeslee said: "Okay with me. Go to Goxhill, get some transition time in 51s and report back."

They did, remarking later, "We wouldn't have had the nerve to do that if we'd known what a famous group it was."

The three did 250 hours of combat flying in Mustangs and wondered how they could ever have been happy in bombers. A bomber pilot would never admit that a fighter could compare with the big stuff; yet I've never been up with one who didn't buzz clouds and pretend he was a fighter plane hedge-hopping. But you have to give the bomber boys this: they were the ones who fought the toughest part of the air war. No matter how fierce the flak or how surrounded by Jerry interceptors, they had to hold it on that bombing run for about five minutes. The Jerries were after the bombers, not the Mustangs, so the Mustangs could boogar off any time it got too hot. Fighters attacked; bombers defended, and there was no sustaining sporting element in it. Forts stumbled through the sky ambushes at 160 m.p.h., while the fighters could do 400, weaving, diving and climbing to dodge the flak puffs. The bomber crews fought oftener than infantrymen and under equally severe conditions. Nobody ever heard of a fighter pilot who wanted to fly bombers. If so, he was sent to a flak shack until it could be determined if he met the requirements for a Section 8 discharge.

In May even the Russians were satisfied that the Second Front was about to be opened. Every time pilots were briefed they were given certain areas on the English coast over which they must not fly at any altitude for any reason: ack-ack gunners fired at all planes over these restricted areas, whether theirs or ours. These were the marshalling areas for the invading armadas and no chances were to be taken with German reconnaissance. Nevertheless, pilots often caught glimpses of vast war games on the ground.

The Germans were nervously carrying on large-scale movements along the coast of France. On May 21 the group attacked these movements, damaging 28 locomotives pulling troops and supplies with which to repel the invasion, seven barges and 13 trucks. "Cowboy" Megura and three other pilots in his section stopped five German trains. Every pilot in the group fired his guns.

Kid Hofer had exhausted his ammo when he came on a flock of Jerry trainers. Hofer played tag with them, seeking to panic the Jerry cadets and force them into a tree.

Another day Blakeslee sighted a long German convoy. He ordered the three squadrons to race him back to Debden. There, 500-pound bombs were slung under the wings and the group took off again to find the convoy. There was a single hole in the dense overcast, but it happened to be directly over the convoy. One by one, the Mustangs winged over and swan-dived through the hole and unleashed their bombs.

"We didn't wipe it out completely," Blakeslee chortled, "But we sure did shake hell out of 'em."

And there were strafing missions over Germany. Then one day Debden heard the Berlin radio snarl:

"You North American gangsters in red-nosed Mustangs will be prosecuted in the People's Court as war criminals."

Some pilots thereupon ordered their crew chiefs to remove the red paint from the nose of their Mustang.

The pilots were living the most memorable period of their lives as they raced over Europe in their silver warplanes, reveling in the quiver of the plane as the guns blazed, slaughtering German troops, stopping trains and watching the boilers geyser gray steam, dive-bombing railroad stations. People seem to have an inherent love of destruction, but it's repressed in normal times. This was a chance to tear up things with impunity. But the turbulent conflicts of March and April, the everyday missions of six and seven hours and the strain of dodging flak were exhausting the pilots.

Millikan, a man of tough mental and physical fibre and one who held fast to a regimen of rest and sleep, was one on whom fatigue showed. He had more than 400 hours of uninterrupted combat flying, about twice what was required for a rest, and he was white, listless, hatchet-faced. Blakeslee's "women and fighter pilots don't mix" was mocked by Millikan's example. There never was a pilot in the 4th with more zest for combat than Millikan. His determination to keep after the Jerries was so unassailable that his wife, Ruby, the first girl he met in England, had long since despaired of persuading him to take a rest at a desk as other husbands had done.

Millikan was carrying his tracer-loaded automatic on the May 30th mission. Intelligence couldn't seem to make up its mind whether a pilot had a better chance with or without a gun if shot down. Deep in Germany, Millikan took his squadron into a climb to rescue "Deacon" Hively from 30-plus Jerries and chased them to the deck. It was near an airdrome and the flak came up hot and heavy as Millikan and Lt. Sam Young, of Dallas, Tex., swooped down.

Young instinctively turned his head sidewise to protect himself from glass and metal shards as flak shattered his windscreen. The nose of his Mustang rammed Millikan's. The impact was shattering. Millikan was knocked about in the cockpit like a tenpin. He had no controls left. The rudder pedals collapsed and sank in the floorboard. The stick flopped around. His Mustang had been cut in half, leaving Millikan to fly a craft with no tail section.

The bisected Mustang went into a high speed spin towards earth, two miles below. Millikan jettisoned the canopy, and the wind pinned him against the seat of the spinning plane. He prepared to jump, pulling the oxygen line out of the socket and casting off helmet and goggles. With its tail section missing, the craft spun in such fashion as to catapult Millikan into the clouds when he released the belt about his legs.

Next Millikan knew, he was on his back falling through space. He put his hand on the ripcord and was about to pull it when he became aware of a plane roaring so loud it might have been over him. And that's where it was. His Mustang was directly above him, engine throbbing, its vivid red spinner whirring—chasing him down.

Blossoming the chute would have cut his falling speed. The plane would overtake him and the prop would grind him to pieces. It was nightmarish. Millikan felt as one does in a dream when he tries to hit a monster and his fist is a powder puff.

The plane was slowly gaining on Millikan in their fall to earth. He saw the big white star on the wing just above his head. Millikan turned his face and writhed. The plane roared past him. As Millikan looked down to watch the Mustang, he saw his dinghy, candy and chewing gum falling after it.

He pulled the ripcord and the chute opened with a jerk. He floated leisurely down on Germany. He could hear the receding drone of the bombers he had been escorting. Then everything was amazingly silent. The air was still. Dangling in his chute, Millikan could hear but one faint sound—blood dripping from his head on his leather jacket.

As the meadow below came up to meet him, Millikan could hear birds singing and he was so tired and lonesome he felt like crying baby-like. The cumulative, punishing fatigue spilled over the dam. Millikan felt it was almost a relief to be ripped out of his gruelling life at Debden, even though it meant imprisonment.

He collapsed on the ground, but struggled to his feet because Germans had no business seeing an American officer that way. The Germans soon ringed him. He panted and waited to see what they would do. One struck him from behind.

His anger was an injection of strength. Millikan raged: "You goddamn miserable son-of-a-bitch!" He clouted his assailant. This display of fury intimidated and quelled the Germans, though they forced him to lug his chute as they marched him to Magdeburg. Their treatment of him improved when they learned he was an officer.

17
D-Day

Every person in the U.K. felt that they would have to pull the lanyard on the invasion of Europe if for no other reason than the soldiers would unravel and snap under the taut expectancy. Washington brass told the U.S. to steel itself to a tremendous casualty toll. Gen. Bradley wisely said: Nuts.

March, April, and then May, with favorable weather spells, came and went. Now it was June. Almost daily the group was escorting bombers to the Pas de Calais area, 25 miles across the Channel.

Blakeslee and his pilots watched great fleets of bombers dump their bombs on this small coastal rim, but they could never see any targets. It appeared that the bombers were dropping their bombs aimlessly. No Hun fighters came up and the pilots wearied of these short, uneventful escorts. But regardless of weather, large formations of bombers continued the bombing. One day the overcast was so thick over England that Blakeslee delayed the take-off, expecting any minute to learn that the mission had been scrubbed. Word came to take off.

"Damn 'em!" said Blakeslee. "The bombers have already broken through the overcast—it's no trouble for them now."

Bombers and fighters alike lost their formation in the soup over the Pas de Calais. The bombers just circled, unable to find whatever it was they were looking for.

"Little Friend," said the leader of a bomber wing on the fighter-to-bomber channel, "can you tell us where the target is?"

Blakeslee exploded: "Did you hear that son-of-a-bitch ask *me* where the target is?"

Later in June they learned why the bombers were bombing fields and woods—to get at the buzz bomb launching sites which British intelligence had discovered.

Every day armadas of unprecedented size were dispatched to pulverize the Pas de Calais and other sections along the French coast with the exception of the Normandy beachhead. Eisenhower had said they would fly night and day. The fighters practiced night-flying. "Deacon" Hively was sent to a school where fighters practiced glide-bombing on brand new Churchill tanks. The Mustangs went into a dive at 4,000 feet and released two 500-pound bombs under the wings at 100 feet.

There were several false alarms. A teletype would come down restricting all personnel to the station, then the restriction would be lifted. Several times Blakeslee and the 14 other group commanders of the Eighth AF were summoned for invasion briefings, only to have them scrubbed because of bad weather.

On June 5th Debden was sealed again; only official phone calls could be made to the outside and these were monitored. The father of one of the waitresses called to ask why his daughter intended to spend the night on the station and was told, "Not why you think." Blakeslee was summoned to Ajax again. This time Maj. Gen. Kepner unrolled the invasion maps and said, "Gentlemen, the invasion begins tomorrow."

In the late afternoon of June 5, Blakeslee strode with running steps into the Officers' Mess. Pilots connected the big sealed envelope clutched under his arm with his tight-lipped tenseness. Some rightly guessed that the envelope contained the secrets of the invasion of France, but the urgency of secrecy was so great that no one commented. Every time somebody mentioned the word invasion, Blakeslee's belly jumped (he told me later).

The bombing attacks had been switched over to the Normandy area. In the late afternoon some 2,000 RAF and AAF bombers dropped 9,200 tons of bombs on the Normandy beachhead area, the first time they had hit this particular sector with great force. Ground crews at Debden were assembled by squadron engineering officers and instructed to place two 500-pound bombs beside each plane and to paint large black and white stripes on the wings and fuselages. Eagle Squadron alumni recalled that the same thing had been done on the eve of the Dieppe Raid.

Special guards were posted about the planes as the Germans were supposed to have 6,000 paratroops poised to make suicide attacks on airfields in England. All personnel carried carbines. Pilots were locked in the station cinema house and saw a secret film showing the glide-bombing of targets which duplicated those they were to hit in France on D-Day.

As Blakeslee briefed the pilots at midnight, the invasion was already in motion. Airborne divisions were already crossing the Channel to Normandy. Deacon and Jimmy Happel were asleep on a sofa. Blakeslee couldn't find them. He thundered: "How could they have failed me at a time like this?"

Blakeslee told the pilots at the briefing:

"I am prepared to lose the whole group."

At 3 o'clock in the morning the pilots walked to their planes and were strapped in by their crew chiefs. No stars were visible because of a solid cloud-layer. It was not the clear blue they had associated with D-Day. They taxied out in the darkness and took off behind Blakeslee. The mechanics could see their red and green lights moving across the field like comets as they formed up. Despite darkness, clouds and tautness, Blakeslee got the group formed up over Debden in record time.

There was no sleep for anybody in East Anglia that

night because of the endless roar of aircraft overhead. Groups of bombers and fighters were rising from nearby fields the same as the 4th. Something like 3,000 aircraft were forming up in the black clouds. The 4th almost collided with Duxford's Thunderbolts. The tremendous fleets kept out of each other's way only by following ground markers to the coast.

The 6,483 invasion ships had already set out in the stormy Channel from Portland, preceded by squadrons of destroyers and minesweepers. Three hundred Lightnings formed an umbrella. When the troops swarmed ashore across the iron pikes, the debris was still dry-heaving dust from the great bomber blow the afternoon before.

The Ninth AF was assigned to maintaining a fighter umbrella immediately over the beachhead. Eighth AF fighters were to form a wall, south, east, and west to prevent Luftwaffe craft from penetrating to the beachhead. The 4th's assignment was to sweep the area around Rouen, France. The Germans were supposed to have about 2,000 aircraft to protect the Atlantic Wall.

At 7:05 A.M. pilots heard Kid Hofer blurt:
"Whoo, a train!"
He tore down to strafe it. It was one of the first shots fired in the invasion.

A 190 slipped into the net. Capt. Shel Monroe, who hailed from Waycross, Ga., pounced and chased the 190 all the way to Paris, up one street and down another, skimming rooftops. He nailed the Jerry on the outskirts of Paris.

The Pole, Maj. Mike Sobanski, was getting his own back on the Germans for what they had done to him and his home in Warsaw in 1939. Raging down to strafe a train, Sobanski damaged his plane on some electrical cables. He asked his No. 2 to look his plane over. Told that the plane was not badly damaged, Sobanski reported that he was going after a second train.

Kid Hofer was likewise leading a section of Green-belt squadron, among them McGrattan. McGrattan had finished his tour of ops and had his B-4 packed to go home. But this was the historic D-Day and he decided to fly one more show before departing that afternoon. Hofer, McGrattan and the other two in the section were suddenly bounced by 15 Hun fighters. Hofer alone escaped. McGrattan and two others* were killed.

A few minutes later pilots heard Lt. Edward Steppe, of New York, say to Sobanski, "Watch those behind you, White Leader."

Late that afternoon, Capt. K. G. Smith, of Boise, Idaho, who had been in a German hospital since being shot down in March, had a phone call from a German officer.

"K. G.," said the German, "I've got some bad news for you. Mike Sobanski was killed this morning."

By this time the group was hopelessly split up in the cloud banks, and Blakeslee and Deacon were trying to get back together to return to Debden. They were talking over the R/T, flying this vector and that in an effort to join up.

"Don," said Deacon finally, "I believe if you'll turn left by that rift of clouds you'll find me."

Blakeslee banked left and there was a QP kite.

"I told you you'd find me," said Deacon.

"Find you?" replied Blakeslee softly, "Hell, Deacon— I *smelled* you."

---

*One was Lt. Harold L. Ross, Jr., Greensboro, N.C. An infantryman later wrote Ross' father: "A Canadian had parachuted from his burning Spitfire and was being strafed in his chute. Lt. Ross was on a dive towards the strafing plane when his plane broke in two. I counted 57 bullet holes . . . Hal was buried in the village cemetery of Bacquepuis, France by the mayor, with most of the village population present. It was considered an honor by the villagers who have him there and that is the reason . . . that it had not been reported . . . Flowers have been placed there every two days by Mme. Cordet. The people of the village wished for his body to remain in their cemetery . . ."

That was the first of three missions flown by the 4th on D-Day. They took bombs over at 12:20 P.M. on a second mission and again at 6:20 P.M. They were discharged on German troop trains and the bridges they had to cross, holding the Wehrmacht at bay while Allied soldiers and their battle gear were moved ashore. All the German commanders said at the Monday morning quarterback sessions after the war that it was this inability to move troops that prevented them from repelling the invasion.

Blakeslee and the group returned after midnight. As he taxied down the runway the wheels on his plane collapsed, as if from fatigue. The pilots gobbled more benzedrine tablets and gathered around Blakeslee in the bar. Red-eyed and numb, Blakeslee was nevertheless full of steam. He sent for the Ordnance officer, a little Philadelphia banker who jumped about like Jenny Wren, Capt. Walter Orenshaw.

"Orenshaw," said Blakeslee, "I want the fuses on those bombs changed from 11 seconds to 4 seconds."

"You what, sir?" Orenshaw blinked.

"You heard me—4 seconds delay."

"But, Colonel, that teletype from Ajax said all fighter groups would use 11 seconds delay," persisted Orenshaw.

"Orenshaw."

"Yes, sir."

"Four seconds."

Higher headquarters had directed the groups to use 11 seconds delay in glide bombing. That much delay was regarded as essential to guard against the chance that a bomb would skip along and explode before the low-flying fighter could race out of blast reach. But they were not as accurate for the reason that they did bounce and skid so long before detonating. There was an element of risk in dropping a 4-second bomb—in fact, it was just too bad if plane and bomb happened to go the same way.

"But that," Blakeslee observed, "will happen to

only one out of ten pilots. Four-second fuses for tomorrow's show, Orenshaw."

On D plus 6 Deacon was leading 334th Squadron in a bombstrafe attack before American troops advancing in Cherbourg Peninsula. A German soldier, firing his rifle, punctured an oil line in Kid Hofer's kite.

"I'm going down," Hofer reported to Deacon.

"Which side of the lines are you on?" asked Deacon.

"Our side."

"Okay, fella, see you tomorrow. And get me a helmet, too."

At this time, on the whole European Continent, there was but one Allied landing field. Hofer, whose luck was partially evidenced by the fact that five planes of his had been destroyed while other pilots were flying them, found himself immediately over this emergency landing strip when he broke out of the clouds. He landed and was received by no less than Maj. Gen. Ralph Royce of the Ninth AF. Hofer was provided with rifle, helmet and jeep for a tour of the battlelines. At one blasted pill box, Hofer stepped over some dead Germans and helped himself to the helmet Deacon had requisitioned. Also a canteen and a copy of *Mein Kampf*, drawn from a circulating library Jan. 3 by a departed soldier named Rudy.

The Ninth AF, which did not have a consistently cordial regard for the Eighth, helped Hofer to a libation of grapefruit juice and hospital alcohol, repaired his oil line and saw him off to Debden. At Debden he was received by Robert A. Lovett, Assistant Secretary of War for Air. Hofer stuck close to Secretary Lovett as that spared him the bother of sharp questions from certain superiors who wanted to know if it was an oil leak or just whimsy that caused him to land in France.

In all, D-Day and the days immediately following were immensely disappointing to the pilots; it was a grand anticlimax. In May, when German fighters abruptly became scarce, when the AAF could parade over Berlin without molestation, it was assumed that Hitler was conserving his fighter strength for all-out use D-Day. An aerial conflict dwarfing everything before was assumed. But on D-Day the 4th destroyed but three planes.

The 4th carried on with its drudgery, paralyzing German troop and supply movements in bomb-strafe attacks. Train engineers were as much in the firing line as Panzer Grenadiers. After the war Goering said:

"Without the American Air Force, the war would still be going on elsewhere, but certainly not on German soil."

The 4th, however, was presently to be released from short-range tactical operations to fly another spectacular mission . . .

18
Khotchetsya Pit

Jerry's failure to come up D-Day was like Harvard failing to show up for the Yale game. Pilots were disgusted. Infantrymen were naturally pleased when they stormed a beach unopposed, but war for fighter pilots, don't forget, was a "grand sport."

Their spirits got a lift when rumor spread of a sensational unprecedented mission, highly secret but near at hand. Everybody knew something was up when Kid Hofer had his trouble with the needle. The medics were inoculating pilots and certain crew chiefs with typhus and other strange shots. Hofer, the boxing champ, who thought it was sport to attack flak towers, who was so eager he slipped off on missions by himself—he just wasn't going to have that needle jabbed in him.

Blakeslee popped it to Hofer where it hurt most. He put him back to flying in a No. 4 position where it was hard to get a bounce on Jerries, he barred him from participating in the secret mission and he forbade him to enter the bar for two weeks.

At this point, Virginia Irwin of *The St. Louis Post-Dispatch*, the most personable and ablest news-hen I met, arrived to do a feature story on Hofer, "the last of the screwball pilots." Virginia kept saying that she had heard that the Debden bar had the only potable beer in the U.K. Hofer, with shy reluctance, finally told her that Blakeslee wouldn't let him go in the bar.

"I guess," Hofer said wretchedly, "you'd better go in with the other boys."

Virginia said, "I'll be back in a couple of pints."

It was too much, Hofer went to Deacon and promised to take the needle if they'd let him go into the bar and fly the mission. Hofer, with his incapacity for fear and his score of 27½ enemy planes destroyed, was too good a hand to leave behind on the kind of a mission this was to be. Deacon relented.

Maj. Goodson, the jocular, ribald Canadian who spoke Greek, German and French, was to lead 336th Squadron on the mission and he was as elated as Hofer. He always met such interesting people on his trips. For example, when he was in Italy breaking in a new Mustang group, he was asked what kind of plane he flew.

"Mustang," Goodson said, "and you?"

"Lightning."

"And you?"

"Thunderbolts."

"And you?" asked Goodson of a rather silent character.

"Messerschmitts," replied the German prisoner.

On the day before the secret mission was flown, Goodson, a top-ranking ace with 15 destroyed in the air and 15 on the ground and the newspaper sobriquet "King of the Strafers", was leading Shirtblue Squadron deep in Germany near Neubrandenburg Airdrome. Goodson was in unusually high good humor that day because of the impending mission, but also because his girl in Canada, after trying for more than two years, had finally been able to join the Red Cross and was due to land in England in a few days to be with him.

Goodson's squadron circled the drome, saw some planes and tested the flak. Goodson said: "Anybody who wants to go down on this drome, feel free to do so." With that Goodson split-essed and streaked over the airfield, guns blazing. Flak punctured his cooling system and the plane began smoking as the gylcol streamed.

Flak, not a German pilot, was bagging another in a

338

long series of outstanding aces—Beeson, Glover, Garrison, Evans, and many more to come. Goodson said over the R/T with curt detachment:

"Goodbye, boys. Keep up the good work."

Goodson was too low to bail, so he bellied in and unhurriedly left his ship, as though he didn't care if it did explode. The squadron came down and blasted his plane to keep it from the Germans. The last they saw of Goodson, he had his hands in his pockets, head down, glumly kicking things as he walked towards a wood. The girl from Canada had missed him by three days.

On the morning of the longest day of the year, June 21, Blakeslee briefed the pilots. To the 4th Group and Blakeslee had come the distinction of being picked to escort Forts on the pioneer Britain-to-Russia shuttle mission. Blakeslee, who had begun his career in Spitfires that could stay aloft for an hour and a half, was now going to lead single-seater fighters the 1,600 miles from Debden to a dot on the Russian Steppes, engaging any Jerries that might appear along the way. It was an aviation milestone; the War Department ordered a classified newsreel made of the historic briefing.

Blakeslee was impatient with any kind of affectation, but for this occasion he was wearing a white scarf. Holding the wand to the glazed briefing map, Blakeslee began in a voice which the sound recorders said sounded something like Gable's:

"Now look, before we all get excited about it, I'll say the whole trip is about 7½ hours. We've done 'em that long before. We'll be throttled back, so Christ, we could stay up for eight hours. There'll be 1,001 bombers acting as diversion for our 104 bombers!"

The pilots roared at this, but it was a reasonable arrangement. It was 15 days after D-Day and it was desirable to do all things possible to destroy the German will to resist. The demonstrated ability of Allied bombers to shuttle between Russia and England with fighter escort was calculated to daunt the Germans. Further, it would have a favorable effect on Russia. But it would all boomerang if the attempt were thwarted by German fighters. Hence, 1,001 bombers were sent over Berlin to occupy the Jerries while 104 bombed an oil refinery south of Berlin and shuttled on to Russia.

"We'll take the bombers up to the Russian frontier," Blakeslee continued. "From there it's 258 miles to base. We should be met by Russian fighter planes—Yaks. I'll be leading with 336th Squadron.

"On the way to Russia—we will not—we will *not*—do any fighting on the way over. You will not drop your tanks. If you're attacked, go into a turn with 'em. If for any reason you should have to drop tanks around Berlin—you've had it. You'll have to return to Debden.

"I want to land 68 aircraft at this place" (pointing). "You're safe here if you're not straggling. The Russians are sensitive to stragglers. Several reconnaissance craft were shot up recently. You don't have to worry about Russian fighters over 15,000 feet— that's their ceiling.

"If you have to identify yourself, it will be done by rocking your ship three to five times and dipping your right wing three to five times. They've got a homing station here, but they may as well shove it up their——. It only has a radius of 15 miles.

"Once we make a rendezvous with the bombers, there will be absolutely no radio conversation. If you see a man's wing on fire—just be quiet, he'll find out about it himself after a while.

"Let's make a pretty landing, a pansy landing, bang, bang, bang. We want to make the thing look like a 7½ hour trip is nothing to us. There are no replacements, so if you crack up your plane, that means you probably stay in Russia for the rest of the war.

"For Christ's sake, no landing errors. The Russians

340

shoot the men who make mistakes—when in Russia do as the Russians do.

"No one will take a gun. If you're forced down—a gun is a death warrant. No guns at all. I don't know whether I'd even let them catch me with a knife. Too much like a weapon. Now these guerrillas are trying to recruit men to fight with them. If you're captured by them, throw up your hands and do as they say, but tell them, politely, no you're a pilot and fight differently from them. They're almost savage, so if they insist, you'd better be still."

The pilots were raptly intent as Blakeslee wound up.

"No one will abort because of lack of oxygen. You'll be at 15,000 feet. You don't need it. You have no business in the 4th Group if you have to have oxygen at 15,000 feet. If you get dizzy, go down under the bombers for a while. Over Russia we will be over 1,000 feet and below 6,000 feet. If your glass elbows break (gas line on wing drop-tanks), pull off to the side, have them fixed and catch us.

"One more thing. If you've got to drink while you're there, for Christ's sake, don't get drunk. Be careful how you appear to the Russians with your crew chiefs. None of this 'okay, Joe' stuff. You treat Russian officers like brother officers—or rather, *not* like brother officers."

He grinned and wound up.

"This whole thing is for show. That's why everything must be pansy. Cheers."

Crew chiefs and mechanics* were to go along on this mission as gunners in the bombers in order to service the Mustangs when they sat down in Russia. For two years the crew chiefs had had only the second-hand thrill of watching the planes take off and return.

---

*For roster of officers and men participating, see Appendix.

Many were rebellious at their remoteness from the dangers their pilots faced and belittled their own part in the war; they were all eagerness. Others went because they were soldiers. The only non-flying officer to go was the group intelligence officer, Maj. Baldwin M. Baldwin, a resident of Reno. Baldwin, a splenetic, snarling man with a thyroid expression, was a rich man's son whose civilian career had been managment of his father's California fortune. Baldwin and his I. O. factotums kept close to the isolated Group Intelligence building, from which Baldwin carried on a sort of guerrilla warfare against Lt. Col. Clatanoff, the ground exec. Clatanoff, able, tactless and domineering, forewent few opportunities to harass the thorny Baldwin clique. Each was out to get the other, and most personnel wished both of them good luck in their aims.

The ground personnel received a brief instruction in aerial gunnery, were equipped with chutes, dinghies, candy, cigarets and toilet paper. As Blakeslee hastened from the briefing to his plane, we saw the engaging spectacle of a full colonel carrying two rolls of tissue.

The whole field turned out to see the 68 Mustangs take off, though their destination remained, theoretically, a top secret. Blakeslee had an alternate plane ready so that if for any reason WDC developed engine trouble, he could land and take off again in the other craft. As he was being strapped into the cockpit, packed with dress clothes, cigarets, tissue, etc., he was examining his Very pistol. A photographer's flash bulb exploded and Blakeslee virtually broke the safety belt.

He carried with him no less than 16 maps to get to the place where no other Allied craft had flown. As he cranked his plane off, he looked quizzically at the men clustered about him. Nobody ever knew for sure what the inscrutable Blakeslee was thinking, but his expression appeared to read: "Don Blakeslee and the

4th Group are about to do it again."

Blakeslee and his No. 2 were first off. They took most of the runway, as the drop-tanks for the trip weighed 108 pounds. Near the end of the runway they pulled the stick and were airborne over Mr. Kettley's farmhouse. The wheels were sucked into the ship bellies and they banked left, circling until the other 66 craft* got up. Blakeslee set course over the field in a rain and was off for a dot in the wilds of Russia.

On the way across Germany Blakeslee was unable to see the ground through the cloud-layer; a cloud-layer, he thought, wasn't going to help him find the roost in the Ukraine. They passed south of Berlin as the 1,001 bombers assaulted Berlin in the diversionary attack. An unusually intense flak barrage came up, one of the heaviest the 4th ever experienced. Lt. Grover C. Siems, Jr., of Woodside, N.Y. squeaked:

"I'm hit, Deac!"

The flak had turned him over like a flapjack and he was flying upside down.

Bombers and fighters entered Poland and dropped their wing tanks. Goodson, shot down the day before, was still at large in Germany and, he said after the war, the sound of the planes going to Russia without him drove him wild.

Having met the bombers at the appointed time and place, it began to look like an uneventful trip. What the pilots didn't know until Goering disclosed it after the war was that a Heinkel bomber had slipped into the formation unobserved and was flying along in formation with the Forts.

Near Warsaw 10 to 15 black-nosed 109s made a head-on attack on the bombers. Five of them were shot down for the loss of one. One of the bombers was shot down, the one in which Goodson's crew chief, S/Sgt. Robert L. Gilbert, of Saginaw, Mich., was flying as waist gunner. Gilbert bailed and stayed

---

*A squadron of planes from the 352nd Fighter Group flew with the 4th.

on for some weeks fighting in the company of Russian guerillas.

At 7:15 P.M. Blakeslee looked apprehensively at his watch, at the timetable strapped to his leg and at several of his 16 maps. The group had parted with the bombers, which were to land at Poltava. The 1,600-mile flight should be ending in 20 minutes. Fuel was getting low and pilots began considering that bailing out over these wilds would be rough as the well-known cob.

Suddenly a volley for flares came up, fired by the Russians. Lt. George H. Logan, Jr., of Montclair, New Jersey, flying on Blakeslee's wing, saw the Colonel rapturously throw his 16 maps into the air. He turned towards Logan and blew kisses at him. Blakeslee, the man who boasted he couldn't fly a course in the link trainer and never went near one, had flown 1,600 miles and found the camouflaged airdrome as though he had a rope tied to it.

Blakeslee jubilated over the R/T: "The end of a perfect show."

It was either 7:35 or 7:36. If it was 7:35, as Blakeslee always insisted, then the group had arrived on the minute of the E.T.A. (estimated time of arrival). Deacon, however, always insisted that the group was one minute late.

The Mustangs roared low over the up-looking Russians. In sections of four they honked up in steep port banks, pressed the buttons to let the wheels down and bounced across the taxi strip at Piryatin. Sixty-six of the original 68 planes landed, of the missing two, one had been shot down and the other was flown by Kid Hofer, who, as usual, was off on a show of his own. Nobody worried when the teletype reached Debden asking for the number markings on the Kid's kite. He had landed at Kiev and the Russians were checking to see if he was a masquerading German.

The Russians hurried to Blakeslee and presented a large bunch of flowers. Whereupon, he was whisked off to Moscow to make a broadcast to America. Maj. Pete Mahan, of Montgomery, Ala., had been sent ahead by Spaatz to make the arrangements. The AAF was resourceful that way.

The pilots stepped out on the wings, surrounded by chattering, cheering Russians. The Russian mechanics had never seen a Mustang, so all they could do was polish them, and this they proceeded to do with a vengeance. One picked up a Very pistol, fascinated. The pistol went off and the flare exploded on the canopy of a Mustang. Two Russian officers, one clutching a pistol, ran up and dragged the nonplussed Russian G. I. off. Deacon later talked them out of executing the oaf, but next day he was sent to the front.

With Blakeslee gone to Moscow, the Deacon was pretty much the chief cook, a role to which he took as a duck to the water. A Russian officer in a white helmet came to Deacon's plane, all smiles and cordiality. In the siege of Stalingrad he had been one of those fabulous airmen who had flown over the German-held part of the city and cascaded hand grenades down from a fragile Tiger Moth, a deadly but fantastic operation. More officers drove up in a '32 model Ford. Deacon couldn't get off the wing of his ship for saluting and being saluted.

"Kommandante, kommandante?" the Russians jabbered. Deacon got out his phonetic spelling card.

"Da, da," Deacon replied. What was needed was food and a bath. He perused the card. It was full of such as how to say in Russian, "Where is the Soviet front?", "North, South, East, West," and "I am wounded", etc. But nothing about how to ask for food and bath. Nearest Deacon could find was, "I am thirsty." It was a fatal selection.

"Khotchetsya pit," quoth Deacon in phonetic Russian.

"Da, da. Schnapps, schnapps?" asked the Russians, quivering to please.

"Da, da," answered Deacon. The Russian gestured

the question whether he also wanted schnapps for all the pilots with him.

"Da, da."

They made off to the hospital to freshen up, Deacon proceeding with the high Russian brass in a Ford, the Junior Birdmen following in a Studebaker. Lt. Donald Malmsten, of Burwell, Nebr., found what he thought was a latrine and proceeded. Some Russian nurses inadvertently walked in, put their hands to their mouths and tittered as they retreated. Malmsten was using a wash sink.

Comrade the Deacon and his fellow-flyers were ceremoniously led to the banquet hall as the sun set on Russia. The hosts brought him a great bunch of red roses and the Russian soldier kissed Deacon full on his lips, as they do in Russia. A balalaika orchestra played American tunes, the pilots dancing with the Russian men as well as the women, also customary.

There were more floral offerings as pilots and hosts sat down to banquet. The piercingly hot vodka was drunk in toasts; you swallowed the full glass of white fire in one fell gulp, then placed the glass on the table upside down. They toasted Marshal Stalin, President Roosevelt, the death of Germany—each with a full glass of white fire. Eyes took on an oyster murkiness, tongues thickened. Deacon saw how things were shaping up and he said, as might a captain abandoning a sinking vessel:

"Hey, fellas, eat all you possibly can—thish stuff is pow'ful potent."

Glasses up, glasses down, quickly filled by alert waiters. Lt. Jack Simon, of Long Beach, Calif., slipped a glass of water in a Russian colonel's place. On the next toast, the Russian drained the glass. The blandness of the water was fire in his mouth. He spat the water out and rolled his eyes ominously, if not with intent to liquidate, at the innocent waiter.

Presently it was made known to Deacon, as the leader of the squadron, that the Russian general was prepared to receive him in his quarters. With Capt. William E. Hedrick, of Denver, Colo., on his left in tight aide-de-camp formation, Deacon was led to the General, who was seated with his staff. The Russians popped to with a twang and saluted the American and his aide. Deacon returned the salute. More food, more vodka toasts and Deacon was held up only upon the thin reed of formality.

Deacon handed the Russian general, who had been chief of air operations at Stalingrad, an American cigaret. The general handed Deacon a Russian cigaret. Deacon signed a $5 bill and handed it to the general. The general handed Deacon a 100-ruble note. Blakeslee had said put on all possible military dog, so Deacon thought he'd better carry on as long as it gratified the Russian.

Accordingly, Deacon took off his belt, a beautiful silver-buckled cowboy belt specially fashioned for him in Oklahoma. This he proffered to the general. The general's eyes widened; he and his staff popped to with a twangy-twang-twang. Deacon wondered if he had committed some sort of an Asiatic *faux pas*. He and Hedrick stood at attention opposite the rigid general and his retinue. Whereupon, the general removed his own belt, kissed it and handed it to Deacon. Deacon kissed it and strapped it around his pinks.

Deacon and the general kissed goodnight, as staunch allies do in consonance with Russian folkways. The C.O.'s straw bed was given to the *Americanyetss* flyer, whose military punctilio and vodka, swilling above and beyond the call of duty had endeared him to his hosts. Next morning the pilots discovered that in Russia every day started with a haircut and shave. Deacon gave his barber a cake of Palmolive soap which the barber handled as though it were a hunk of platinum from the Urals, frugally shearing flakes off with a razor.

The Heinkel bomber which had flown for a time unseen in the Fort formation on the way to Russia had returned to its German base and the pilot reported where the Americans landed. The Germans tailored a bombing attack. On the second night the Luftwaffe sent a fleet of bombers, which destroyed a very large portion of the Fort squadrons, and some JU 88s to strafe and bomb the fighter bases.

Deacon was standing in front of his tent relieving himself when a flare illuminated the camp. Forty-mm. cannon whizzed through the tents.

"Jesus H. Christ, they're strafing us!" bellowed Deacon.

Not so. It was Russian anti-craft coming from the low ground over which the tent-site looked. Most ran to cover, but others could only hop as their feet were in sleeping bags. Deacon grabbed his boots and hat and, along with the others, took a running jump into some holes. They quickly discovered that the holes had been dug for purposes other than shelter. But none stirred.

The attacks of the German fighter bombers continued and Deacon got permission from the Russians to set up an interception system. The Russians were delighted with the ingenuity displayed in removing some crystals from Mustang radios and installing them in the control tower radio. This change of crystals placed the ground radio and the Mustangs on the same frequency. This made it possible to direct the fighters from the ground as they sought the raiders.

Deacon, acting as controller, scrambled a section of four Mustangs to 4,000 feet as soon as Russian spotters phoned in a flash that some JU 88s were heading for the field. Trying to interpret the Russians' English and their gestures, Deacon feverishly dead-reckoned where the 88s could best be intercepted and gave the Mustangs a call on the blower:

"Nuthouse here. Bandits coming in at angels four. Vector 260. Vector two-er-six-er-zero. Over."

"Roger. Out."

The section missed the 88 and it came streaking across the field and was nailed by a Russian Yak. Another attack was made and this time, though no kills were made, the attack was beat off.

Deacon and the other pilots were eager to arrange a show wherein they could fly to the German base, which was loaded with aircraft, and beat it up. The Wolfpack was crowding the 4th again for first place and this appeared a likely opportunity to take a long step ahead. But despite the most importunate entreaties, the Russians would not permit the Americans to launch the attack, explaining:

"You are our guests. We protect *you*. If you did this, Goebbels would say you had come to fight for us."

The Debden mechanics, who had experienced the thrill of seeing their Mustangs beat off the attack en route to Russia, got the ships in shape and after five days, during which the Russians extended the utmost cordiality to the Americans, the Mustangs took off on the next leg of the triangle mission. They flew from Russia to Italy. The bombers pasted an oil refinery at Drohobycy, Poland on the way. No German attacks were made and the 4th broke escort at the Yugoslavian coast. Mustangs of the 15th AF, based in Italy, came in to provide withdrawal support for the bombers. Not knowing anything about the D-Day zebra stripes painted on the Eighth AF planes, the 15th AF pilots made attack gestures, but no shots were fired. The group landed at Lucrera near Foggia.

One day Deacon started out to see his brother, Sgt. Bill Hively, of Columbus, Ohio, who was stationed with the AAF on Sardinia. Accompanied by Siems, he developed engine trouble on the way and landed near the Anzio beachhead amid the 109 and 190 wreckage.

"Say, Grover," said Deacon as they taxied, "you don't think—"

"Think what?"

"—They forgot to clear the mines here?"

"*Whot?*"

With that they taxied back, taking great care to follow the same path out. On Sardinia, Deacon was told that his brother was on location about 30 miles away at a direction finding post atop a mountain crag. Because of the elevation of the mountain and the winding road leading to it, Sgt. Hively and his three friends could see a car coming up the mountain for an hour before it arrived, but they weren't looking this time.

Most of the population of Bosa, men, women and children, followed Deacon and Siems as they sought out Sgt. Hively in a wine emporium. The village was ancient and Deacon walked over dusty cobblestones up one alley, turned left, turned right, then into a still narrower alley and up some steep stairs. Deacon kept his head down as he mounted the creaking stairs so that Sgt. Hively saw only that it was an officer. To his companions, the sergeant said, "Okay, pop to." Deacon got right up in his brother's face and abruptly lifted his head.

"Me older brudder!"

"Me younger brudder!"

Deacon always said that the thrill of this meeting with his brother surpassed any other of his life as combat pilot.

Sgt. Hively sent for the mayor, and with the entire ambulatory population following, they repaired to what appeared a garage. The mayor of Bosa, Sardinia opened the portals and there stood cask on cask of wines, the dust on which was older than the oldest peasant in his entourage. Deacon and Siems did their duty with the wine, as with the vodka. For the sake of the mayor and his constituents, Deacon and Siems gave the place a dust-swirling buzz job.

Kid Hofer, having talked the Russians into servicing his plane at Kiev, took off with Lt. Willard (GI) Gillette, of Homeward, Kans., and Lt. James F. Callahan, Inkerman, Pa., with a view of rejoining the group in Italy. Hofer was not the best of navigators and the other two pilots became anxious.

"I'm flying 280°," Hofer said.

"You're wrong," said Gillette. "See you later."

Gillette left Hofer and started out on a new heading. He made Italy; Callahan landed on Sicily; Hofer, on Malta. But they got to Italy in time for the next mission.

Now the spirited, swashbuckling hot rocks of the 4th were never once accused of even false modesty, and presently, in between swims in the Adriatic and visits to Rome, they pointed out to the 15th AF pilots that they were having the edifying experience of associating with the hottest outfit in Eighth AF, and probably any other.

The 15th AF pilots took about as kindly to this swaggering as you would suppose. They said: "If you're so keen, why don't you show us?"

To which 4th pilots responded, "Cheers, friends, that's what we've been waiting for you to say."

It was thereupon arranged that next day (July 2), the 4th would go along as part of the fighter escort for the 15th AF bombers attacking targets in Budapest, capital of Hungary. So the fleet started out for Budapest on the mission, in which the 4th was to exhibit the fashion in which the masters clobbered the wily Hun.

Everything snafued from the start. The 15th AF pilots were maliciously pleased as they heard 4th pilots on the blower calling Horseback to say they had to abort on account of motor trouble. The planes were malfunctioning because they were unequipped with the dust filters necessary in the Mediterranean theater and because the nozzles on the belly tanks were of different size and were starving the cylinders. Thus, by the time the bombers and fighters reached the river separating Buda from Pest, the 4th was more the size of a squadron than a group. 334th Squadron, for example, had but eight planes left.

The 4th had been assigned the "free lance" type of support, which meant they were not encumbered with protection of any one box of bombers, but were free to roam in search of enemy fighters. They were weaving high above the bombers and other fighters, but the flak came up fiercely.

"Just like back home," said Blakeslee. He decided that no Jerries were coming up and was leading two of the squadrons down in search of ground targets for strafing. Just then Deacon shouted:

"Pectin leader to Horseback—here comes the Luft-waffe!"

It did look like it, with between 50 and 60 Me. 109s coming in to smack the bombers at 30,000 feet. All that stood between them and the bombers were 20-odd Mustangs. The boasting mood was gone now. The 4th made frantic calls to the 15th AF pilots below to come up with some help. Whether the S.O.S. was unheard or ignored, the result was the same: the 4th was left on its own. Pilots who dived after the 109s would bawl:

"The bastards are down here flying formation!"

The 109s pulled a boner which nullified their numerical advantage. They turned their backs to the fighters to launch the attack on the bombers. Emerson found a 109 flying along with a section of Mustangs. As Emerson attacked, the 109 went into a steep climb. Emerson had the pieces flying when his fuel feed failed; he stalled and spun out. But the Jerry came spinning down with a wing off.

Blakeslee downed one. Capt. Frank Jones, of Montclair, N. J., who always flew with a teddy bear in his cockpit, got another, but his roommate, Lt. George I. Stanford, of Southport, Conn., was shot down. Shel Monroe and his section pitched in to break up a formation of some 25 of the 109s.

Deacon got on the tail of another 109 and began blasting. At the same time a 109 was blasting Deacon; Siems was blasting that one; Siems was being blasted; Hedrick was blasting that one; and yet another in this deadly tandem was blasting Hedrick.

The 109 at which Deacon was firing exploded after a four-second burst, but the one on his tail was pumping cannon shells into his Mustang. One exploded the glass canopy over Deacon's head. His right eye was bloodied and he lost control of his plane. Despite this wound in one eye and blood-dimmed vision in the other, Deacon rejoined the fray and shot down two more 109s, for which he was awarded the D.S.C.

A cannon shell ripped into Siems' shoulder and took away part of his neck and chin. Gasping with pain, Siems managed to get his craft back to Italy and landed in the middle of a vast bomber drome at Foggia. Nobody saw him land. Sitting helplessly on the ground in his cockpit, filling his flying suit with blood, Siems failed to get control tower on the radio, and he was too badly wounded to walk. Fearing he'd bleed to death, Siems flipped on the gun switch and began firing his guns. He was never told whether it was the sound of the firing or the tracers flying over the buildings which brought help.

Despite the numerical odds, the attack on the bombers was largely frustrated. When Blakeslee counted noses back in Italy, however, he found that Hofer was among the missing. Little thought was given to it at first as it was logically assumed that the Kid had simply goofed-off somewhere on the deck by himself. Probably in a couple of hours he would return, or phone up from Cairo or Shangri-la, or somewhere. But he didn't. How, when and where nobody ever learned, but Kid Hofer, "last of the screwball pilots", was killed over Budapest. The Budapest mission was the frolic from which Hofer

353

didn't return.

Weeks later the Germans reported through the Red Cross that Hofer had been identified by his dog tags and was buried in Hungary. It was the end of one of the AAF's most colorful, engaging fighter pilots, the end of an almost fantastic career which began when he entered the RCAF enlistment office in Windsor by mistake. He had destroyed 27½ enemy aircraft—perhaps he got one or two more before being shot down—and had been the first flight officer in the E.T.O. to qualify as ace. He was a vividly smiling boy who appeared to have no appreciation of danger, one who joyously romped about the deadly skies over Europe with a "Gee, ain't the Alps pretty," and a "Let's go clobber 'em!"

The action over Budapest had swept the group score past the 600-mark and already the pilots were talking of the party that would be thrown on their return to Debden. Under treatment for his face wounds, Deacon chafed at remaining behind in an Italian hospital when the others left. But the medics kept him confined and Blakeslee forbade him to fly with his injury.

The group did one more show, taking the bombers on an uneventful mission to the marshalling yards at Arad, Rumania, and prepared to fly back to England on the third leg of the triangle. Meanwhile, Deacon encountered a doctor in the hospital who had studied under his father at Johns Hopkins. Deacon induced his father's whilom protege to take him to the eyesight surgery room. He memorized the chart and thus was able to pass an eye test next morning. But Blakeslee was adamant: "You're grounded, Deac."

When the day came to leave, Deacon, abetted by Col. Ben Kelsey, of Waterbury, Conn., a widely known test pilot, sneaked out of the hospital on the pretext of seeing the group off. He hitch-hiked a ride to the drome in the pickaback P-38 and arrived just before take-off time. Hiding from Blakeslee, Deacon confided to his squadron that he was going to stowaway on the flight.

"Now listen," Deacon said to Shel Monroe, "I'm going to fly on your right so I can use my good eye to keep from ramming you. If we get in a fight, don't anybody get excited and go saying 'Deacon' on the R/T. Don would clobber me."

On July 5 the group crossed over Corsica and made rendezvous over the Mediterranean with the bombers, which were to bomb railroad yards in France along the route from Italy to England. No fighters appeared and the group was relieved by the Wolfpack, over Chauearoux. Everyone at Debden turned out to receive the returning pilots, Blakeslee having announced their arrival over the R/T. The pilots raced low across the hangars at the end of the famous mission, but they were too worn out for the stunting one expected.

Over a beer, someone idly remarked to Blakeslee, "Deacon landed in front of you."

"Oh, no," Blakeslee corrected, "Deacon is in Italy in the hospital."

Blakeslee turned and saw Deacon. His eyes snapped, but he shook his head resignedly and smiled, "Deacon, I don't know whether to court-martial you or give you a medal."

Next day Blakeslee and Deacon journeyed to London for some high octane relaxation after the arduous mission, which had taken them in a great 7,000-mile triangle from England to Russia to Italy to England. It was mid-July and the buzz-bomb bombardment of London was at its height. Thousands were evacuating London to escape the devastation, which arrived at five-minute intervals on cloudy days. The siren sounded, there followed the unforgettable throb of the bomb coursing just over the roof-tops trailing orange flame, and you held your breath to see of the motor would cut off before it passed over. It was in this explosive inferno that Blakeslee and Deacon sought rest and recuperation. They rented several furnished flats in the Mayfair district and stocked them with enough spirits to float a PBY. On the third day, Deacon liked to relate, he came up in Marble Arch Pavilion, the feature being Danny Kaye in *Up in Arms*. Deacon guffawed at a sequence. He felt a hand on his shoulder—Blakeslee's. In the world's largest city they had become separated, but had ended up in the same place, the same as on D-Day in the overcast.

The Russian do was one of the 4th's prime triumphs. The brilliance of Blakeslee's leadership was recognized with a second Distinguished Service Cross, second only to the Congressional Medal. But the pilots were dispirited when they considered they had flown 7,000 miles over enemy territory and had been able to bag but 9½ Jerries (the 352nd Group element got 5½). No one could fathom the paucity of German planes as intelligence reported that the Luftwaffe had plenty of them left.

The pilots went on flying every day in the wake of the invasion, wish-thinking that the Germans were simply hoarding their fighters for a supreme throw of the dice. Strafing and dive-bombing every day as the AEF advanced, the pilots got an especial kick out of dropping wing tanks on an installation and igniting the gasoline vapor with incendiary bullets.

But even though the pickings were slim as far as dogfighting was concerned, Godfrey returned from the States to demonstrate that a pilot of intense combat ardor and superior prowess could still find targets. By now he was among the very few left of the Old Guard, most of the others having rotated stateside or gone down.

Godfrey had gone home with Gentile in April for a 30-day leave. Gentile had received an ovation which was epitomized by the fact that Gen. Arnold sent him about over the country in his own transport. Gentile made rhetorical speeches to bond rallies, was photographed with his mother kneeling in prayer, kissed babies, became engaged and resigned himself to the role of national celebrity at 23.

Godfrey also received a heady acclaim as Gentile's wing man; together they had destroyed 56 enemy planes. The AAF was pleased as punch to have this Damon-Pythias angle exploited, for it brought home to thousands of fledgling pilots that survival depended greatly upon No. 1 and 2 sticking together in combat. Gentile and Godfrey mugged the part cheerfully and wholeheartedly. They did New York in the visiting fireman tradition and were genuinely surprised to find, as they shuttled between the Stork Club and Toots Shors, that the taxi drivers not only recognized them from their pictures, but refused to accept the fare, a forbearance which I do not for a moment think depressed the frugal Gentile. The girls crowded about the table of Maestro Gentile and wing man.

"In what part," asked one girl, "of Gentile's wing do you fly?"

Godfrey explained that flying Gentile's wing didn't mean he was in the plane with him. He said: "Look, Mustangs are operated by one man. Just him alone."

"Ooh," she cooed, "you fly all by yourself in a plane?"

Despite a superficial cheerfulness in the sister act with Gentile, Godfrey was growing a little weary of the wing man angle. He didn't question Gentile's greatness as a fighter pilot—he had seen it in action more than anybody else—but he knew he had the stuff to run up an equal score. He aimed for 50 destroyed.

At Debden Gentile and Godfrey were expected any day. Gentile dropped a line to say he was touring the country in an Oldsmobile and asked if his promotion to major had come through: he knew the recommendation had started up through channels to Pinetree before he departed. Blakeslee told me to write Gentile that his promotion had bounced, probably because

358

Gentile had failed to show the proper viscosity of humility in explaining to Buck Gen. Auton how he came to prang that Mustang.

But Gentile was not destined to fly combat again or to return to Debden. With his stature as an AAF celebrity, Gentile now belonged to the Ages.

Last Debden heard of him was his marriage, in which The Greek participated as best man. Gentile was assigned to test jet planes at Wright Field. Soon thereafter the *AP* reported that Gentile denied that he had buzzed Columbus. At Debden they said: "We believe you, Don, 'cause you say it's true."

Godfrey's return to England was followed very soon by a cable from Washington. The War Department wanted to know if Godfrey was familiar with the army regulation—No. 600 dash something—that governed clearance of public statements by army officers. I calculate that Godfrey had given out 25 to 35 newspaper interviews at Debden and nobody had said anything, but now he had struck a wrong note and they excavated a regulation (oh, yes, the Air Corps had many things in common with the Army). The *casus belli* was a newspaper story appearing all over America.

Capt. John T. Godfrey, Rhode Island's leading fighter ace, is "burned up" by what he calls America's present policy of "spoon-feeding" its thousands of future combat pilots.

"I stood six days of their constant silly restrictions at Hillsgrove, R. I., and then I said to hell with it and went back home." he told a *United Press* reporter.

"They won't let the kids fly when it's cloudy. They won't let them do this or that—until it makes you ill. They wouldn't let me fly the Ohio River with a 2,000-foot ceiling. I can remember taking off in England when you jumped straight into overcast and stayed that way up to 30,000 feet or more," Godfrey added.

He expressed the opinion that a kid-glove policy by "brass hats" in this country is endangering the lives of all youngsters now in training camps . . .

"I figure it's a lot better to take risks and get better pilots," he said. "If the boys are spoon-fed at home it makes it mighty tough fitting them into combat outfits."

It appeared that the least Godfrey could get was a stiff dose of the 104th*, but his status as outstanding AAF warrior evoked the quality of mercy and it fell as a gentle rain: Ajax directed a post-graduate course in the proscriptive regulation for Godfrey and told him to go and sin no more.

On the morning of Aug. 5 the canvas tent-tops at the Newport general hospital developed a high sea as *Reggie's Reply* roared over a flagpole level. Godfrey gave the three loud throttle razzles to let Charlotte know that he and the group were forming up for the day's work.

Six hours later the Mustangs came in over the hospital with all the zoom derived from letting down from 15,000 feet, and the tents all but collapsed in the suction of the plane's wake. Godfrey racked the craft about in some spectacular snap rolls. Charlotte knew from that he had had a good day. Specifically: a 109 destroyed in air combat; three destroyed by strafing; three more damaged; eight locomotives, pulling Hun soldiers up to the front, shot up and halted. This brought Godfrey's score to 30, with 17 in the air and 13 on the ground, and tied him with his quondam mentor, Gentile. That night Godfrey brought Charlotte over to Debden for dinner and told her his score

---

*Under the 104th Article of War, officers may waive trial by court-martial and accept punishment such as a fine at the discretion of a general officer.

would soon be 50.

Nobody doubted Godfrey's will and skill to destroy 20 or more Jerries, but they wondered, on an actuarial basis, if his luck at surviving the hazards would endure long enough. As Godfrey sat by the rose arbor on the greensward in front of the mess that soft summer night, he thought about the marks on his plane, parked out there in the darkness.

That morning, in clobbering the 109, he had almost chewed the 109's tail assembly with his prop, so close did he press the attack. His guns shredded the craft and then it blew to pieces. Godfrey had too much zoom to leap-frog the flaming debris and his Mustang was scorched black as he flew through the fire.

Although airborne Jerries were becoming as scarce as hen's teeth, every pilot in the group was getting to fire his guns at ground targets. On one mission the group poured armor-piercing incendiaries into 88 German locomotives, 24 box cars, two roundhouses, four flat cars, 5 trucks, 1 transformer station, a staff car, 35 oil tank cars and 2 water towers. Once they exploded a trainload of buzz bombs en route to the French coast where they would have been launched over Debden towards London.

Godfrey's crew chief, who called him Johnnie the same as McKennon's called him Mac, cleaned the black blisters from the belly of his kite and the next morning he was off with a three-razzle salute to Charlotte.

Godfrey and three others were scouring the environs of Berlin for Jerries when Godfrey, as usual, was the first to spot the speck which grew into an enemy plane.

"I'm going down at 3 o'clock to us," Godfrey said over the R/T. "I see a Jerry at 4,000."

Godfrey rolled her over and roared down on the Me. 410, followed by the other three in his section. Godfrey trained his guns on the twin-engine fighter bomber and squirted. At 75 yards, first the starboard and then the port motor, began smoking. Godfrey saw the German jump from the clobbered plane. His chute did not open and the German splattered on the rocky earth beside his plane.

Flying on east of Berlin and then southwest, Godfrey sighted two more German craft. He said: "Godfrey here. Two 109s landing on that drome. Let's go down and see how the flak is."

A brilliant white flare was fired on the airdrome, presumably to alert the German ground-gunners to the presence of the American fighters. Intense fire came up. The Jerries were good with flak; they'd been practicing for five years. A burst belted Godfrey's plane.

Freddie Glover, the hoarse-voiced, bellicose delegate from Asheville, N. C., sprayed a 109 on the ground. The pilot was trying to jump from the cockpit. He slumped back down in the plane and his plane flamed.

"There, you cotton-knocker," growled Glover.

Godfrey set fire to another and said: "Let's make one more pass at that 88 over there." Flying in a treetop zig-zag, the Mustangs rifled over the hangars. The golf balls sprayed up. One exploded the glass windscreen. Godfrey felt like an ice pick had been jabbed in his forehead. A shard had wounded him. The wind came in through the jagged rent in the windscreen. It clotted the blood.

"Flak's pretty wicked," Godfrey said. "We'd better get back up."

The flak had also perforated the cooling system in Godfrey's plane and the engine, through loss of glycol, was running a temperature. Godfrey pulled up to 2,000 feet and his Mustang began bleeding glycol profusely.

Godfrey's voice was wavy. He said: "This is Johnnie. Afraid I'll have to bail out. Best of luck to you."

Godfrey jettisoned his canopy so he could bail out. Glover came back sharply. "Don't jump, Johnnie!

Don't jump. Just hold your water now, lemme tell you what to do."

"Okay, Freddie."

"You can make it. Are your r.p.m.s falling?"

"No."

"Well, stick to it, goddamnit! Start pumping that primer and don't stop for hell. Pump that primer handle. Pump it!"

Godfrey commenced pumping, though for a moment he wasn't sure why. This sent raw gas into the pistons; raw gas doesn't burn as fast and thus doesn't give off as much heat as the explosive lean mixture. The glycol stopped leaking, the temperature receded.

"I think you can make it, Johnnie," Glover soothed. Godfrey and Glover had been flying together for a long time and they were among the few of the old-timers left in the 336th Squadron. Glover was ferocious in combat, often stormy and quarrelsome in personal intercourse, but given to strong personal attachments.

"How is it?" Glover asked.

"It depends on how long my arm will hold out on this pumping, Freddie."

The arm was aching and corded by the time they reached Hanover, but Godfrey knew that once he stopped pumping, he would have to bail. Hanover flak came up and rocked Godfrey's plane. They had to turn back and go around Hanover. The thought of going back deeper into Germany drove Godfrey crazy. He was scared and rattled. He thought that if he saw another Jerry he would just jump anyway.

By the time Godfrey reached Amsterdam on the coast, the constant pumping of the primer had caused the handle to gouge through his leather gloves and his hand was raw blisters and blood. As they started across the Channel, Godfrey found he had but 25 gallons of gas. After all he had escaped, it appeared that he was going to have to jump in the killing drink. He began transmitting distress signals, from which ground stations could take a bearing which would locate him and make rescue possible.

"May Day, May Day, May Day," Godfrey frantically shouted. "Engine cutting out. Will probably have to jump . . ."

"We have a fix on you," the ground stations came back. "Friends will pick you up . . . Keep talking, keep talking . . . Give us another voice fix . . ."

Godfrey's earphones were loose and flapping around. He had left his canopy in Germany and the wind made so much noise he couldn't be sure he heard the controller's message correctly. He was flying his plane with his left hand, pumping the primer with his right and trying to find a third hand to hold the earphone closer to his ear.

"Are you sure friends are near?" he bleated. He knew controllers were always reassuring in any event, because a quiet, confident word could mean the difference between panic and self-possession in a pilot. But before the controller could answer, Godfrey shouted:

"There it is, there it is! Jesus, it looks good."

It was England.

He didn't buzz Charlotte that day. His nerves were shot. He just telephoned that he'd be over later and how was the supply of spirits.

Ajax stopped the press release which rehearsed the manner in which Glover had nursed Godfrey back to England. The P.R.O. said the engineering section was skeptical about the pump-priming preventing the plane from overheating, which is a footnote, incidently, on the care Gen. Kepner took to see that press releases in his command were accurate. An engineering officer was dispatched to Debden; after an investigation, the release became such and a teletype went to all fighter groups instructing pilots in the use of the primer. Goodson had been the first to use it, Glover remembered, and Godfrey was back at Debden, shaken but ready to go.

Like Godfrey, the other pilots saw dogfighting at altitude as neat fencing and drome beat-ups as bare-knuckle brawls. They dreaded the strafe jobs, and none more so than the mission they undertook in conjunction with the RAF's celebrated Beaufighter attack on German naval vessels berthed in Norwegian fjords.

Blakeslee briefed the pilots to fly to a neighboring base over which the rocket-firing Beaufighters were circling to make rendezvous. They coursed out at 1,000 feet across the North Sea, keeping low to avoid radar detection. The Beaufighters made a successful attack on the vessels, destroying 4 of 14, and started back to England.

The Mustangs, however, flew inland over the rugged crags to attack German planes parked on three fields, each with 60 to 80 flak emplacements. The planes were so well protected in the revetments the pilots couldn't fire them, and a murderous miasma of the orange golfballs corkscrewed up. Capt. Jones, the Montclair, N. J. pilot who always took his teddy bear on missions, and "Lum" Blanding, of Sumter, S. C., were badly hit as 335th Squadron made a pass at a drome with 60 heavy flak guns and an untabulated number of light guns. They quickly pulled up and made for the North Sea in an effort to get home.

Jones had flown 290 hours of combat operations; 10 more hours and 9 more days and he would be married to a Red Cross girl on duty in England and on the way home. He headed his limping Mustang out over the white-capped sea, but soon saw he would have to jump.

"I've got to get out," Jones shouted. "Tell Pidge I'll be back, though. Don't forget, tell Pidge . . ."

Jones' No 2 circled the spot off the Norwegian coast where the plane splashed; all he could see in the water was the tail assembly sinking beneath the waves. He was sure Jones had perished. His parents were informed and the girl returned the engagement ring. Months later we heard that somebody, perhaps Norwegian patriots, perhaps the Germans, had rescued Jones. Although this was difficult to believe in view of the fact that his No. 2 had found no trace of a dinghy, we had seen so many pilots erroneously reported dead that the information was credible. Jones' fiancee came to a Debden party later and was the gayest girl there. "He said that he'd make it back, didn't he?" she said. But as it turned out, and much sadder, Jones did die that afternoon in the bleak North Sea.

Blanding likewise set out for England across the sea, trying to fly a tricky fighter craft with a fractured skull and body wounds. The pilots on each side of him saw the sun sparkling on the blood-drenched canopy. Groggily fighting the impulse to give up, Blanding trimmed his craft up and ripped strips from his trousers to keep from bleeding to death.

England was two hours away over the sea, and Blanding felt faint and sick. Blanding, a powerful, amiable hulk of a man who was nicknamed Lum because he had an incisor missing, had been clobbered some months before. On that occasion he jettisoned the canopy and was rising to bail, when he saw that the damage did not warrant bailing. Blanding was unnerved. He said: "I'm too old for this game." Blakeslee posted him to Atchem to duty as instructor. After exactly one day of this life, Blanding phoned Blakeslee: "Colonel, I can't stand it—send for me, please."

Blanding made it back to an RAF base in north Scotland, Acklington, with two other pilots on each side. One landed in front of Blanding to point the way; Blanding tailed him in. He was lifted from the cockpit into an ambulance. The RAF types couldn't believe that a man in his condition could discipline a Mustang from Norway to England. The British placed his helmet in a museum.

The desolate North Sea and the choppy English Channel were as hateful to pilots as the golf ball flak. If they were not forced down in the drink, then the monotony of flying across the sea, with each wave looking like the other, made them want to bail out. They were always thrilled to make landfall, and none more so than Lt. Earl C. Walsh, of Goshen Springs, Miss. Walsh was with the group as it bombed and strafed German troops in the Scheldt Estuary. His motor being rough, Walsh unloaded a 500-pound bomb near a large barge and turned for England. Twelve to 15 miles from the coast of Holland the motor coughed and died. As Walsh floated down towards the water, another Mustang orbited overhead radioing a bearing on his position.

The water was running rough and Walsh had trouble in slipping out of his chute harness and inflating the dinghy lashed to his hindside. The waves tossed him out of the dinghy several times, but in 40 minutes a Walrus seaplane came in for a landing. As it was settling on its pontoons, a wave raised up and slapped part of a wing off. As the Walrus taxied up to Walsh in his little rubber boat, it ran over him and knocked him back into the icy drink. Walsh swam towards the tail of the plane and the British crew gallantly tossed him the only dinghy aboard the plane.

As Walsh climbed into his second dinghy a second time, the seaplane ran over him a second time and a sharp piece of the plane punctured the dinghy. As Walsh sank and was losing consciousness, the Limeys got a rope about him and reeled him in. At which time the rough sea snapped the other wing off the Walrus and carried away one float. Walsh and his would-be rescuers thereupon jumped into the water and watched the Walrus sink. His head kept above the water by his Mae West preserver, Walsh passed out again and didn't come to until 2:30 that morning off the coast of England. A motor launch had happened by and rescued the men who had flown to rescue Walsh.

As August wore on, a few airborne Jerries were flushed and the pilots nailed them as the advancing Allied armies watched and cheered below. Lt. Donald Perkins, of Palos Park, Ill., attacked three near Paris and watched one spin down 5,000 feet to crash near American troops. The soldiers waved to Perkins, as did a throng of Frenchmen watching the soldiers march on Paris. A large gaggle of Jerries bounced four other Mustangs, piloted by Lt. Preston B. Hardy, Dillon S. C.; Lt. Ira Grounds, Talpa, Tex.; Lt. William E. Whalen, Hamilton, N. Y.; and Lt. Logan. Each got a Jerry. Whalen's victim crash-landed, got out of his smoking plane and waved to Whalen according to the vagaries of the Teutonic warrior code. Whalen returned the salutation with gunfire. All the while a French farmer was stacking hay, not looking up as the warplanes churned over his head in spectacular combat. The Jerry crashed near the farmer, but he went right on stacking his hay.

On another mission, Hardy and two others—Lt. Robert A. Dickmeyer, Ada, Ohio,; Capt. Robert H. Kanaga, Harbor Beach, Mich.—brought back the news to Debden, which was the first the outside world knew of it, that the Germans were flooding the Low Countries to obstruct the Allied Advance, with no remorse that the salt water would leave the land barren for generations. Hardy was the first to see it when he looked down from 14,000 feet and saw water where his map showed land.

The Mustang sucked the tent-tops and made the grass lie down. It was 8 o'clock in the morning and Charlotte was just coming off night duty. She ran outside and waved to Godfrey as the Aug. 24th mission got underway.

Lt. Melvin N. Dickey, of Tampa, Fla., set three

JU 52s on fire on his first pass over the drome. The flak was coming up through the black smoke plumes as the Mustangs zig-zagged in. Holding the throttle to the firewall and fish-tailing his craft to disconcert the ground-gunners, Godfrey held his forehead to the gunsight and blazed away, destroying four JUs to bring his score to 36 destroyed, the most planes a U.S. pilot had destroyed as of that time.

He was rocked about in the cockpit and his craft wobbled as a burst of flak riddled it. Godfrey shrank from looking at his instruments as he guessed the motor was catching fire. "Oh, what the hell?" he said to himself. That was a memorable feature of Godfrey's combat personality. He could get rattled and frightened to the point of panic, and at the very same time shed it and demonstrate a remarkable degree of reckless, careless aggressiveness. He had returned from America exhausted by the activity attendant upon bond rallies and night-spotting. He had flown every mission since returning; he was oppressed and worn by the repeated sight of his friends being maimed and drowned. His six feet two inches were gaunt, his long fingers had a tremble, his eyes were tired, but he kept spearing himself back into the muzzle of the German guns. Combat was a tar baby he couldn't let go of. He was so exhausted, as sometimes happened to pilots, that on occasion he wanted to cry. Getting shot down would be virtually a relief, a way to escape the crazy pattern of living that enmeshed him.

So to hell with whatever might be wrong with his plane. He made three more attacks on the burning drome as the group criss-crossed the field and yelled. Godfrey saw the smoke billowing back from his plane. Pumping the primer wouldn't keep it alive this time. He had been operating on borrowed time. This was the default.

"Johnnie here," they heard him say. "This is it . . . Tell Charlotte . . ."

369

Godfrey's plane stalled out a bare 30 feet above the ground and as it bellied into a meadow, his forehead banged against his gunsight, knocking him out. He groped for consciousness, instinctively fearing he would be burned in the plane. He had the impression that he was in a two-seater plane. Why didn't the other fellow get out?

"Get out, get out!" he was mumbling. Consciousness returned. But his hand trembled so much he couldn't at first operate the catch to pull the canopy back to escape. Dickey buzzed Godfrey in a farewell salute. His plane sounded like a giant lawn-mower as it thundered over.

Godfrey staggered to a nearby wood and blacked-out again. He took benzedrine tablets and ran most of the day, quenching a thick thirst by sinking his feet in mudholes to squeeze the water out. At midnight he was trudging towards France, but he had to halt on account of foot blisters. He gave himself two jabs of morphine from his escape kit and lay down to rest or die, he didn't much care which.

Next morning his head was clearer and he lay in the heart of Germany thinking along the same lines as the others before him. He looked at his watch and speculated. "The boys have been briefed and they're just about crossing out over the Channel now." All through the day he would look at his watch to mark the events at Debden: "They're in the bar now . . . Everybody buying beer because it's the end of the month . . . They're walking down by the Aero Club to the cinema . . ." He thought back over the days, which now belonged to another period of his life, of buzzing Newport Hospital, of the acclaim he and Gentile had received in New York.

He lay concealed beside a railroad track, planning to conceal himself in the tinder beneath the coal of a France-bound train, but a trail of blood led a German farmer to him.

Back at Debden, no one said much about Godfrey

being shot down. It was expected. Chaplain Edgar Brohm, of St. Louis, Mo., was delegated to tell Charlotte. He naturally hated the job of telling her. He didn't have to. A nurse went to Charlotte's room and said:

"The chaplain from Debden is here to see you."

Charlotte passed out cold.

20
Fighter Pilots and Women?

They came and they went, they bloomed and they faded, but Blakeslee appeared timeless. His steel was of a little bit harder temper than the rest. It seemed that he was as much a fixture over Europe as the overcast. Virtually all the RAF-trained pilots had gone their ways, but Debden was so accustomed to these twin-winged characters that when AAF-trained replacements arrived, it was said, "We're getting some *American* pilots."

There was curiosity to see how the American-trained pilots stacked up with the RAF types. Blakeslee and the few remaining RAF elders were quick to find that they had superior training and were keen to have at the "wily Hun," a phrase, incidentally, that came as naturally to pilots as *damnyankee* to a Southerner. Sad to relate, most of these pilots never got an equal opportunity to run up large scores, as the air war was petering out. In April, for example, the group had destroyed 207 aircraft, but in August, only 28. Luftwaffe fighter strength had been trampled by the Eighth AF.

By September there was sound reason to expect that the Germans would surrender (after all, you know, history shows that the Germans always surrender before fighting on their own soil), and Blakeslee was already talking about getting the hell out of England and colonizing another Debden in the Pacific. Despite three years of uninterrupted combat operations and more than 1,000 combat hours, Blakeslee resolutely resisted all suggestions that he go home on leave. But with the war folding, Blakeslee gave in with the thought that he might be away for another three years in the Pacific or in Germany.

His anxiety was that once he set foot in America, the AAF might intern him. This they had done to Col. Zemke, but he had simply hopped a ride back to England and brushed aside Lt. Col. Schilling, of Traverse City, Mich., who had been appointed C. O. in his place. Zemke visited Debden and explained that he was A.W.O.L., but he was also Zemke and orders were cut confirming and making of record his trip back. After all, the A.W.O.L., article of war really wasn't fashioned to punish men who went over the hill to seek hazardous duty. Blakeslee was reassured when some medium-high brass told him to do as Zemke had done if they tried to corral him.

"Deacon" Hively was already in the States on leave and Blakeslee cabled him to hold the phone in the Sherry-Netherland until he could get there. When Blakeslee departed, the see-saw rivalry with Zemke's Wolfpack had seen Debden slip back into second place. The Wolfpack had been the first to pass the 100-, the 200- and 300-marks, while the Blakesleewaffe had been the first to pass the 400-, 500- and 600-marks.

Lt. Col. Claiborne H. Kinnard, Jr., a rugged six-footer from Franklin, Tenn., took over as C.O. in Blakeslee's absence. He came from the 355th Group at neighboring Steeple Morden and was possibly the outstanding strafing technician in the business. Beginning its third year of operations, the 4th, led by Kinnard, destroyed 11 parked planes to regain the lead from the Wolfpack, 687 to 684. Two weeks later the 4th got five in air combat to become the first to pass the 700-mark.

At the same time War Department orders announced that the 4th had received the Distinguished Unit Citation, the equivalent of the Navy's Presidential Unit Citation and the highest unit honor that can be awarded. The citation read:

The 4th Fighter Group, VIII Fighter Command, Army Air Forces, United States Army, is cited for outstanding performance of duty and extraordinary heroism in action during the period of 5 March to 24 April 1944 . . . The 4th Fighter Group, displaying determination, aggressiveness and will to seek out and engage the enemy, destroyed 189 enemy airplanes, probably destroyed 9, and damaged 41 in the air, and destroyed 134 enemy airplanes, probably destroyed 6, and damaged 99 on the ground.

This group suffered 44 casualties, including pilots killed in action, missing in action and prisoners of war. On 21 March 1944, a day in which no operations were scheduled, knowing of a concentration of enemy aircraft in the Bordeaux area of France which had been detrimental to military operations, the 4th Fighter Group requested permission to attack this target and voluntarily executed an attack in a determined effort to seek out and destroy the enemy air force . . . The daring and skill displayed by the group in this voluntary venture inflicted irreparable damage to hangars, airdrome buildings, wagons and airdrome soldier personnel in addition to the enemy airplanes destroyed.

On 8 April 1944 the 4th Fighter Group, in its continued aggressiveness and determination to free the skies of enemy aircraft, destroyed 31 enemy airplanes . . . thus breaking the record for the largest number of enemy planes destroyed in the air in one day by any one group of the VIII Fighter Command.

The extraordinary heroism, gallantry, determination and *esprit de corps* in overcoming unusually difficult and hazardous conditions reflect highest credit on this organization of the Army Air Forces.

The citation entitled all members of the group, flying and non-flying, to wear a gold-bordered blue plaque over the left tunic pocket.

Blakeslee was flown back to the States and rendezvoused with Deacon in a suite atop the Sherry-Netherland. The alert, and I hear, pretty, lady press agent of the hostelry soon had the New York press in to meet the 26-year-old colonel who listed to port with 16 U.S. and British decorations. *The New York Times* headlined, "Hero of 500 Missions Flinches at Camera" (it was ever thus among head writers).

The Communist-hating *Daily News* had printed a story some time before saying that when the pilots landed in Russia, they were provided with Russian prostitutes. So the Left-loving tabloid *PM* was on hand at the press conference to check *The News'* allegation with a man who was there. He was a full colonel and if anyone were provided with a trull, surely it would be he.

"Not true at all," Blakeslee told *PM*. "Somebody just shooting their mouth off."

Naturally the news-hawks asked the handsome young colonel about his love life, assuming same. He disavowed even an academic interest in any girl and observed:

"Fighter pilots and women don't mix."

He meant by that, without remembering such uniformly ardent warriors as Millikan but thinking of others, that pilots had a way of getting cautious after cupid bit. It was a fetching quote. The press services pounced on it. The quote became a box insert on the front pages of papers from coast-to-coast.

Almost immediately Blakeslee was deluged with letters from all over the country from young ladies who had fighter pilots for husbands, fiances or friends, and had always understood that they were, far from a combat opiate, the sustaining inspiration to the pilot in his mortal struggles with Axis monsters. And now this iconoclastic, outrageous "fighter pilots and women don't mix" from this, this—whatsis name?—Blakeslee. Blakeslee had clobbered the female vanity of America. Debden, when it saw the clipping, was one big belly laugh. "Look who's talking!" they roared.

Fairport Harbor, a suburb of Cleveland, hadn't seen Blakeslee for three years and eight months, but they had kept up with him and 6,000 turned out for his parade. The Diamond Alkali Company, once his employer, gave Blakeslee a wrist watch and the vice-president and general manager said, "You are the symbol of everything we have worked and striven for since Pearl Harbor," and Blakeslee and Deacon praised the contribution of the Home Front and decided to hasten back to the less rarified atmosphere of fair Debden.

Somewhere between Cleveland and New York Blakeslee and Deacon conceived a notion that it would be nice to fly the Atlantic from New York to Debden in a Mustang. A TWA navigator had put it in their heads.

"That would shake 'em," ruminated Deacon. "Just call the tower and say it's Horseback and his No. 2 requesting landing instructions after flight from New York."

"Well, look, why th' hell not?" said Blakeslee. They understood the crossing record was about six hours and was held by a Mosquito. Inasmuch as the 4th had proved the Mustang the world's greatest combat plane, they reasoned, it should also cop the crossing record. They began to plot. They would fly via Canada, Newfoundland, Ireland.

The chief test pilot for North American Aviation, Inc., Mustang manufacturers, knew the two pilots and thought it was a pregnant idea. He would provide them with Mustangs stripped of armor and equipped with special radio. They calculated that at this time of the year they could catch a 75 m.p.h. tailwind at

30,000 feet and make the hop in about four hours and a half. The AAF, of course, forbade the attempt.

Blakeslee returned to Debden. First thing he did was to make a flat-footed denial that he had ever really said "fighter pilots and women don't mix". He now said: "You can't fight the war without 'em!" This was a laugh, as everyone could remember having heard him mouth the statement until it was a Debden cliché. For example, a few days before Clark was to wed Lady Bridget-Elliot, daughter of a British earl, Blakeslee emitted an elaborate disquisition on just how the marriage would cause Clark to lose his vinegar. We assumed Blakeslee's disavowal of his favorite maxim grew out of his sobering experience with the wounded girls who wrote him the biting letters. Later we learned the reason why Blakeslee was so purposeful, if not systematic, in disowning authorship. In the States he had been secretly wed to his old hometown girl.

Blakeslee had returned, nevertheless, with zest to take him through another 3½ years of combat. He ordered a new log book and said, "Well, I'm glad this is a thick one. I'm good for two more."

"When are you going to quit?"

"Quit?" he said, "Why, I'm just learning to fly."

But as Maj. Gen. Kepner had remarked the day Eisenhower pinned the D.S.C. on Blakeslee, "Don lives in constant dread that some so-and-so is going to stop him from flying." To avoid it, Blakeslee kept his flying time secret. On missions he began logging the time only from cross-out over the Channel to landfall on the way back, eliminating the time between Debden and the coast. This contrasted with others who, returning with say a couple of hours of their tours uncompleted, orbited over the base to fill it out to avoid going on another mission. When borrowed to lead other groups, he didn't log the time at all. So nobody really knows precisely what the total was, only that it was well above 1,000 hours of combat operations.

Finally the blow came: Blakeslee was told he was too valuable to be risked any further over Germany. He was to be relieved of his job as commander of the 4th and return to the Z. of I. to fly a desk. It was probably the only time Blakeslee ever felt sorry for himself.

The only consolation was that Col. Zemke was to go off ops with him. Both, however, were to be permitted to fly combat until they received movement orders. Blakeslee had it in mind to see Gen. Kepner and talk him out of the transfer, but Zemke moved first and got such a firm "no" that Blakeslee recognized it was no use. The day before Zemke was to report for duty as executive officer of the 65th Fighter Wing, he went on his last mission. Zemke's* plane iced up in a cloud and he parachuted into Germany. A very few minutes after Wing received this news in the Wolfpack's mission summary, Gen. Auton called Blakeslee and said: "You're grounded."

Blakeslee looked wilted as he waited around Debden for his orders. One day he decided to slip off on a show despite the fact that German skies were now off-limits to him. It appealed to his sense of whimsy to fly in No. 2 position. However, Glover, on whose wing he was flying, forgot to open the radiator doors and his engine overheated, forcing them to abort.

Blakeslee had WDC harnessed for a short trip to Paris, directing his crew chief to remove the guns from the plane's wings to make a place for the champagne he meant to fetch. He returned in a few days, saying he had a pretty poor time. The flavor was going out of everything for him.

His rebellion at the idea of leaving his life at Debden was further inflamed by the emergence of a challenging new menace of the Luftwaffe: the jet-

---

*Zemke told me at Maxwell Field in March, 1946 that the Germans said: "Ah! Col. Zemke. Now when we get old Blakeslee, the war will be over!"

propelled fighters. They had the RAF and the AAF anxious. Their speed was vastly superior to all conventional-type craft and they were viewed as a great threat if the Germans could get them up in force, although it had been demonstrated that Mustangs, in certain circumstances, could outfight a jet. Red Dog and Glover each shot down one, among the first bagged by U.S. pilots.

Glover slipped up on his victim and exploded it before it could turn on the fan. Red Dog found one making tight, leisurely spirals some 1,800 yards away. Red Dog gave his Mustang full throttle as he dived down on the jet and opened fire at 1,500 yards, but the range was too great. However, the jet—blow jobs, they called them—made a port turn instead of outdistancing Red Dog, which required him to slow down. This enabled Red Dog to close the gap and clobber the jet, which crashed into a railroad station.

The AAF, nervously seeking the answer to jets, ordered the 4th to do some experimental flying with RAF jet fighters. Lolling about the group operations building one morning, Blakeslee, a forlorn fighter emeritus, considered how he would handle the jets and listened to Kinnard in the next room briefing the pilots—his pilots—for a practice escort with the RAF jets trying to hit the bombers. Kinnard was saying:

"We were chasing some German jets the other day over a drome and it was just like a lot of poodle dogs chasing a fox, getting in each other's way. You can't catch 'em in level flight, but you can turn in a tighter circle and you can use your zoom to bounce 'em from above."

The floorboards of the building vibrated as the Mustangs and RAF jets taxied by to take off. Blakeslee stared at them through the window with a pronounced wistfulness. He said with a flash of enthusiasm, "Say, I'd like to go back to the States and form a new jet group for the Pacific with 4th Group personnel." But the enthusiasm sounded hollow.

"Monty" Montgomery was helping the I.O.s preparing the map for a beat-up mission. The day before he had spotted a concentration of German planes in an air park and the 4th had permission to attack it. The concentration had been reported on the mission report the day before and there was nervous speculation that another group, likely a Wolfpack, might get there first.

"Now wouldn't that be a dirty trick?" said Blakeslee.

Take-off time was advanced as word arrived that a front was moving swiftly down from Ireland. Blakeslee watched McKennon come bouncing into the room, saying, "What's the show, what's the show, fellas?"

"You can't go," said the group surgeon, Maj. Nathan Lippman, of Atlantic City, N.J.

"Why in the hell not?"

"Because that wound will open up and start bleeding at altitude," the medic said.

McKennon and Deacon, who roomed together, had been throwing a sword into the wall a week before. It bounced and the tip pierced McKennon's cheek.

"What kind of drip would my boys think I was if I didn't make a tough show like this one?" McKennon demanded.

"Now look, Mac, I don't want to ground you but—"

Blakeslee interrupted the medic. He said gently, with a twinkle: "That flak's after you, Mac." McKennon had been shot down by flak recently, but escaped back to England.

McKennon ignored both, and immersed himself in a new shoot 'em up saga, *Singing Guns*.

This was the life and these were the characters that bound Blakeslee to Debden. With a few days left at Debden, Blakeslee embarked on a series of sentimental sorties, leisurely cruising over the green and tan countryside to places he associated with some phase of his nearly four years in the U. K. His companion was Maj. John D. McFarlane, of Calais, Me., who had arrived in England with the RCAF about the same time as Blakeslee. The two flew to an RAF base, Biggin Hill, at which both had once been stationed. They landed and walked to the tea room they had frequented in RAF days and recalled that in those days the favored few could slip down to the kitchen and obtain real eggs. The French lady remembered them, but only vaguely. They found a few RAF officers they knew, but most long since gone their ways. Of the 150 pilots with whom Blakeslee had sailed to England, only three were still around.

The time was nearly come for Blakeslee to depart the 4th's ancestral home, Debden. The officers presented a loving cup to him at an informal session in the bar. He said exactly what everybody knew he would say:

"You all know how I feel about leaving. Debden—well, it's been home to me . . . I guess I'd better shut up now before I start blubbering . . ."

That's about all the sentiment Blakeslee ever let anybody see at Debden. Possibly that's all he had in him. He failed to take the loving cup with him when he left England.

Next day Blakeslee made for another airfield by himself, lost in his reverie. The fighter pilot who had survived 1,000 combat hours neglected that little essential of letting the wheels down for a landing. He crash-landed. It was like Buffalo Bill missing a buffalo.

That night in the bar I said by way of jest:

"Well, Colonel, how about your rule that he who prangs—"

Blakeslee finished it for me:

"—Goes home."

They say old soldiers never die. Nor pilots, who just fly, fly away.

At Debden they say Don Blakeslee's vapor trails will never fade from the skies over Germany. And that high winds at angels 30 are actually echoes of: "That'll be enough of that go-o-damned R/T chatter!"

By January 1945 the three squadrons of the 4th Group had destroyed more enemy aircraft than the entire U.S. Air Corps did in World War I (763 to 755).

But the effort had cost heavily. In fact, at one time pilots arriving at a replacement pool in England rebelled at assignment to the 4th because the savagery of its attacks resulted in such a high loss rate. Dozens of its pilots had been shot down, chiefly by ground fire, and were German prisoners.

As prisoners, they called themselves *Krieges*, and settled down to the suffocating monotony of life in a prison camp, there to fight the sternest part of the war—the fight to avoid loss of their minds, or, as Kriege parlance had it, to keep from "going 'round the bend." The Krieges all remembered the little booklet of instructions about their rights and obligations as prisoners of war and the line about "your government has not forgotten you." But the assurance seemed meaningless, if not a mockery, as the barbed wire months dragged on.

The treatment accorded pilots by the Germans varied with the stage of the war and according to the element which took them prisoner. Generally, the best treatment was at the hands of Luftwaffe personnel; Wehrmacht troops were fairly correct; civilians were entirely unpredictable.

When Capt. K. G. Smith was shot down in March, 1944, he was badly burned about the face and placed in a hospital where a German surgeon did a brilliant, painstaking job of plastic surgery—everything except restoration of the eyebrows, a point on which K. G. was firm.

"No thank you," K. G. demurred. "No German eyebrows for me. I'll wait and get some American eyebrows."

When he had convalesced sufficiently to face a German intelligence officer for interrogation, the German said, "Ah, K. G., we've been expecting you for some time." This, of course, was calculated to disarm the prisoner, foster the idea that German intelligence knew all about him and the group anyway, and thus move him to spill additional information the Germans didn't have. It was a simple technique, probably evolved by a suspicious husband a few generations after the Garden of Eden episode, but it was nevertheless impressive and often productive. For that reason, soldiers of all armies were drilled from induction day on to give only the information "name, rank, serial number"—that and nothing more.

The Germans, pursuing the we-know-anyway line, next showed K. G. a photograph of the ace board which hung in the Debden bar, leaving K. G. to speculate that somebody who had visited Debden, probably somebody's date, was a spy.

K. G. was put on duty as an orderly in the *dulag luft* and received treatment that was altogether correct. They told K. G. about a lone Thunderbolt pilot with some unaccountable grudge against a railroad station nearby. Every day this pilot buzzed the station and if he saw one single thing moving, gave the station a frantic beat-up with his machine guns. This pilot, because of the regularity of his inspections, the Germans nicknamed the "American officer-of-the-day".

Every time a 4th Group pilot was shot down and captured in the vicinity of the hospital, the Germans would make a gossipy call beginning: "K. G., guess who's here from Debden."

When Godfrey was captured and led through a

small town, angry Germans stoned and spat upon him. Godfrey stood at attention before the German interrogator, as the little book said to do. The German had spent enough time in America to affect a Brooklyn accent.

"Now look," he said, "I'm Hans and you're Johnnie. You're a captain in the American Air Force and I'm a captain in the Luftwaffe. We both know why I'm here talking to you.

"What we want to know is how you Americans spot those airdromes. Now take the one over which you were shot down. We had 12 JU 52s parked on it. Recently some so-and-so came along and destroyed three of them. Then you come along today and get eight."

Godfrey didn't think it wise to disclose that he happened to be the "so and so" who had done both jobs. He struck to the name, rank, serial number response, and the German strove to break him down by showing him that he knew all anyway. He asked first about the family of a fellow pilot.

"Was Bob Mirsch's baby born on time?" he asked casually. "You know we've been sweating that out."

Then he asked Godfrey if he had delivered the message from Lt. Bob Wehrman to his uncle in Connecticut.

"What message?" asked Godfrey. This did startle him.

"Oh, well," said the German, "that night before you left Debden to go to the States on leave, you told Wehrman at the bar that you'd take a message to his uncle, didn't you?"

The questions were adroit and might well have confused a prisoner, still shocked by having been shot down and rattled through being surrounded by the enemy, if he had not been fortified by the name, rank, serial number drill. For example, the location of Debden was supposed to be secret and all correspondence was censored to prevent personnel from disclosing it. It was forbidden in fact, to name a town within liberty run distance of the station. Of course, when an enemy agent saw 100 soldiers getting off the train at Audley End he was free to conclude that there must be a station nearby. RAF practice was contrary.

You could get in trouble for giving the Debden phone number (Saffron Walden 3164) in a letter, although no one considered the rule in the light of the scores of phone calls received nightly from girls in London.

Godfrey was taken aback when the German threw his Sunday punch: "Now, Johnnie, the plane you were shot down in was marked VF F. Why weren't you flying your own Mustang, VF P?"

But as the war ground on, the German interrogating officers became less persistent and painstaking in their questioning. They asked just enough routine questions to avoid being sent to the Eastern or Western Fronts. When Maj. George Carpenter, of Oil City, Pa., was shot down in an air duel, he was austerely uncommunicative and the Germans let it go by nicknaming him "Major Can't-Say."

Ordinarily the prisoner was brought in and shown a dossier in book form on the 4th Group, containing decorations, promotions and, usually, photos of the pilots. They even had names of some non-flying personnel, such as Clatanoff. If they were a few days behind on a promotion or award of a cluster to D.F.C., then they shrugged it off as if to say it was just clogged up in the message center.

But this was not the Mata Hari stuff it might appear, for the body of what they had was information the AAF employed a high-powered staff of P.R.O.s to put out to hometown papers. All the Germans needed was a newspaper clipping service and a subscription to *Stars* & *Stripes*. This is not said to belittle the German intelligence system, for it did have some information on the 4th which apparently could be obtained only by an agent visiting Debden.

Frequently they placed the Kriege in solitary confinement for a week to soften him up for a subsequent interrogation, after which he was herded into a stockade to begin his struggle to keep from going 'round the bend. Most 4th Group Krieges were imprisoned in compounds at Barth, on the Baltic coast, or in southern Germany at Moosberg. A prison organization was established on a basis of rank. Col. Zemke was the Kriege commandant at Barth and Maj. Beeson was appointed his S-4. S-4 is army for supply, and considering the lack of supplies in Kriege camp, Beeson's appointment was more sardonic than purposeful.

Beeson paced the floor with slue-footed gait, fretting like a baby with starched diapers because he had missed the invasion. He called a German a Hun and was placed in solitary confinement.

The camps were crowded and bleak; the food was better than that in a Belsen or Buchenwald, but it was only the Red Cross food parcels that kept meat on the prisoners' bones. Even so, many digestive systems were temporarily, perhaps permanently, deranged, by sawdust bread, etc.

The Krieges were cut off from Allied news sources and had only the fabrications of Goebbel's propaganda. This isolation was one of the most maddening of Kriege privations because news suggested the answer as to how many more centuries must pass before they were liberated from their barbed wire durance.

The pilots, so abruptly swept from the thrill and pageantry of life at Debden into this squalor and bleakness, slept away as many of the four-dimensional hours as they could and lay about in despairing idleness the rest of the time. Some of the most sunlit personalities grew dark. Nerves unravelled. A new inmate would arrive and begin, "There I was at 20,000 feet . . ." A book would be slammed on the floor, or the old inmates would stalk out of the room with a "Who th' hell cares?" Morale was balanced on a razor's edge. The failure of an Allied offensive would produce dejected scowls. A new inmate bringing some news of some big show would make them fretful.

A package of cigarets would bribe a Kraut guard to bring extra food. Next day the Kriege would put the squeeze on him in this wise:

"You brought us some stuff yesterday. Right?"

"Ja, ja," the guard would say, eager for more cigarets.

"Bring more today or we'll tell your commander."

Daily and nightly the Krieges saw or heard the Allied air armadas overhead, and they learned more about precision bombing as the bombers pinpointed targets close by but never hit the compounds.

The Krieges in Bunte's camp tried to dilute the monotony with some homemade booze. Each prisoner kicked in from his Red Cross parcel until they had 150 boxes of prunes and 150 pounds of sugar. This they slipped into a G. I. cooking vat and let it ferment. They got drunk all right, but it was only briefly, as the prison diet had so weakened their stomachs that they straightway vomited.

Some, to keep from going 'round the bend, played cowboy and Indian like children. Col. Zemke, a former amateur boxer, and a West Point paratrooper, Maj. Cyrus Manierre, put on a three-round boxing match for the Krieges. The Germans were right proud of having Zemke* as a prisoner and treated him with a good deal of admiring deference. A number of high-ranking Hun officers came to see the bout. Zemke was ahead in the second round when a U.S. bombing attack nearly broke up the match.

Thrown together at Barth were Krieges from both the Wolfpack and Debden. Each new pilot would bring them up to date on the see-saw scoring rivalry. There were some crackling debates over the relative merits of the two outfits, but the pilots kept it fairly amicable, for the prime fact now was their common misery.

Millikan bit into a piece of black sawdust bread and $350 worth of dental work, for which he had borrowed money to qualify for cadet training, was punched out. Millikan, of tougher fibre than many, resolved that he was going to wring some profit out of his desolation. With a few books available, he laid out a college course and ground it into his head, which was overcrowded with thoughts of his wife and daughter in a thatched-roof cottage in Essex County. Others tortured themselves thinking of food and recalling the succulence of the steaks at Debden. Millikan, however, resolutely talked himself into believing at each meal of sawdust bread, prunes, turnips, etc., that he was sitting down to a banquet. He knew enough physiology to recognize that the scant diet was shrinking his belly, so he ate his hot food first and saved the meat shreds for last.

Millikan learned that the Luftwaffe had a pronounced respect for the 4th and once or twice talked to pilots who had fought the "Red Noses." One was a Jerry credited with destroying 80 Allied planes. He belonged to that group around Brunswick which had the ace of spades on the spinners. The pilot told Millikan that this 109 outfit was the 4th Group of the Luftwaffe and Millikan, reflecting on his experiences with them, doubted him not at all.

---

*After his capture, Zemke was being taken under guard to Berlin on a civilian train. A Ninth AF Thunderbolt group strafed the train. Zemke ducked. A German girl about 11 years old was sitting by him. A machine gun bullet took the top of her head off. It fell in Zemke's lap.

For most of the day Zemke was held with the train passengers. The Germans looked at him and his U.S. uniform with hatred, as a member of a race that could be so barbaric as to strafe women and children. They forgot how German pilots in 1940 strafed French civilians to clog roads and impede movement of the French army.

The train stopped, passengers got out. The Thunderbolts attacked them. The American pilots did not know how close they came to killing Zemke.

Goodson was gratified to find that he had been written up in a Luftwaffe service magazine. Two of Germany's outstanding aces flew to an airfield once to meet him. One, credited with 300 Allied planes, came in over the field in an FW 190 flying upside down a few feet off the ground. Goodson doubted if Gentile or even Kid Hofer would try that one.

The days came and went, bringing shattering Allied successes, but no end to Kriege life. Millikan* lay in the sun one day as a flight of Hun fighter pilots buzzed the camp to tantalize the Americans. Millikan held his hands up in pretense that he was laying off a ring of deflection and heard himself shouting with frantic anger, "Spin in, you son-of-a-bitch, spin in!"

German officers after the war disclosed that at one time Hitler had ordered the execution of all American airmen in the Kriege camps, but that the professionally correct Wehrmacht refused to carry out the order. However, the Germans did make an attempt to hold on to the prisoners and moved them about to stall their liberation by the advancing Allied armies. Herded into box cars, the Krieges were transported hundreds of miles with no opportunity to relieve themselves. Finally there would be a halt in some town. The Krieges, in their discomfort and anonymity, would swarm out to establish themselves on lawns, sidewalks—anyplace. Indignant hausfraus came charging out with broom handles flying to abate the nuisances in the process of commitment. The Krieges just snarled and nonchalantly motioned them to go away. It was also a vivid way for the Krieges to express their feeling for Germany. One train-stop was, therefore, worth 10,000 words.

---

*After the war, Goodson and Millikan began work with Goodyear's aviation division.

22
Swede Carlson, Scrapper

So far we've dealt mostly with the great days of the 4th Fighter Group, but since this chronicle is most certainly not intended as a rah-rah, yea team vapor, it ought to be said with some emphasis that there were dispirited interludes of mediocre performance. There were times when it seemed the 4th lost too many bombers and others when Jerry gaggles flew underneath the group and were gone before anybody called a bounce.

To win its Distinguished Unit Citation in March and April of 1944 the group had lost almost all of its top-ranking aces. Either through enemy action or rotation to the States, almost all of the old hands, in whom so much invaluable combat experience reposed, had departed. The replacements were keen to become Gentiles and Beesons, and they had the stuff to do it, but first they had to become seasoned. Rivalry with the Wolfpack, which had been similarly but not equally denuded of its star performers, prodded the group to limp along.

A series of spirited engagements with the Jerries would have done wonders, but the Jerries came up so infrequently that the missions became tiresome exertions in which the pilots froze and dragged themselves across Germany in the overcast as targets for the heavy flak. Some pilots flew more than 100 combat hours without seeing anything that corresponded with the cardboard silhouettes of a 190 or 109. It was one of England's severest winters and the group droopiness was compounded by long stretches in which the pilots couldn't even practice-fly.

Non-flying officers and men, who had been with the group from the start, reminisced about the great days and the feats of the departed stars.

"Trouble with this group is," the new arrivals would say, "it's living in the past."

Which brought the tart reply: "Sure we're living in the past—we don't have any present."

Kinnard consequently took over from Blakeslee at an unfavorable time and, despite a demonstrated capacity for leadership, wondered if he could regenerate the 4th. For example, the 4th still fired its guns by pressing the tit on the stick and jettisoned its wing tanks by pulling the trigger on the stick. It was a carryover from RAF days. Every group in the AAF save the 4th had precisely the opposite arrangements. Thus, new pilots often dropped their tanks when they had meant to fire. An old pilot, flying a Mustang which had not been adapted, would pull the trigger and get rid of his tanks and find himself blazing away at his flight leader. But Kinnard could never persuade them to change willingly.

He brought in some of his associates to install as squadron commanders and operations officers, with a view of revitalizing the outfit and bringing it to his way of doing things, which is a C.O.'s prerogative. But pilots like McKennon, Red Dog and Glover, who had already shot down more Jerry planes than these candidates for their jobs had ever seen, and who had almost as much combat time as the others had cross-country time, were not so easy to be rid of. It was a tough set of circumstances for any commander to buck. The 4th Group was in the Horse Latitudes and Kinnard doubted that he could put enough wind in the sails to get it going again.

When Kinnard left to command another group, which he did creditably, Lt. Co. Harry J. Dayhuff, of Ogden, Utah, came over from the 78th at Duxford and took command briefly. He was a personable, likeable fellow, but Debden was accustomed to the firebrand Blakeslee and Dayhuff was a little "nervous in the service" as C. O. of the celebrated 4th.

Dayhuff was succeeded by Col. Everett W. Stewart, who hailed from the same town as Eisenhower, Abilene, Kans. Stewart, a veteran of both Pacific and European wars, was an olive-skinned, soft-voiced pilot who got things done without shouting. He believed that the most important part of an officer's equipment was not necessarily knowledge, but ability to get along with others.

In a short time Stewart established himself with the 1,500 officers and men of the 4th as perhaps the best-liked C. O. they had had. He impressed on the non-flying officers, who saw to it that personnel was fed, paid, clothed, that their services were patently indispensable and that he regarded them highly. He didn't care how the previous C. O. and his ubiquitous ground exec, Clatanoff, had rated them; their sixty-six dash ones would be graded according to their performance from that day on. He not only gave the enlisted men the usual blah about having their interests at heart, but proved it.

Not least in Stewart's roster of reforms was, according to Debden sentiment, his choice of a new ground exec to administer the non-flying sphere. Clatanoff was going to 2nd Air Division Headquarters. First it was Maj. V. V. Mitchell, Jr., of Tallassee, Ala., and then, disregarding a lot of majors and seniority to get the talent he wanted, it was Capt. Kenneth G. Patton, of Winchester, Va. Stewart told them to let the adjutants do the paper work, that they should concentrate on being a sort of mayor at Debden.

"I'm not interested," Stewart told Patton, "in making any records for using the least petrol for liberty runs. I want the officers to bring to our parties the best-looking women in England, I want them to drink as much as they wish short of being asses, I want them to play hard and fly hard. I want the G. I.s looked after. In short, I run a 'happy ship' and I mean for the 4th Group to get back where it belongs."

Everybody took a new lease on life. Nobody questioned that Blakeslee was the daddy of them all as an air leader. But there was general resentment that he was so immersed in flying that he turned over all non-flying personnel to Clatanoff on a memorandum receipt. This created a festering circumstance in which Blakeslee commanded the pilots and abandoned some 1,500 non-flying officers and enlisted men to the dubious mercies of Clatanoff. Stewart, contrarily, made himself boss of the station to the satisfaction of all hands. He succeeded in restoring a deteriorating *esprit de corps*. The experience level had risen and the 4th was ready to ride again.

The war, unaccountably, went on, and in December there was the Ardennes breakthrough. Some enlisted men left to train as infantry replacements. RAF and AAF went on pulping Germany with bombers and perforating the pulp with fighter strafing.

Jan 17.—Lt. Van Chandler, Waxahachie, Tex., was leading Green Section of 336th Squadron when he reported to Maj. Glover, who was leading the group:

"I see planes on a drome."

"Well, go down and test for flak," Glover directed.

"Shall I drop my tanks?"

"Hell, yes, drop your goddamn tanks!" Glover shouted in his rusty-hinge voice.

"No flak here," Chandler reported back.

"Well, make another pass," Glover ordered.

"No flak, I've made four passes," responded Chandler, and the squadron clobbered 25 parked planes. Three German mechanics were tugging a plane. Green Section allowed one to escape.

Over Folkstone, England on the way back, Lt. Harry Hagan, Yorkville, Ohio, gave out of gas and bailed out over a forest, landing in a tree. Hagan made his way to the highway and found it alive with ambulances, police cars and air raid wardens.

"A buzz bomb has just dropped," they said.

It was Hagan's abandoned Mustang crashing.

Jan. 28— Glover briefed the pilots and took off. He finally broke through the overcast into the blue at 6,500 feet. He had the sky all to himself, for a snow squall had come up so suddenly the rest of the group couldn't get off.

Jan. 29—The group saw more V-2s (rockets) spiralling up from Germany towards England. Glover said after the mission, "The heavy flak hadn't changed a bit. Big black and orange puffs all around. If it's making a sort of *womp* noise, then it isn't going to hit you. But if it makes a crackling sound, like balling up cellophane in your hand, then, brother, it's close."

Feb. 6—Every pilot in 335th Squadron fired his guns as they destroyed 15 railroad cars and ammunition train. Flying with 336th Squadron, "Swede" Carlson called up to ask, "Mac, can I come and bring my section?" To which McKennon said, "Sure, sure." Carlson found a military truck being towed by a horse. They were seeing a lot of that these days, eloquent testimony that the AAF was drying up Germany's oil supply. The pilots had already begun to suspect that the real reason the Huns had stopped coming up was lack of fuel, because every day they saw dromes loaded with aircraft. Carlson clobbered the truck and let the enemy horse off with a nervous breakdown.

Lt. Charles E. Konsler, Utica, Ky., flew over a German village, which were coming to look like ghost towns. Konsler dipped his wings and some German children shook their fists.

Lt. Wilbur B. Eaton, Portland, Ore., and Lt. Robert Buchholtz, Oklahoma City, streaked over a small car and saw three German officers jump out and flee. The Germans scanned the dense clouds to make sure the two Mustangs had gone their way, cautiously backing towards their car to make sure they weren't doubling back. Hidden in the overcast, the two pilots had made

394

a circle and came back from behind. The three officers backed into a firing squad of 12 half-inch machine guns.

"I don't think," Eaton said to Buchholtz, "that they'll make it for supper tonight."

Buchholtz rocked his wings.

Feb. 21—Carlson and Lt. B. O. Brooker, Columbia, S. C., routed a swarm of German soldiers off a train. They assumed the position in a ditch where 50-plus were left lying.

Feb. 22—Of 80 million Germans, most must have seen Allied planes this day. As Freddie Glover said at the briefing, "It looks like they mean to wreck Germany today." Four air forces—8th, 9th, 15th and RAF—attacked from half their normal altitude. Glover got a jet in his K-14 sight, but the jet just walked off and left him.

The group caused a traffic snarl on the fast autobahn between Berlin and Leipzig. To Berlin were going lorries of supplies needed in the impending siege, and from Berlin, lorries of civilians with household effects. Berlin was being evacuated.

Returning from some formation-flying over Berlin, Blue Section of 334th Squadron—Capt. Thomas R. Bell, Shawboro, N. C.; Capt. Carl G. Payne, San Antonio; Lt. Gordon A. Denson, Rockville, Conn.; Lt. Arthur R. Bowers, Tiskilwa, Ill.—spotted a jet fighter flying low over a highway.

Payne dipped down and decommissioned a port jet unit, which left the jet slowed down to the speed of an all-out Mustang. The jet streaked along on one unit and Bowers bounced it, but forgot to set his K-14 for the wing span of the jet and his bullets went wild.

All the time Bell and Denson flew above the jet in case the pilot tried to escape in a sudden climb, but the jet pilot, apparently in panic, just scooted down the highway and made the turns as though driving a car. Payne made a second attack and the jet exploded.

Blue Section flew on to destroy six more planes parked on a grass airdrome and exhausted their ammo. Flying back towards England at 11,000 feet, Bowers caught sight of a gaggle of Jerries at 12 o'clock and above. The Jerries climbed and came whizzing in for a stern bounce.

They began firing on the four Mustangs before they got within range. Blue Section pilots could see the cannon falling in an arc behind them. Helpless without a bullet in their guns, the pilots developed an intense curiosity as to what they were going to do when the Jerries got within gun range.

The Jerries, for some inexplicable reason, crawled up on the starboard side of the four Mustangs and flew fraternally along with them in string formation. They were mixed 109s and 190s.

"What the hell is this?" asked Payne.

"Ask the man who owns one?" answered somebody.

Blue Section tried to get an expression out of the Germans by rocking wings. The Germans rocked wings back at them. The pilots decided to turn into the Germans as if they were going to attack.

The result was that Payne found himself with two wing men, instead of the usual one. On his left was Bowers. On his right, about 50 feet away and in excellent formation, was the 190 pilot, dutifully flying along as though bucking for promotion. The German looked over at Payne. Payne glanced over at Bowers, then quickly back at the German.

Bell likewise found a dependable Jerry to cruise along on his wing. Germans and Americans flew along for a few minutes thus, each waiting for someone to drop the other shoe.

If sweat were gasoline, Blue Section pilots might still be flying somewhere with their 109 and 190 pickups, but it's not and they decided to make a break for it. They whipped into port turn for England and the Germans continued on without them, reconciled, it would seem, to the fact that the best of enemies must part.

The seven aircraft destroyed by Blue Section brought the group score to an even 800. But once again the Wolfpack had spurted into first place and was well on the way to 1,000 destroyed, which had become the goal of both outfits. But for all the Germans who came up to fight in these closing days of the war, it would have seemed that Jerry thought you could take it with you.

For sheer scrappiness, the way in which "Swede" Carlson, the Red Bluff, Calif. delegate, slipped over into the M.I.A. column is unexcelled in the annals of the 4th.

Carlson was one of the few remaining old-timers. He was one of the eight who broke out of an ambush of 60-plus Huns the day the first Berlin raid was attempted. Stocky, sandy-haired and emotional, Carlson, whose business had once been ferrying want-to-be-divorcees to Reno, had been bested and rattled many times, but he kept boring in with undiminished combat ardor. His father once ruined a horse galloping him 20 miles to show a neighboring rancher his son's D.F.C. That had a lot to do with Carlson's will to combat.

On this particular day Carlson clobbered a four-engined bomber as he joined in a wild, disorderly attack on a drome near Berlin. He got too low, his Mustang mushed and bellied in near the drome.

Carlson sat and blasphemed in his cockpit, looking around to determine the best direction in which to flee. The group was still criss-crossing the drome in hell-for-leather passes, to each his own traffic pattern, 300 machine guns blinking orange on the wings. Billows of smoke coiled up, so dense that pilots could hide in them from the orange golf balls.

Carlson still hadn't jumped from his crashed ship when he heard someone say over the radio:

"We'd better strafe that pranged Mustang."

Carlson roared: "No, hell you don't—I'm still in this kite!"

In all the confusion of dodging the golf balls and each other's plane, amind the smoke cones, nobody but Carlson saw the two 190s trying to slip in for a landing.

"Hey, Mac!" yelled Carlson to McKennon, who was leading the group in this mission. "Get those two 190s! Get 'em!"

McKennon's eyes darted about. He answered: "Don't see 'em. What's your damn altitude?"

"Altitude?" screeched the exasperated Carlson.

"Hell, yes—your damn altitude," said McKennon.

"Hell, Mac, I haven't got any altitude—I'm on the ground!"

Carlson was standing in his cockpit. He slipped off his parachute preparatory to fleeing the vicinity where an angry German mob might lynch him, as they had others. These first moments after crashing were the golden moments for escaping. But Carlson, although the war was over for him, hadn't shed the psychology of those still streaking about in the clouds. He couldn't think of letting these easy-meat 190s get away.

"Mac, Mac! . . . Get the bastards, get 'em, I tell you!" bawled Carlson, putting one trembling leg over the cockpit side to get out.

"Where are they, Swede? What's their altitude?"

"They're at 7 o'clock to you. They're in the circuit . . . They're going south now . . . Now they're turning . . ."

"I see one, I see one!" That was Lt. Paul M. Morgan, Lexington, Ky. He fell on the 190 and shredded a wingtip, but overshot. Brooker came in behind and gave the 190 a shattering burst of fire and the 190 crashed with its pilot.

"Cheers, fellas," panted Carlson.

He jumped from the wing and fled to escape the inflamed German civilians, but some soldiers corralled him. The German soldiers from the drome angrily rebuked Carlson, for they had heard him giving directions over the radio.

"The war," they fumed, "is supposed to end for you once you're on the ground."

The dead 190 pilot happened to be a man named Hoffman, commanding officer of the drome.

Maj. Pierce W. McKennon, the long-legged boogie-woogie virtuoso whose cowling featured a painting of a tusky Arkansas razorback hog running across a row of 19½ swastikas, had become C. O. of 335th Squadron, for, while in his earlier combat days he had revealed a Hoferian tendency to boogar off by himself, he was one of the most gifted pilots the 4th produced. The AAF washed him out of primary.

Four times McKennon grounded Lt. George Green, of Whittier, Calif, for such transgressions as using the deputy C. O.'s jeep without permission and for pranging a kite. And about twice that many times McKennon threatened to purge Green from his squadron.

Green, who had once done some tumbling in a circus and sulled up when told he resembled Victor Mature, had been on probation. It was observed that however late he caroused in the bar of nights, he was always up and beaming at the dispersal next morning, whereas lesser men slept in. One day he was flying Red Dog's wing and they bounced two Jerries. Red Dog clobbered his, but when he looked about for his wing man, Green was nowhere about. The Jerry had eluded Green. Red Dog looked down and saw Green scudding along on top of a great white cumulus cloud, which position was an entreaty for a Jerry to roar down and knock him off. Red Dog was incensed. He split-essed and and roared down in a power dive on the hapless Green. As his plane all but grazed Green's, Red Dog shouted: "Break, you silly bastard—break!"

Lt. Col. Sidney Woods, Somerton, Ariz., has just shot down on one mission as many Germans as you see fingers on the right hand. Lt. Richard Moore, Barstow, Ill.
Lt. Millard Jenks had said he would, when the Germans gave in, take his first drink, an 8-ounce slug of Scotch. He did V-E night. See?

Upper left—McKennon, shot down near Berlin, is—he hopes—going to be flown bac[k]
McKennon. The group is circling low overhead. Their guns slaughter approaching Germ[an]
Upper right—Green at controls; McKennon sitting.
Inset—The way they looked as Green prepared to give 'er the gun. Note parachute[s]
Lower left—En route back to England, Green has to share oxygen with McKennon[.]
Lower right—They land at Debden.

n by Green, who landed to pick him up. Green cooly sheds his parachute to make room for
log.

heel. Green had to sacrifice it. If he has to bail . . .

VICTORY IN EUROPE

The 4th Group forms on parade ground to return thanks to God for the victory. Flag at half mast for President Roosevelt.

PARLEZ-VOUS FRENCH?

Here's opportunity to sport your French knowledge. If you've forgotten it, let it be known that after the war the French government put Maj. Godfrey's Mustang on display under Eiffel Tower. The 4th had shot down Huns over Paris. Parisians had helped 4th fliers escape back to Debden. Liberte! Equalite! Fraternite!

A United States cemetery in the university town of Cambridge, 15 miles from Debden, where some members of the 4th Group lie.

Thereafter, Green was glue on his No. 1's wing. He was a crack flier, always ready to have at the wily Hun, and McKennon decided to give him just one more chance. And before the sun set March 18, McKennon rejoiced in his clemency.

McKennon was leading the squadron in an attack on Prenzlau Airdrome, some 40 miles from Berlin. The flak spewed and crackled. McKennon said: "Everybody check his kite to see if you're hit."

He then found that a burst had smacked his own craft and he saw the needle bounce on zero oil pressure. It meant bailing. Better than most, McKennon knew what that meant. Flak had slapped him out of the skies the preceding summer over enemy-held France. But he had escaped and made his way back to Debden, reasoning with pilot logic, "I've had my bad luck now. I'll be okay from here on." Soon he was hit again, this time slightly wounded, and he barely made it back to Debden. As Blakeslee had said, "The flak is after you." Now, as he prepared to bail the third time, McKennon was convinced.

Acting on experience gained the first time he bailed in enemy territory, McKennon quickly looked around for a place to land near some woods or other concealment, some place to hide until dark. He saw a farmhouse and banked away: its German occupants might see and report him.

At 4,000 feet he let the canopy fly off the plane, pulled the stick back and awaited the reaction. But he didn't fall clear, as his G-suit became entangled with the canopy apparatus. Half-in and half-out, McKennon's spine was all but cracked as the powerful prop wash arched him nearly double against the seat.

Green's reaction to seeing the flak cripple McKennon's plane was a flash of anger. Had he been more reasonable he never would have even considered it—the others didn't—because he knew that many had tried the same thing and had gotten ignominiously stuck in the mud, or otherwise captured. Only one pilot had ever carried it off, and that was in the larger cockpit of a Thunderbolt. Moreover, there was a standing order against making the attempt. He'd be court-martialed if he succeeded; a German prisoner if he failed.

Green and the other 24 pilots watched McKennon fight clear of the spinning Mustang and parachute to the ground. He and the plane fell nearly together, about six miles from the drome.

Green circled with the other pilots and noticed a factory near the small field in which McKennon was running about. Probably a whole posse of *Volksturm* would soon be pouncing upon McKennon. But the 24 Mustangs circling with Green gave him courage. Green abruptly decided to have a go. He was going to land in that field and pick McKennon up and take him the hell back to Debden.

Green made two passes over the field and by observing the direction in which smoke from the crashed plane was blowing, knew which direction to land in. As he made the landing approach, the other pilots assumed that he, too, was being forced down by flak stings.

The Germans were already after McKennon. Green saw several Germans, presumably soldiers, running towards McKennon. They held a calf-size Dalmation dog on a leash.

Green screamed: "Strafe those Huns!"

A Mustang came barreling in, guns flashing. Germans and dog were slaughtered.

Green figured that once on the ground, he could hold any other Germans off with his Mustang guns until McKennon could get in the cockpit. He didn't have time to figure that, in the landing position, the Mustang's guns would be pointed upwards, and thus useless for firing at ground targets.

He was too busy considering that McKennon's burning plane was in the middle of the field. That would necessitate landing the short way across the rectangular meadow instead of the longer way, diagonally. Further, he was still carrying the heavy wing tanks on his craft and that meant stalling out at an unpredictable speed. Green just let the flaps down to the maximum and hoped.

McKennon came sprinting up to the Mustang as Green began to shuck off his flying gear to make room in the cramped cockpit. No word passed between them, just labored breathing. McKennon released the wing tanks to lighten the plane and reached in the cockpit to adjust the flaps for a short take-off.

Green stood on the wings as he shed his chute and dinghy, keeping an alert eye on the factory a few hundred yards away. Green hurled his chute and dinghy on the ground, and as they flapped in the slipstream, he realized with a twang that no matter what happened, it would be impossible to bail out. The thought was all the more unpleasant as he had once been forced to ditch in the Channel and had developed a well-known water phobia. But space had to be provided. He had come too far to tell Mac he had changed his mind. The roar of the motor kept McKennon from hearing Green murmur, "Jesus, I'm crazy!"

The 24 mustangs orbited overhead to provide top-cover against anything trying to get at the two pilots. There was no argument about who would fly the craft. McKennon, six feet one, lifted himself into the cockpit and Green sat in his lap to do the flying. They were more crowded than they would have been in a barber's chair. McKennon's cheek was pressed flat against Green's shoulder blades and his feet were partially on the rudder pedals because there wasn't any other place in the barrel-size cockpit for them. Still, it felt good to be close to someone after thinking he was alone in Germany.

So far, the rescue effort had required some skill, but mostly audacity and disregard for army rules, both of which came natural to the thick-maned Green. Now came the tough part—getting the craft off the ground in a bumpy meadow with a short run.

Green pulled the canopy forward over his head and his leather helmet touched the top. He held the wheel brakes down and gunned the motor. He registered 60 inches of mercury, whereas the instructions said never more than 35. The Mustang quivered and pranced against the powerful airflow. The trim tabs were still adjusted for landing and the tail tattooed the ground like a woodpecker.

The air wash made the grass lie down flat. Green released the brakes and the Mustang catapulted forward. Green ordinarily used 800 to 900 yards of Debden runway to get off, but if he was to make this one, he had to do it in 200 to 300 yards of bumpy meadow.

The plane raced forward towards a patch of woods. The tail left the ground. As the plane charged over a rise it felt like they were getting airborne, but the wheels found the ground again and the craft lurched. The pilot heard a metallic tattoo and thought the prop had been fouled. But it was only the safety belt buckle—left outside when they closed the canopy— beating against the metal fuselage.

The red nose of the craft raced forward at the trees. Green liked a take-off speed of 150 m.p.h., but he pulled the stick into his belly when he got it up to 80 m.p.h. The plane sluggishly wobbled and wallowed as it groaned off the ground.

"Pull your wheels up!" a pilot cried from above.

The wheels came up and the craft climbed. The pent-up jabber of the 24 pilots who had watched the rescue in gooseflesh suspense burst forth.

"Goddamn, he made it!"

"Inky" Davis said: "I've sure as hell seen everything now!"

Green gasped: "God, we're going to get home!"

McKennon, who loved his showmanship, said casually to his squadron:

"Horseback is airborne again."

410

The pilots whistled and roared. On the last play of the game, Green and McKennon had run the length of the field from behind the goal posts for the winning touchdown.

"Okay, fellas," said McKennon paternally, "form up and let's go home."

But that was all the calmness left in McKennon. The reaction to his deliverance set in. He pounded Green on the back for miles as they raced homeward, repeating over and over, "Oh, you crazy bastard, you crazy bastard you!"

They had a trip of two hours and 35 minutes to make, most of it over enemy territory, McKennon's feet kept hitting the rudders and the craft bounced about in the sky, so he threw his boots overside to make his feet smaller. His knees were painfully pressed against the magneto switches and his legs went to sleep under Green's weight.

McKennon laughed, gurgled like a baby, and kept banging Green's back. In cadet school you didn't smoke within 50 feet of an aircraft, but the two smoked Green's half-package of Chesterfields and then went through McKennon's Lucky Strikes.

Shooting across Germany the plane hit a dense haze. Green couldn't fly through it on instruments because, sitting in McKennon's lap, he was too high to see the instruments. Green began climbing over the haze. Ten thousand feet is the altitude at which flyers are supposed to go to oxygen, but they had to climb to 18,000 to leap-frog the haze.

McKennon's skin began to itch. This was the symptom which always told him when he needed oxygen. His jabber ceased. Green turned his head and saw that McKennon had passed out. McKennon had thrown his oxygen mask out with his helmet when he bailed from his ship. Green, the junior birdman McKennon had not kicked out of his squadron, took the mask from his own face and held it to that of the unconscious McKennon. McKennon revived. From

411

then on they took turns sucking at Green's mask.

You might have expected them to land in France to pick up chutes and dinghies, especially the water-fearing Green. But they had just one motive in this life as they raced along in the late spring afternoon—Debden and a bottle, one each.

The Mustang hit the coast of Dunkirk and Green gave it full throttle so that in case of motor failure, there would be some chance of gliding to the English coast. But the Mustang, named *Suzanne* after Green's wife, rocketed them to Essex County. Green picked out the cluster of white houses at Newport in the shape of a "6" with tail pointing to Debden—a reference point used by 4th Groups pilots for three years.

Green whooshed over the Officers' Club and the hangars and honked it up in a sharp peel-off. The pull of gravity multiplied his weight about four times and McKennon gasped. Green, his fright supplanted by friskiness, looked back and grinned. McKennon just shook his head groggily.

Green called the watchtower and said, "Clear the runway."

"Is this an emergency landing?" asked the tower.

"I guess so," said Green, "we've got two pilots in this kite."

"You wha-a-at?" asked the tower, piping the one-seat Mustang.

"Come on," Green said, "landing instructions—for two."

24
One Grand

By late March, 1945, the AEF and the Russians were piledriving the Wehrmacht into an even narrower space and U.S. and Russian fighters were encountering each other. Once they exchanged shots before nationality was mutually recognized.

On March 22 the pilots were briefed by Lt. Col. Sidney Woods, of Somerton, Ariz., who was deputy group commander, to rendezvous over Germany with 15th AF bombers which would fly up from their bases across the Alps in Italy.

Having escorted the Liberators to their oil refinery target uneventfully, Woods cruised towards Berlin and crossed its northern fringe in search of Jerries. On a drome between Berlin and the Oder River battle lines, where the Russians were preparing to uncork their final drive on the capital, Woods peered down from 11,000 feet and spotted a gaggle of some 15 FW 190s.

"Horseback here." Woods said. "Let's bounce 'em."

Some of the 190s were still taking off as the Mustangs powerdived. The 190s had bombs slung underneath—two on the wings and one on the fuselage. The ensuing massacre, which raged from the deck to 5,000 feet and lasted half an hour, was one of the neatest actions ever fought by the 4th. It revealed what the third generation of Debden pilots could do when they did encounter Jerries.

Woods, a taut, assertive, tigerish little man who had been a football star, maneuvered on the tail of a 190. He pulled the trigger on the stick to jettison his

413

drop-tanks in preparation for combat. But only one tank fell. Resistance to the slipstream of the 190 offered by the remaining tank flipped Woods' Mustang on its back like a flapjack. But Woods kept right on firing from the inverted position and the 190 ploughed into the ground.

With Lt. Richard E. Moore, of Barstow, Ill, sticking close on his wing, Woods pulled up into a 190 which was firing a deflection shot at him from above. The 190 flamed and crashed.

Capt. William (Buzz) Riedel*, of Ault, Colo., who had finally escaped training command duties ("get one for me") in the States and was having the time of his life, clobbered two more, one of which was dogging Moore's tail. One each was destroyed by Lt. Hagan, Lt. R.O. Davis, Morrow, Ark.; Lt. Jerome E. Jahnke, Los Angeles; and Lt. Fred Farrington, Falls City, Nebr. Lt. William Antonides, Carbondale, Colo., probably destroyed two more, but couldn't watch them crash as he had to break away from a flak barrage.

Woods, who had destroyed some Jap planes in the Pacific, went after a third Jerry in workmanlike manner. Flying a bare 50 feet off the ground, Woods focused the magical K-14 gunsight and squirted a short burst. The canopy and bombs came off the 190 and it crashed with its pilot.

Woods then saw a 190 firing at a Mustang. Woods clobbered this one, his fourth. The next 190 he went after was flying in a section of four. Woods fired a little ahead of the plane and saw tracers, which told them he had little ammunition left. Woods corrected his aim slightly and fired his last tracers. They were enough. The 190 banged into the meadow, Woods' fifth victim.

The remaining 190s were so rattled by the deadly

---

*His mother wrote recently that he was killed on Nov. 15, 1945 in a C-64 accident over Germany.

onslaught that one, to lighten his craft for fleeing, exploded his three bombs on his own drome.

In all, the pilots had shot down 10 of the 15 Jerries. But the more significant fact was the stride the encounter marked in fighter operations. In the Battle of Britain, Spitfires could operate in combat for an hour and a half. But now they could sweep eastward beyond Berlin, take 10 FW 190s by the scruff of the neck and boot them out of the sky, and return to England.

As Goering moaned: "Mustangs made a playground of Bavaria."

The German war machine was becoming disorganized and there was less reason to be wary of Luftwaffe tricks and ruses than in former days when pilots didn't even know who was talking to them over the radio. Deacon had been leading the group over Germany one day when the ground station called up to say:

"Nuthouse here. Horseback, your part of the show has been scrubbed. Go to M for monkey and sweep the area. Steer 124 degrees."

"Horseback to Nuthouse. Okay. Steer 124," said Deacon.

The voice came back: "Steer 242."

"Did you say 242, Horseback?" asked the controller.

"Roger, Nuthouse, 242."

"This is Nuthouse, Horseback. Don't steer 242. Steer 124."

The voice came back: "Steer 170."

Deacon looked at his map and saw that a course of 170° would take him over the sea.

Deacon was exasperated. He said: "Horseback to Nuthouse. Did you say steer er-one-seven-er-zero?"

Nuthouse answered: "Disregard all vectors."

The "170°" voice was a German radio tuned to the 4th frequency to cause confusion, and perhaps get the group lost over the North Sea.

But this phase was over now. It was just a question of seeing how many arrows had to be shot into the writhing German body before it ceased to move. Churchill had already said, "One more good heave all together and it will be over." On March 24 came the weather SHAEF had awaited to press the button for the crossing of the Rhine River.

It was just like D-Day except for the sparkling blue weather. We heard the RAF coursing out over Debden during the night to paste the Rhine defenses. The sun came up and there were hundreds of gliders being towed over Debden at low altitude towards Germany. There was not a single cloud puff in the sky. The sky sparkled with the sun glints from hundreds of silver Forts and Libs lumbering along.

Col. Stewart was ordered to make a "maximum effort," which meant a group of approximately 70 Mustangs instead of the usual 48. Stewart briefed the pilots to patrol an area 30 miles long and 30 miles wide east of the Rhine near Osenbruck.

"Stop everything that moves, in the air and on the ground," Stewart ordered. "Nothing is to get through to attack these airborne troops."

There was no doubt that the Allied Armies would successfully buck the line and pour over the Rhine into Germany. Stewart said: "If you are forced down, dig into the ground and wait. Our infantry will be right along and pick you up."

For days the pilots had flown over German fields jammed with aircraft. They knew the Germans had them. Both sides knew this was the last critical struggle. The Germans were showing a complete willingness to sacrifice everything, even though the end was plain as a pikestaff. This, surely, would be the day on which they would at last throw up all their fighters. The greatest air battle of the war was indicated.

Stewart taxied out and waited for the three squadrons to draw up behind him. The pilots had their canopies drawn forward and their oxygen masks attached by the time they wheeled past the watchtower, a sure sign that a hot time was expected.

The group patrolled the sector all morning and was relieved by another group when it returned to Debden for lunch. The pilots refueled and returned to patrol the area all afternoon. They saw not a single Jerry. The group needed 133 planes to bring the total to 1,000 destroyed, and it didn't appear the war was going to last long enough to clobber them.

April 4—The group destroyed three jets and damaged three more without loss. Lt. Raymond A. Dyer, of Glassport, Pa., dived on one which was ripsnorting into the bombers, opening fire and watching him crash. The Wolfpack got one jet, leaving the 4th with a lead of 15½ Jerries.

April 10—The Wolfpack attacked a drome and destroyed 41 to sweep into the lead, 911 to 893.

April 11—The field order sent the group to Czechoslovakia and it flew over packed dromes on which the 4th might have regained the lead. But Patton's armies were advancing so swiftly that the field order forbade all strafing lest it menace U.S. troops. The best of Philadelphia lawyers couldn't read the injunction any other way.

Free Germany was becoming a smaller and smaller corridor into which German planes were being moved and compressed. The jackpot was there if only Pinetree would sanction an attack.

April 13—The group escorted bombers to Denmark and attacked some moored seaplanes, which wouldn't burn as they had no fuel in them. The Wolfpack swept far into the lead by destroying approximately 90 parked planes.

Every night the P.R.O. broadcast a communique over the station blower on the day's operations. Of course it got out anyway and everybody was sick. It was too much of a lead to overcome.

April 16—Lt. Col. Woods was grim at the briefing.

417

Probably he was regretful for not having ignored the no-strafing order, as another group had done, and maintained the 4th's leadership. Woods obviously meant to make it up to the group, especially to the all-enduring line crews who were so disconsolate. They beat the Wolfpack at football and baseball and they had expected the pilots to carry the ball in the air.

"We will begin," said Woods, "by knocking out the flak emplacements."

They all knew that meant some were not going to return to Debden that night.

Woods himself was shot down, as he had expected to be. But the attack was a brilliant one and the pilots returned with approximately 100 planes destroyed. It put the 4th back in the running, but the Wolfpack maintained a slight, but winning edge.

April 17—The Wolfpack boys prayed for the war to end right away while they still had the lead. Whereas, the 4th—well, if the war just *had* to go on for a few days more . . .

Glover led a squadron through a wall of flak to destroy four more.

Woods and several other pilots who had been shot down on the jackpot mission, were liberated by Patton's tanks and returned with 15 additional claims for planes destroyed, the Russians took Berlin, Himmler took poison, Hitler married Eva Braun, Germany surrendered, Tiny Tim said God bless us every one, the war was over and *The New York Times* reported:

LONDON, May 13— The Eighth Air Force's 4th Fighter Group, commanded by Col. Everett W. Stewart . . . grabbed off top honors of the European war for destruction of enemy planes.

Stewart's group blasted 1,016 Nazi planes— 550 in aerial combat and 466 on the ground.

Runners-up in the record race were the fliers of the 56th group (Wolfpack) with 1,006½ enemy planes to their credit including 680 in the air.

418

So that's the way it was. The ornery, ranchy characters from Debden out-gunned the pedigreed Wolfpack. The Wolfpack was a great outfit—no doubt about it—but then 4 is supposed to come before 56, isn't it?

Yes, the 4th—red-headed stepchild of the AAF— outdid the vaunted Wolfpack. The victory margin was 9½.

If, for example, Godfrey had not returned from the States and destroyed 10 more planes—the two groups would have tied. In which case, I take it, the 4th and the Wolfpack would have adjourned their contest to the Pacific to play off the tie.

Cheers.

- *Off* -

BASIC GIBBERISH

Abort: Turn back.

Ammo: Drop-tank.

Baby: Drop-tank.

Beat-up: *n.*, thorough buzz job or strafing; *v.t.*, ground attack.

Big Friends: Bombers; fighters were Little Friends.

Blower: Supercharger; also telephone, Tanoy or radio.

Browned-off: Vexed.

Bug: Cluster to a decoration.

Buzz: Fly low over a ground object; also *buzz* job.

Circuit: RAF equivalent of AAF's landing pattern.

Clobber: To splinter; attack; rend; cripple e.g., blasting a German plane was *clobbering* it; Monty *clobbered* Rommel at El Alamein; FDR said of the enemy: "We'll hit him again, again, and again." He might have said: We'll *clobber* him." Marshal Stalin ended his orders of the day with, "Death to the Nazi invader!" He could have said, "*Clobber* the Jerry!"

Deck: Flying just off the ground.

Deflection: Shooting from an angle to the target.

Dispersal: Squadron huts on fringes of field in which pilots donned flying gear, reported for interrogation, and swapped salaries at penny-ante between missions.

Do: Any arranged event, such as a wedding, dance or mission.

Do.: Dornier, German-make plane.

D/S: Detached service, which was an acceptable austerity substitute for leave or furlough.

Eager: A pilot who wanted to fly every rough mission

was *eager*. A girl who called several times to remind you that you had invited her to the dance was *eager*. A girl who—well, that was *eagerness*.

ETO: European Theater of Operations; also, ETO-happy.

Flat-out: Full speed; *full-bore*.

FW: Focke-Wulf.

Gaggle: A cluster; pack; a *gaggle* of FWs might range from 10 to 50.

Gen: Information; the dope.

Goat: Any inhabitant of the British Isles. Also, *goat mail* for a local letter; *Goatland* for England. An American going steadily with a Limey girl was referred to as a *goat lover*. The longer the soldier stayed in England, the more securely did the idiom become lodged in his speech, the inferences of which we leave to historians of Goat-American Relations and to Mr. Mencken.

Gong Ceremony: Decoration ceremony on the parade ground.

Group: A fighter group had three squadrons; bomber group, four.

Had it: Finished; washed up; over with.

Immelman: A combat maneuver devised in World War I by the German ace, von Immelman. He would let an Allied plane get on his tail, pull up suddenly and swoop down.

I.O.: Intelligence officer. A peculiar breed and generally tiresome, they associated themselves with the pilot gentry and sought to pick up a sun-tan in the reflected glory. Nice boys—before their names were drawn out of a hat and they were sent to Harrisburg.

Kite: Aircraft.

Kriege: Prisoner of war.

Let Down: Reduce altitude gently, as distinct from a dive.

Local: Neighborhood pub.

Lufberry: A defensive maneuver, a hand-me-down

from World War I. Beset by a superior force, a squadron would form itelf into a tight ring and circle. Thus, any attacker trying to crash the ring would necessarily expose himself to fire from the revolving noses.

May Day: "I have to bail, plot my position for rescue."

Me.: Messerschmitt 109, 110, 210, 410, etc.

N.Y.R.: Not yet returned. Pilots were not immediately listed as M.I.A. (missing in action) as they might have landed at a forward base or be floating in the drink.

O.D.: Officer-of-the-Day. A 24-hour tour of duty as a kind of sheriff of the station, during which period the O.D. was fall guy for anything that went wrong. A warrant officer always seemed to hit it on dance nights and Christmas.

Ops: Operations.

Pinetree: Code for Hq., Eighth Air Force, located at High Wycombe.

Poon: A British pound sterling; often used by Americans as dollar bills.

Prang: to crack up.

Press: RAF for start engines.

P.R.O.: Public Relations Officer; expatriate of a newspaper city room lent-leased to the army to serve as a reporter and press liaison officer. By those whom he has gotten into print, his name is called blessed. To those clients he has failed to get in print often and elaborately enough to square with their usually varicose estimates of their own newsworthiness, the P.R.O. existed as "that newspaper type who puts out all that bull." By himself, the P.R.O. is called a man who's going to return to his city room loom, requisition a couple of barracks bags and blow like all get-out. Meanwhile, he timidly associates himself with Tom Paine, who after all, was the original P.R.O. in light of his services to Washington and the Revolutionary Army.

Oh, yes, and the army was the same in '76 as now—there was no T.O. spot for Public Relations Officer Tom Paine.

Queue: A line; also *queue up*.

SCORES*

Name	Air	Ground	Total
Maj. John T. Godfrey	18	18	36
Maj. Don S. Gentile	23	7	30
Maj. James A. Goodson	15	15	30
1st Lt. Ralph K. Hofer	16	11½	27½
Maj. Duane W. Beeson	18	7	25
Maj. Fred W. Glover	11	13	24
Lt. Col. Claiborne H. Kinnard	6	14½	20½
Capt. Nicholas Megura	13½	6	19½
Maj. Pierce W. McKennon	11½	8	19½
Maj. George Carpenter	14	4	18
Capt. Charles F. Anderson	11	7	18
Col. Donald J. M. Blakeslee	15	2	17
Maj. Gerald E. Montgomery	3	14	17
Lt. Col. James A. Clark	11	5	16
Maj. Louis L. Norley	11	5	16
Capt. Willard W. Millikan	13	2	15
Maj. Howard (Deacon) Hively	12	3	15
Capt. Albert L. Schlegel	10	5	15
1st Lt. H. Thomas Biel	6	7	13
Capt. Joseph L. Lang	8½	4	12½
Lt. Col. Sidney S. Woods	7	5	12
1st Lt. Paul S. Riley	8	3	11
Capt. Kendall E. Carlson	7	4	11
Capt. Shelton W. Monroe	6	5	11
Col. Everett W. Stewart	9	1½	10½
Capt. Frank C. Jones	5	5½	10½

*Officially confirmed by War Department.

Ground Name	Ground	Total	Air
Capt. Donald M. Malmsten	1½	9	10½
Capt. Ted E. Lines	10	0	10
Capt. Victor J. France	5	5	10
Capt. Donald R. Emerson	5	5	10
Maj. James R. Happel	4	6	10
Capt. Joseph H. Bennett	9	0	9
Capt. Bernard L. McGrattan	9	0	9
Lt. Vermont Garrison	8	1	9
Capt. David W. Howe	6	3	9
Lt. Col. Jack Oberhansley	5	4	9
1st. Lt. Grover C. Siems	5	4	9
1st Lt. Van E. Chandler	5	4	9
Capt. William B. Smith	3	6	9
1st. Lt. James W. Ayers	1	7	8
Capt. Carl R. Alfred	0	8	8
1st Lt. Joe H. Joiner	3½	4	7½
Col. Chesley G. Peterson	7	0	7
Capt. Raymond C. Care	6	1	7
1st Lt. William O. Antonides	0	7	7
Maj. Henry L. Mills	6	0	6
Capt. Kenneth G. Smith	6	0	6
Maj. Winslow M. Sobanski	5	1	6
Maj. Michael G. H. McPharlin	5	1	6
1st Lt. Clemens A. Fiedler	5	1	6
Capt. Archie W. Chatterley	5	1	6
1st Lt. Robert F. Nelson	1	5	6
1st Lt. Frank E. Speer	1	5	6
1st Lt. Douglas P. Pederson	0	6	6
1st Lt. Arthur R. Bowers	0	6	6
Capt. Carl G. Payne	2	3½	5
1st Lt. Gilbert L. Kesler	½	5	5½
Capt. Thomas P. Bell	0	5½	5½
1st Lt. Loton D. Jennings	0	5½	5½
Lt. Col. Roy W. Evans	5	0	5
1st Lt. Spiros N. Pissanos	5	0	5
Maj. Gerald C. Brown	5	0	5
1st Lt. Alex Rafalovich	4	1	5

Capt. Vasseure H. Wynn	3	2	5
1st Lt. Jack D. McFadden	2	3	5
Capt. Robert D. Hobert	2	3	5
Capt. Nelson M. Dickey	0	5	5
1st Lt. Kenneth G. Helfrecht	0	5	5
1st Lt. Gordon A. Denson	0	5	5
F/O Donald P. Baugh	0	5	5

GROUP SCORES*

Group	Air	Ground	Total
4th**	550	466	1,016
56th**	679½	327	1,006½
355th	356	504	860
352nd	493½	273	766½
353rd	340	405	745
357th	586½	110	696
78th	330	343½	673½
339th	234	399	633
55th	305½	255	560½
364th	261	194	455
20th	205	227	432
479th	155	277	432
359th	247½	110	357½
361st	219½	132	351½
356th	193	77	270

*Of the 15 fighter groups of the Eighth Air Force.

**Scores of the 4th and 56th Groups are final and officially confirmed. The other 13 group scores may vary slightly from the final, official tally, but very little.

4TH'S SQUADRON SCORES***

Squadron	Air	Ground	Total
334th	210⅙	185¼	395⁵⁄₁₂
335th	165⅙	97⅓	226½
336th	174⅔	183⁵⁄₁₂	358½

***In addition to those destroyed, the 4th probably destroyed 64 and damaged 461.

Lt. Anthony J. Seaman, Greenville, S. C. . . . . Oct. 20, 1942

Capt. Richard D. McMinn, Salt Lake City, Utah . . . . Apr. 15, 1943

Capt. Stanley M. Anderson, Indianapolis, Ind. . . . . . . Apr. 15, 1943

Lt. John F. Lutz, Fulton, Mo. . . . . May 4, 1943

Lt. Robert A. Boock, Springfield, Ill. . . . . May 18, 1943

Lt. Gordon H. Whitlow, Denver, Colo. . . . . May 21, 1943

Lt. LeLand L. McFarlane, Sacramento, Calif. . . . . May 21, 1943

Lt. Dale B. Leaf, Marshalltown, Ia. . . . . Sept. 2, 1943

Lt. Ivan R. Moon, West Palm Beach, Fla. . . . . Nov. 3, 1943

Lt. Mark H. Kolter, Lima, Ohio . . . . May 30, 1944

Lt. Harry B. Noon, Indianapolis, Ind. . . . . June 11, 1943

Lt. Ralph K. Hofer, Salem, Mo. . . . . July 2, 1944

Capt. Joseph L. Lang, Hyde Park, Mass. . . . . Oct. 14, 1944

Lt. John L. Childs, Floral Park, N.Y. . . . . Nov. 6, 1944

Maj. Winslow M. Sobanski, New York, N.Y. . . . . June 6, 1944

F/O William D. Bates, Cullman, Ala. . . . . Feb. 6, 1945

Lt. Chester P. Grimm, Farmington, Ill. . . . . Jan. 21, 1943

Lt. Ward K. Wortman, Spokane, Wash. . . . . July 14, 1943

Capt. William P. Kelly, Saratoga, N.Y. . . . . Feb. 2, 1943

Lt. Frederick D. Merritt, Rockland, Me. . . . . July 30, 1943

Lt. Burton C. Wyman, Englewood, N.J. . . . . Jan. 29, 1944

Lt. Richard I. Reed, St. Petersburg, Fla. . . . . Feb. 20, 1944

Lt. Joseph W. Sullivan, New York, N.Y. . . . . Feb. 25, 1944

Lt. Edward P. Freeburger, Edgewood, Md. . . . . Mar. 18, 1944

Lt. James H. Brandenburg, Cincinnati, O. . . . . Mar. 21, 1944

Lt. Clemens A. Fiedler, Fredericksburg, Tex. . . . . Apr. 10, 1944

Lt. Ralph W. Saunders, Pekin, Ill. . . . . Apr. 13, 1944

Lt. William W. Hunt, Pinos Altos, N.M. . . . . May 21, 1944

Lt. Harry E. Jennings, Buffalo, N.Y. . . . . May 24, 1944

Lt. Robert H. Homuth, Chicago, Ill. . . . . May 31, 1944

Capt. Bernard J. McGrattan, Utica, N.Y. . . . . June 6, 1944

Lt. Cecil E. Garbey, Tulsa, Okla. . . . . June 6, 1944

F/O Walter Smith, Birmingham, Ala. . . . . June 6, 1944

Lt. Harold L. Ross, Greensboro, N.C. . . . . June 6, 1944

Capt. Frank C. Jones, Jr., Montclair, N.J. . . . . Aug. 8, 1944

Lt. Stephen R. Boren, Marinetta, Wisc. . . . . Aug. 13, 1944

Lt. Bernard J. Rosenson, Monessen, Pa. . . . . Aug. 18, 1944

Lt. Leo Dailey, Hornell, N.Y. Aug. 18, 1944

Lt. Dean J. Hill, Los Angeles, Calif. . . . . June 19, 1944

Lt. Jap A. Powell, Indianapolis, Ind. . . . . Feb. 13, 1943

Lt. Robert H. Richards, Walden, N.Y. . . . . Mar. 4, 1944

Lt. Peter G. Lehman, New York, N.Y. . . . . Mar. 31, 1944

Capt. Robert D. Hobert, Woodland, Wash. . . . . Apr. 5, 1944

Lt. Robert S. Tussey, Altoona, Pa. . . . . May 11, 1944

Lt. Kenneth B. Smith, Watsontown, Pa. . . . . June 7, 1944

Lt. Harvie J. Arnold, Oklahoma City, Okla. . . . . June 18, 1944

Lt. Ferris S. Harris, Houston, Tex. . . . . Aug. 28, 1944

Lt. Robert W. White, Fort Worth, Tex. . . . . Sept. 10, 1944

Capt. Donald R. Emerson, Pembina, N.D. . . . . Dec. 25, 1944

Lt. Frederick D. Hall, Coopers Plains, N.Y. . . . . Jan. 16, 1945

Lt. Harry L. Davis, Cotulla, Tex. . . . . Mar. 26, 1945

Lt. Earl F. Hustwit, Pittsburgh, Pa. . . . . Mar. 26, 1945

Capt. Victor J. France, Dallas, Tex. . . . . Apr. 18, 1944

Capt. Albert L. Schlegel, Cleveland, O. . . . . Aug. 28, 1944

Capt. Frank Boyles, Mt. Vernon, N.Y. . . . . Apr. 8, 1944

F/O Frank D. Gallion, Millersburg, Ohio . . . . Nov. 3, 1943

F/O William A. Cox, Houston, Tex. . . . . Feb. 3, 1944

Lt. Edmund D. Whalen, Brooklyn, N.Y. . . . . Mar. 6, 1944

Lt. Robert P. Claus, Bronx, N.Y. . . . . Apr. 8, 1944

Lt. H. Thomas Biel, St. Paul, Minn. . . . . Apr. 24, 1944

Lt. Edward J. Steppe, Woodside, L. I., N.Y. . . . . June 6, 1944

Lt. James F. Scott, Brownwood, Tex. . . . . June 8, 1944

Lt. Leon J. Cole, Nashville, Tenn. . . . . June 11, 1944

Lt. Thomas S. Sharp, McArthur, O. . . . . July 2, 1944

Lt. C. G. Howard, Tulsa, Okla. . . . . Aug. 18, 1944

Lt. Herbert J. Vander Vate, Buffalo, N.Y. . . . . Aug. 28, 1944

Capt. William B. Smith, Bluefield, Va. . . . . Sept. 13, 1944

Lt. Leonard R. Werner, Mt. Vernon, N.Y. . . . . Nov. 20, 1944

Lt. Carmen D. Delnero, West Springfield, Mass. . . . . Nov. 21, 1944

Lt. Arthur J. Senecal, Worcester, Mass. . . . . Jan. 2, 1945

Lt. John T. Slater, Waverly, N.Y. . . . . Sept. 21, 1942

Lt. George W. Barnes, Canton, N.C. . . . . Mar. 3, 1944

F/O Joseph Goetz, Buffalo, N.Y. . . . . Mar. 21, 1944

Lt. Lloyd F. Henry, Indianapolis, Ind. . . . . Apr. 19, 1944

Capt. Charles F. Anderson, Gary, Ind. . . . . Apr. 19, 1944

Lt. Frank T. Sibbett, San Francisco, Calif. . . . . June 21, 1944

Lt. Kermit O. Dahlen, Thompson, Ia. . . . . July 19, 1944

Lt. Lloyd G. Kingham, Grass Valley, Calif. . . . . July 22, 1944

Lt. Robert G. Fischer, Gotha, Fla. . . . . Aug. 8, 1944

Lt. Robert J. Cooper, Chicago, Ill. . . . . Aug. 18, 1944

Lt. John T. Conley, St. Paul, Minn. . . . . Aug. 18, 1944

Lt. Paul S. Iden, Minerva, O. Sept. 11, 1944

Lt. Nicholas W. Vozzy, Abingdon, Pa. . . . . Sept. 17, 1944

Lt. Ralph E. Lewis, Benton, Ill. . . . . Nov. 18, 1944

Capt. Charles D. Hewes, Biloxi, Miss. . . . . Dec. 18, 1944

Lt. Robert L. Stallings, Andrews, Ind. . . . . Jan. 17, 1945

Lt. Paul G. Santos, New York, N.Y. . . . . Feb. 6, 1945

---

*Some of these were killed, but had not been officially declared so at the time of this writing.

Lt. Herman S. Rassmussen, Oakland, Calif. . . . . Apr. 9, 1945

Lt. Edward J. McLoughlin, Brooklyn, N.Y. . . . . Apr. 16, 1945

Lt. William H. Baker, Jr., Temple, Tex. . . . . Sept. 26, 1942

Lt. Gene P. Neville, Oklahoma City, Okla. . . . . Sept. 26, 1942

Lt. Leonard T. Ryerson, Whitinsville, Mass. . . . . . . Sept. 26, 1942

Lt. Dennis D. Smith, Sedan, Kans. . . . . Sept. 26,1942

Lt. George K. Villinger, Palmyra, N.J. . . . . Mar. 2, 1944

Lt. Glen A. Herter, E. Windsor, Ont., Canada . . . . . . Mar. 3, 1944

Lt. Ernest K. Skilton, Hollywood, Calif. . . . . Mar. 16, 1944

Lt. Robert H. Seifert, Oneida, N.Y. . . . . Apr. 15, 1944

Lt. Conrad J. Netting, San Antonio, Tex. . . . . June 10, 1944

Lt. Gerald C. Chapman, Stoughton, Mass. . . . . Aug. 2, 1944

Lt. Henry A. Ingalls, Los Angeles, Calif. . . . . Sept. 11, 1944

Lt. George H. Logan, Jr., Upper Montclair, N.J. . . . . . Oct. 2, 1944

Lt. Henry A. Kaul, Forest Bank, Ill. . . . . Feb. 11, 1945

Capt. LeRoy Carpenter, Jr., Austin, Tex. . . . . Apr. 16, 1945

Capt. Carl R. Alfred, Atwater, O. . . . . Apr. 16, 1945

71st EAGLE SQUADRON*

Maj. Gus Daymond, commander, Burbank, Calif.

Capt. Oscar H. Coen, Carbondale, Ill.

Capt. R. S. Sprague, San Diego, Calif.

Lt. M. G. McPharlin, Hastings, Mich.

Capt. S. A. Maureillo, Astoria, N.Y.

Lt. T. J. Andrews, Costa Mesa, Calif.

Lt. W. T. O'Regan, Los Angeles, Calif.

Lt. H. H. Strickland, Washington, D.C.

Lt. R. D. McMinn, Salt Lake City, Utah

Lt. W. J. Hollander, Raleigh, N.C.

Lt. H. L. Stewart, Raleigh, N.C.

Lt. James A. Clark, Jr., Westbury, L.I.

Lt. W. C. Brite, Evansville, Ind.

Lt. G. C. Ross, Albuquerque, N.M.

Lt. A. H. (Hoppy) Hopson, Dallas, Tex.

Lt. Robert (Junior) Priser, Tucson, Ariz.

---

*That is, those who transferred to the AAF in September, 1942 to form the 4th Fighter Group.

Lt. G. H. Whitlow, Denver, Colo.

Lt. J. F. Lutz, Fulton, Mo.

Lt. Howard (Deacon) Hively, Athens, O.

Lt. S. M. Anderson, Indianapolis, Ind.

Lt. M. S. Vosberg, Azusa, Calif.

Lt. H. L. (Hank) Mills, Leonia, N.J.

Lt. Duane W. Beeson, Boise, Idaho

Lt. R. C. (Bud) Care, Angola, Ind.

Lt. R. A. Boock, Springfield, Ill.

Lt. J. C. Harrington, Buffalo, N.Y.

Lt. A. J. Seaman, Greenville, N.C.

Lt. Victor J. France, Oklahoma City, Okla.

Lt. Vernon A Boehle, Indianapolis, Ind.

Lt. W. B. Morgan, Honolulu, T. H.

121st EAGLE SQUADRON

Maj. W. J. Daley, commander, Amarillo, Tex.

Capt. Selden R. Edner, San Jose, Calif.

Lt. Gilbert (Gunner) Halsey, Chickasha, Okla.

Lt. G. B. Fetrow, Upland, Calif.

Lt. Frank R. Boyles, Mt. Vernon, N.Y.

Lt. E. D. Beattie, Albany, Ga.

Lt. F. O. Smith, Foard City, Tex.

Lt. A. D. Young, Buffalo, Kan.

Lt. B. A. Taylor, Salem, Ore.

Lt. J. M. Osborne, Washington, D.C.

Lt. Cadman V. Padgett, Bethesda, Md.

Lt. Frank M. Fink, Philadelphia, Penn.

Lt. D. K. Willis, Leavenworth, Ind.

Lt. R. G. Patterson, Los Angeles, Calif.

Lt. K. G. Smith, Boise, Idaho

Lt. J. G. Matthews, Wallington, N.J.

Lt. C. A. Hardin, Harrodsbury, Ky.

Lt. George Carpenter, Oil City, Pa.

Lt. Paul M. Ellington, Tulsa, Okla.

Lt. Leon M. Blanding, Sumter, S.C.

Lt. R. J. Fox, Larchmont, N.Y.

Lt. Jimmie Happel, Paulsboro, N.J.

Lt. Roy Evans, San Bernardino, Calif.
Lt. W. P. Kelly, Saratoga, N.Y.
Lt. J.M. Saunders, Nashville, Tenn.
Lt. J. T. Slater, Waverly, N.Y.

133rd EAGLE SQUADRON

Maj. C. W. McColpin, commander, Buffalo, N.Y.
Capt. M. E. Jackson, Corpus Christi, Tex.
Capt. C. A. Cook, Jr., Alhambra, Calif.
Lt. W. H. Baker, Temple, Tex.
Lt. G. B. Sperry, Alhambra, Calif.
Lt. R. M. Beaty, Rye, N.Y.
Lt. L. T. Ryerson, Whitinsville, Mass.
Lt. Don S. Gentile, Piqua, O.
Lt. D. D. Smith, Orlando, Fla.
Lt. G. G. Wright, Wilkes Barre, Pa.
Lt. G. H. Middletown, Visilia, Calif.
Lt. E. L. Miller, Oakland, Calif.
Lt. R. E. Smith, Washington, D.C.
Lt. G. P. Neville, Oklahoma City, Okla.
Lt. Leroy Gover, San Carlos, Calif.
Lt. D. E. Lambert, Exeter, Calif.
Lt. Carl H. Miley, Toledo, O.
Lt. Don D. Nee, Long Beach, Calif.
Lt. G. J. Smart, Solan, Kans.
Lt. H. L. Ayres, Indianapolis, Ind.
Lt. R. L. Alexander, Aylmer, Ontario
Lt. W. C. Slade, Jr., Brama, Okla.
Lt. C. H. Patterson, Forth Worth, Tex.
Lt. Joe L. Bennett, Tusumcari, N.M
Lt. J. Mitchelweis, Jr., Rockford, Ill.

ROSTER, FIRST
BRITAIN-TO-RUSSIA SHUTTLE

Col. Don Blakeslee
Maj. Baldwin M. Baldwin
Maj. Leon M. Blanding
Capt. William F. Hedrick
Maj. Howard D. Hively
Lt. Robert C. Church
Lt. Donald R. Emerson
Lt. John W. Goodwyn
Lt. Robert L. Hills
Lt. Ralph K. Hofer
Lt. Gilbert W. Hunt
Lt. Robert P. Kenyon
Lt. James C. Lane
Lt. Joseph L. Lang
Lt. Ted E. Lines
Lt. George H. Logan, Jr.
Capt. Shelton W. Monroe
Lt. Joseph A. Patteeuw
Lt. Donald D. Perkins
Lt. James W. Russell, Jr.
M/Sgt. Joseph D. Coady
M/Sgt. Paul F. Riddle
T/Sgt. Howard C. Kehrer
T/Sgt. Wilbur V. Ramey
T/Sgt. Chester C. Wall
S/Sgt. Donald E. Allen
S/Sgt. Vincent J. Andra
S/Sgt. Paul G. Fox
S/Sgt. Milton A. Kosmoski
S/Sgt. Joseph S. Waydak
Cpl. Glen K. Roen
M/Sgt. Frank Bonk
T/Sgt. Phillip E. Betz
T/Sgt. Francis P. Farrell
T/Sgt. Earl F. Mart
T/Sgt. Oscar M. Price
T/Sgt. Clarence E. Ziebell
S/Sgt. Ernest D. Cool
S/Sgt. Harry F. East
S/Sgt. Louis R. Gauthier
S/Sgt. Paul I. Grimm
S/Sgt. William Schultz

Capt. Frank C. Jones, Jr.
Capt. Thomas E. Joyce
Capt. George I. Stanford, Jr.
Capt. Neil Van Wyk
Lt. James F. Callahan
M/Sgt. Gerhardt H. Betz
S/Sgt. Warren G. Adams
S/Sgt. Elwood L. Briel
Lt. Zack S. Sensibaugh
Lt. Charles H. Shilke
Lt. Grover C. Siems
Lt. Darwin L. Berry
Lt. Clarence L. Boretsky
Lt. Charles L. Brock
Lt. Richard J. Corbett
Lt. Robert A. Dickmeyer
Lt. Harry E. Dugan, Jr.
Lt. Willard G. Gillette
Lt. Ira E. Grounds
Lt. Preston B. Hardy
Lt. Ferris S. Harris
Lt. Joseph W. Higgins
Lt. Donald M. Malmstem
Lt. Orval C. Miles
Lt. David K. Needham
Lt. J. C. Norris
Lt. Thomas S. Sharp
Lt. Frank T. Sibbett
Lt. Jack T. Simon
Lt. Curtis Simpson
Lt. George C. Smith
F/O Lester B. Godwin
Chief W/O Eddie J. Nassef
S/Sgt. Elwood L. Briel
S/Sgt. Robert L. Gilbert
S/Sgt. Lawrence H. Krantz
S/Sgt. Dorn I. Painter
S/Sgt. Glesner H. Weckbacher
S/Sgt. John E. Wilson
Sgt. George W. Ashton
Sgt. Albert A. Burnham
Cpl. Ellsworth G. Schaldach